Migration, Diasporas and Citizenship Series

Series Editors: Robin Cohen, Former Director of the International Migration Institute and Professor of Development Studies, University of Oxford, UK and **Zig Layton-Henry**, Professor of Politics, University of Warwick, UK.

Editorial Board: **Rainer Baubock**, European University Institute, Italy; **James F. Hollifield**, Southern Methodist University, USA; **Jan Rath**, University of Amsterdam, The Netherlands

The Migration, Diasporas and Citizenship series covers three important aspects of the migration progress. Firstly, the determinants, dynamics and characteristics of international migration. Secondly, the continuing attachment of many contemporary migrants to their places of origin, signified by the word 'diaspora', and thirdly the attempt, by contrast, to belong and gain acceptance in places of settlement, signified by the word 'citizenship'. The series publishes work that shows engagement with and a lively appreciation of the wider social and political issues that are influenced by international migration.

Also published in Migration Studies by Palgrave Macmillan

Bridget Anderson and Isabel Shutes (*editors*)
MIGRATION AND CARE LABOUR
Theory, Policy and Politics

Fiona Barker
NATIONALISM, IDENTITY AND THE GOVERNANCE OF DIVERSITY
Old Politics, New Arrivals

Loretta Bass
AFRICAN IMMIGRANT FAMILIES IN ANOTHER FRANCE

Michaela Benson and Nick Osbaldiston
UNDERSTANDING LIFESTYLE MIGRATION
Theoretical Approaches to Migration and the Quest for a Better Way of Life

Stephen Castles, Derya Ozkul and Magdalena Arias Cubas (*editors*)
SOCIAL TRANSFORMATION AND MIGRATION
National and Local Experiences in South Korea, Turkey, Mexico and Australia

Daniel Conway and Pauline Leonard
MIGRATION, SPACE AND TRANSNATIONAL IDENTITIES
The British in South Africa

Rosie Cox (*editor*)
SISTERS OR SERVANTS
Au Pairsí Lives in Global Context

Saniye Dedeoglu
MIGRANTS, WORK AND SOCIAL INTEGRATION
Women's Labour in the Turkish Ethnic Economy

Catrin Lundström
WHITE MIGRATIONS
Gender, Whiteness and Privilege in Transnational Migration

Amanda Klekowski von Koppenfels
MIGRANTS OR EXPATRIATES?
Americans in Europe

Eric Morier-Genoud
IMPERIAL MIGRATIONS
Colonial Communities and Diaspora in the Portuguese World

Dominic Pasura
African Transnational Diasporas
Fractured Communities and Plural Identities of Zimbabweans in Britain

Helen Schwenken, Sabine Ruß-Sattar
NEW BORDER AND CITIZENSHIP POLITICS

Louise Ryan, Alessio D'Angelo and Umut Erel (*editors*)
MIGRANT CAPITAL
Networks, Identities and Strategies

Evan Smith and Marinella Marmo
RACE, GENDER AND THE BODY IN BRITISH IMMIGRATION CONTROL
Subject to Examination

Holly Thorpe
TRANSNATIONAL MOBILITIES IN ACTION SPORT CULTURES

Vron Ware
MILITARY MIGRANTS
Fighting for YOUR Country

Migration, Diasporas and Citizenship
Series Standing Order ISBN 978–0–230–30078–1 (hardback) and
978–0–230–30079–8 (paperback)
(*outside North America only*)
You can receive future titles in this series as they are 3published by placing a standing order. Please contact your bookseller or, in case of difficulty, write to us at the address below with your name and address, the title of the series and one of the ISBNs quoted above.

Customer Services Department, Macmillan Distribution Ltd, Houndmills, Basingstoke, Hampshire RG21 6XS, England

Migration, Space and Transnational Identities

The British in South Africa

Daniel Conway
Lecturer in Politics and International Studies, Open University, UK

and

Pauline Leonard
Professor of Sociology, University of Southampton, UK

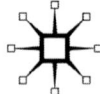

© Daniel Conway and Pauline Leonard 2014

All rights reserved. No reproduction, copy or transmission of this publication may be made without written permission.

No portion of this publication may be reproduced, copied or transmitted save with written permission or in accordance with the provisions of the Copyright, Designs and Patents Act 1988, or under the terms of any licence permitting limited copying issued by the Copyright Licensing Agency, Saffron House, 6–10 Kirby Street, London EC1N 8TS.

Any person who does any unauthorized act in relation to this publication may be liable to criminal prosecution and civil claims for damages.

The authors have asserted their rights to be identified as the authors of this work in accordance with the Copyright, Designs and Patents Act 1988.

First published 2014 by
PALGRAVE MACMILLAN

Palgrave Macmillan in the UK is an imprint of Macmillan Publishers Limited, registered in England, company number 785998, of Houndmills, Basingstoke, Hampshire RG21 6XS.

Palgrave Macmillan in the US is a division of St Martin's Press LLC, 175 Fifth Avenue, New York, NY 10010.

Palgrave Macmillan is the global academic imprint of the above companies and has companies and representatives throughout the world.

Palgrave® and Macmillan® are registered trademarks in the United States, the United Kingdom, Europe and other countries

ISBN: 978–0–230–34657–4

This book is printed on paper suitable for recycling and made from fully managed and sustained forest sources. Logging, pulping and manufacturing processes are expected to conform to the environmental regulations of the country of origin.

A catalogue record for this book is available from the British Library.

A catalog record for this book is available from the Library of Congress.

Contents

Series Preface		vi
Acknowledgements		viii
1	The British in South Africa: Continuity or Change?	1
2	The Historical, Political and Social Dynamics of British Migration to South Africa	30
3	Transnational and Translocal Identities: Settling in South Africa	50
4	Space and Place in South Africa	78
5	Landscapes of Belonging: Negotiating Britishness in South Africa	105
6	The Landscapes of Un/belonging in South Africa	128
7	Narratives of Continuity and Change: British Social and Political Attitudes in South Africa	152
8	The British in South Africa: Conclusion	177
Notes		189
Bibliography		191
Index		205

Series Preface

The British in South Africa are poorly understood and easily dismissed. The journalist Alistair Sparks (whom the authors quote) thought the British played 'a curious role in a drama cast for two'. The 'two' are, of course, Afrikaners and black Africans. Many Afrikaners looked back to the wars of 1880–1881 and 1899–1902, which they remembered as brutal imperialist invasions of the republics they had created to escape British rule. The British in South Africa were a living embodiment of their defeat and oppression. Although the British often described themselves as 'liberals', for the black consciousness leader, Steve Biko, they were hypocrites. At least the Afrikaners would have to face the music; they were there for the long term. By contrast, he averred, the British profited from apartheid, but always had their passports in their back pockets.

One of the most important tasks Daniel Conway and Pauline Leonard have accomplished is emancipating the social category from its caricature. The British in South Africa are a multilayered and complex group. There were some, certainly, who were imperialists and, no doubt, others who were hypocrites. Rhodes was a prime example of the first. In the wake of the Anglo-Boer war, he and Lord Milner assembled a group of posh young men from Oxford, known as Milner's 'kindergarten', to anglicize the country. In trying to impose the English language, Anglicanism, English common law, rugby and cricket, the foundation of schools and universities and much else, Milner's kindergarten made a determined effect to link South Africa to a wider British imperial role. Despite the intense effort at social engineering, the transplant never quite took. Boer obduracy, Zulu military resistance and the sheer numbers of rural Africans meant that South Africa never quite became a culturally defined 'British dominion', a process that largely worked in Canada, New Zealand and Australia.

British South Africans were also not always the best bearers of the imperial mission. In 1820, a group of 5000 settlers were dragooned to stabilise the eastern frontier; they were not sturdy yeomen, but demobbed soldiers (freed from the Napoleonic wars) and artisans, unused to rural life. When gold was discovered on the Witwatersrand, Cornish miners and adventurers of all sorts poured into Johannesburg, many of whom had the barest of links to Britain. Most of the early trade unions were founded by British workers, who opposed the machinations of British capitalists. Again, in the 1950s and 1960s, the Afrikaner government encouraged the immigration of skilled British workers, caught between their old hostilities and their perceived need to augment the white population against the emerging and larger *swart gevaar* (black danger).

As Conway and Leonard note, in the post-apartheid period, new segments have appeared or consolidated. South Africa hosts the eighth largest community of British retirees. There are many 'snowbirds', some evading tax, others taking advantage of the possibility of living a continuous summer in the northern and southern hemispheres. A half-million British tourists, some with family links, visit the country each year.

In their nuanced account, Conway and Leonard deploy the analytical lenses of transnationalism, translocalism and diaspora to pick up the multifaceted character of the British in South Africa. But, above all, they allow members of the British 'community' (a problematic word in itself) to speak for themselves. Working from an already deep familiarity with their subjects, the authors have undertaken 60 interviews in Johannesburg, Cape Town and Pietermaritzburg. Complex, contradictory, self-delusional, nostalgic, smug, fearful and confused voices emerge, but it is important that we can now hear those voices – for they have been systematically or, more often, inadvertently drowned out by the other players in the South African drama.

How are they adapting to the new South Africa? Conway and Leonard conclude that despite encompassing 'a broad range of identities, lifestyles, attitudes and social relations', the participants they surveyed 'were steadfast in their ongoing sense of identification with British nationality and their sense of belonging, if not to the material and political landscape of the contemporary United Kingdom, to an imagined community with some shared characteristics and sense of culture'. No doubt, as the authors acknowledge, there is some self-selection in the people wanting to be interviewed. It is likely that others of British descent have been rendered invisible or absorbed in the wider 'white' category. However, Conway and Leonard have undoubtedly shone a probing searchlight on the many British in South Africa for whom the categories 'white' or 'rainbow nation' are inadequate. They are to be congratulated for their illuminating and sensitive account.

Robin Cohen
Professor Emeritus, University of Oxford

Acknowledgements

We are very grateful to the British Academy for funding the research which made this book possible and to the many people who participated in the project, welcoming us so graciously into their homes and lives. Many thanks also go to colleagues in the migration and whiteness studies research communities who have provided us with insightful inspiration and support along the way. Particular thanks go to Heather Cusden, Melissa Steyn, Caroline Knowles, Charlotte Lemanski, and Karen O'Reilly.

Pauline would like to thank all her colleagues at Southampton for their interest and support: in particular Susan Halford and Derek McGhee; and family and friends – the 'African' Leonards, Guy, Mary and Bill; John and Dorothy; Will, Frances, Ed and Emily; Murray and Molly.

Daniel would like to thank colleagues at the Open University and at Goldsmiths, University of London and the Migration Research Unit, University College London where he had visiting research fellowships; and family and friends, in particular John and Sandra.

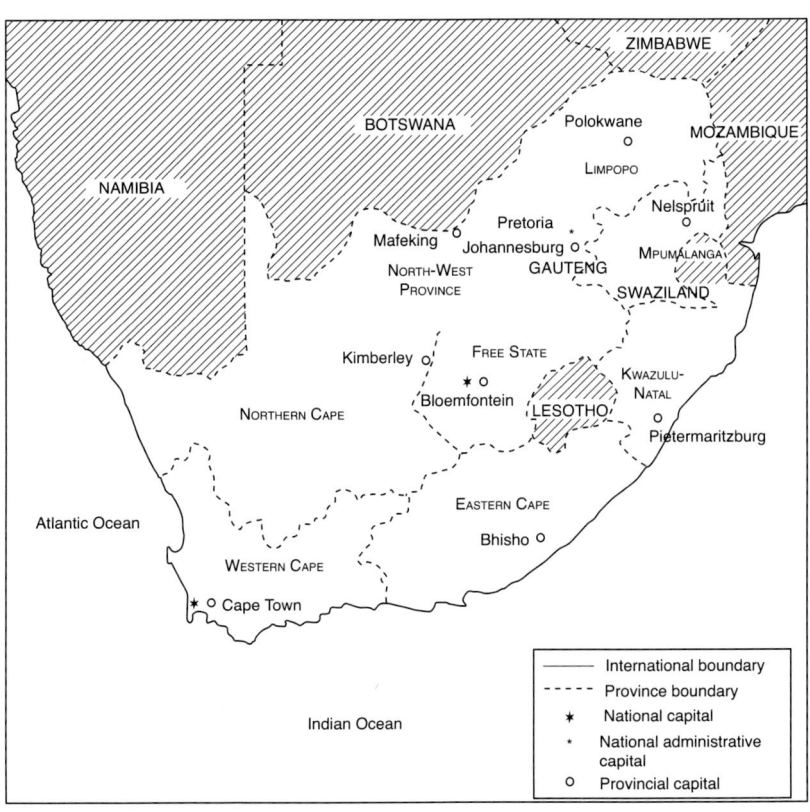

1
The British in South Africa: Continuity or Change?

'But what exactly do you mean by "The British in South Africa"?' Pauline was asked on a hot summer's afternoon in the garden of Claudia's London house in 2010. Now in her 80s, Claudia was born in South Africa and had grown up in the province then known as Natal (now Kwazulu-Natal). Of British ancestry, she identifies as 'white South African', and remembers being advised by the passport office of the new National Party government of 1948 that she should relinquish her British passport if she wished to remain a South African citizen. Although she subsequently came to live in the United Kingdom for most of her adult life, she has continued to make regular visits to the house in which she had lived as a child, in the leafy suburbs of Pietermaritzburg, and still feels that she is, first and foremost, South African. She maintains good contact with her neighbours, an eclectic mixture of white South Africans, Afrikaners[1], British, and mixed heritage Europeans. Many have histories of South African residence spanning several generations, while others have arrived relatively recently, due to the various assisted passage schemes of the 1960s, 1970s and 1980s, which encouraged and eased white immigration. 'I'm not sure the term has any meaning anymore,' Claudia continued. 'We are all just "white"'.

While Claudia may question the salience of nationality, the fact that she chooses to categorise herself as white underscores the ongoing and powerful position of race in the construction of individual identities in South Africa (Distiller and Steyn, 2004). The historical, political and social reasons underlying this distinguish South Africa as a distinctive context within transnational migration flows. Its history of colonial settlement, white minority government, the racially-based socio-economic and political system known as apartheid (literally meaning 'apartness'/'separateness') and 'whites-only' immigration policies mean that being white and English-speaking have long had political and social significance within white society in South Africa. For those whites with British connections, South Africa's chequered colonial past provides a controversial legacy. White British migrants were important for apartheid, and white British settlers were thus often accused of supporting the regime, while much of the rest of the world was indicating its antipathy by subjecting South Africa to a variety of sanctions and boycotts.

With the ending of apartheid and the succession to power of the African National Congress (ANC) in 1994, a new 'Rainbow Nation' was conceptualised. While this discourse can be accused of masking complexity through oversimplification (Nuttall and Michael, 2000), nonetheless the changing multicultural context means that 'whites', including British migrants, have to rethink and reconstruct their identities, relations, performances and attitudes. As Claudia indicates, being 'white' is still very much part of the grammar of South Africa and remains a key marker of identity, even though it 'just isn't what it used to be' (Steyn, 2001).

Yet the representation and imagination of South Africa should not be reduced to the inherited structures of its separatist, apartheid past (Distiller and Steyn, 2004). Albeit in uneven and contested ways, it is a country of plurivocal and multi-layered interpretations, transformations and possibilities (Tomlinson et al., 2003). For the British, while South Africa may present a more complex context than some other popular migratory destinations such as, say, France or Spain, it continues to be an attractive location and the number of migrants is significant: there are an estimated 219,000 British expatriates in South Africa (higher than the number resident in Germany and only slightly less than in New Zealand; Finch et al., 2010). In addition, South Africa has a booming tourist industry, which sees more British visitors to the country than any other group outside of Africa (Laing, 2013). At peak season, there are almost 60,000 British tourists in the country and almost half a million visit each year. Furthermore, with its 'retirement visa' scheme, South Africa is a top 10 destination for British retirees (Finch et al., 2010).

Yet despite these long-established and noteworthy links, South Africa has been surprisingly underresearched in the academic literature on British privileged and lifestyle migration. The reasons for this include the fact that 'in social science research and teaching, the Global South remains a marginal, residual and generalised category' (Williams et al., 2009, p. 1). South Africa occupies a somewhat ambivalent position within the North/South dichotomy; its white communities in particular share elements of the North, yet it also has many features in common with the South. It is still in the process of emerging as a developed economy, as exemplified by its inclusion in 2010 as a developing industrialised economy in the BRICS (Brazil, Russia, India, China and South Africa) classification, although as yet, its growth rates are lower than Brazil, India or China.

This may in part explain the lack of research interest by 'privileged' migration studies in the North, which have tended, to focus on other Westernised/developed contexts. Further, South Africa's history as a one-time political outcast may be an additional reason it has been somewhat avoided by academics in the North. One of our motivations for writing this book, therefore, is to rise to Williams et al.'s (2009) challenge of readjusting the research lens. By making an addition to the rich scholarship on South Africa already existing within that country, not least on the question of changing white identities, we hope to contribute to the communication of some of the diversity and complexity of South Africa.

A second motivation arises from the fact that while until the mid-twentieth century the great majority of English-speaking white people in South Africa were of British origin or descent, and as a group dominated nineteenth-century South Africa politically, they have rather fallen out of the focus of recent research (Lambert, 2009). In 1929, William Macmillan published *'Bantu, Boer and Briton: The Making of the South African Native Problem'* which firmly placed 'The Briton' as one of the three key ethnic groups in South Africa and a critical player in the evolution of 'the native problem'. As the historical standard for many years, Macmillan's work centralised British people within the construction of South Africa's history. However, by the 1950s, John Bond described the British as 'an unknown people' (1956, p. 1), and in the 1970s, Butler suggested that any earlier British sentiment had been 'burned out' (1976, p. 13). Further, Garson (1976) claimed that British identification had been abandoned such that they were now merely part of a broader group of 'WESSAs', White English-Speaking South Africans, that was still developing an identity (cited in Salusbury and Foster, 2004, p. 95).

As such, in the contemporary context, can the British be considered an identifiable 'group' at all? Indeed, both of us have received substantial critique from other academics about the topic of this book: 'There is *no* such group as "The British in South Africa"', it has been claimed. In the light of this, and Claudia's uncertainty, the question of whether the

British in South Africa even have a recognisable identity seems worth pursuing. Further, this potentially ephemeral quality of a British identity problematises the claim made in a recent British think-tank report that the global phenomenon of outward British migration has a progressive and significant ideological and socio-economic impact on the societies where contemporary Britons migrate (Finch et al., 2010).

A third motivation springs from our own personal experiences of being white and 'British in South Africa'. Despite Claudia's ambivalence, from our own engagements and relationships with South Africa, we both feel the term 'British' *does* have traction. Pauline's story is intersected by both colonialism and gender to reveal the complexities and ambiguities of privilege and nation. When she was a child, her father, John, made regular trips to Tanzania, invited through the country's historical links with the United Kingdom for his 'expert' assistance with the training of its teachers. A geographer by discipline, he always returned from his trips with wonderful photographs of the people and landscape and, from a child's perspective, exciting travel stories and intriguing, intricate artefacts.

Pauline longed to visit South Africa, and as an adult, she has been able to establish an ongoing relationship with the country, first through her partner, Guy, a third generation Zimbabwean, whose schoolteacher grandfather had emigrated in the 1930s to teach the children of the white British prospectors, farmers, engineers, navvies and administrators building the new Rhodesia. Originally settling in Southern Rhodesia, the family later moved to Northern Rhodesia. Some years after the country's move to independence and the creation of Zambia in 1963, Guy's father, Bill, now also a head teacher, received a letter from the newly formed Government saying his services were no longer required. The choice was to move to South Africa or return home to the United Kingdom. Disliking the apartheid state, the family chose the latter course, although Bill's qualifications and work experience were derogated by the British educational system, and he had to return to the bottom of the career ladder at the probationary teacher level. However, ongoing connections with those British relatives who *did* decide to move to South Africa, as well as the fact that much of Guy's career has been in that country, have meant that Pauline, Guy and their children have all spent considerable time there over the years, developing a deep familiarity and a great sense of attachment with its people and landscapes. In time, Pauline's own relationship with South Africa has been further developed through her own research and teaching.

Daniel lived in South Africa in the early to mid-2000s while studying for his PhD and lecturing at Rhodes University in Grahamstown, Eastern Cape Province. His interest in the country was also inspired by his family's experiences of living there, which, like many other British migrant families, are deeply implicated in the interrelated historical and socio-political relationship between South Africa and the United Kingdom. Daniel's father, also called John, had been one of the many thousands of British emigrants to use the assisted passage scheme in the late 1960s; as an engineer, he and his colleagues were 'headhunted' by a South African company when the firm they worked for went into liquidation.

Daniel's mother, Sandra, went to South Africa with a group of female friends, intending to live there for a year or so. She had chosen South Africa because of the stories her father had told about the country while he was stationed there for a period during the Second World War, as well as the fact that it was easier to obtain a visa than for continental Europe. Daniel's parents met and married and lived in South Africa for five years, returning to Britain in 1975 due to a combination of homesickness and concern with the country's politics and future.

In the early 2000s, many of Daniel's peers at Rhodes University had British parents or grandparents, had already spent a gap year in the United Kingdom, or were British born. 'Britishness' was a salient identity, distinct, albeit interrelated, from the broader English-speaking white identity that both Rhodes and Grahamstown had a long association with. Yet it was also problematic and contentious; parents of students at Rhodes were often open about wanting their children to leave the country upon graduation, and British residents could appear deeply dislocated in the rapidly changing politics of the country. The university's 'Britishness' was also embodied through its many British staff, its heritage and its claims to a particular British form of education, but this was becoming increasingly controversial and appeared racist in the broader context.[2] The lived reality of this was also complex: the British traditions of the university and the presumed universality of academic practices were not matched by the experience. In everday life boundaries were fluid, and behaviours that would be considered unprofessional in a British context were sometimes latently tolerated. Although a fascinating country in which to study politics and society, the complexities of this academic and social context led to Daniel's decision to return to the United Kingdom.

The continued attachment of those in South Africa of British ancestry to some of the cultural trappings of home, in spite of the dramatic political and social changes marking their country of residence, was an interesting topic of conversation when Daniel and Pauline first met at a Worldwide Universities Network 'White Spaces' Conference in 2009. To what extent, we wondered, were the lives of the white British migrants changing and adapting in relation to the democratic, post-apartheid regime 15 years later? What impact has this had on them socially and economically? How is this articulated on the ground, in terms of their daily practices and the spaces and places in which these are conducted? And how is this affecting their senses of (national) identity and the nature of their engagement with, and contribution to, both South Africa and Britain? Are they, for example, ceasing to self-identify as British and, like Claudia, positioning themselves within the catch-all category of 'South African white'? And indeed, if the meanings of whiteness have shifted in the new, supposedly 'post-racial' South Africa, what does 'whiteness' now mean for the British in contemporary South Africa (Steyn, 2001)? It was through these questions of migration, space and transnational identities that our research project was conceived.

However, Claudia's ambivalence about the existence of a 'British' identity meant that it was with some initial trepidation that we posted a feature on our proposed research on 'The British in South Africa' in the *Telegraph Weekly World Edition* newspaper and the *Daily Telegraph* online in the summer of 2010 (Conway, 26 July 2010). This article was also featured on the *Telegraph*'s expat website and was reposted in a number of other expatriate and other online forums. The FIFA World Cup, hosted by South Africa, was in full swing, although England had just lost their place in the tournament. In our article, we explained that we were about to embark on a funded project[3] to explore the lives of British-born expatriates in South Africa and how they relate both to the dynamic country around them and their former home. We were particularly interested in the expat's sense of change, and how they were experiencing the post-apartheid state. We wrote that we were looking to talk to British residents living in either Cape Town or Johannesburg, and anyone interested in participating in the research was invited to make contact with us.

By midday, our email inboxes were bursting! Messages were pouring in from people identifying as British, some simply insisting that we interview them, others demanding to know why we weren't also coming to the Eastern Cape, Kwazulu-Natal and so forth. The respondents were an eclectic mixture of people who had lived in the country for many years since the 1960s, 1970s and 1980s, as well as those who had moved there more recently, post-apartheid. Some were working and emailing us from their work addresses, others were retired or non-working partners. For all this diversity, it was clear that we had touched a nerve: a good many people wanted to talk about their experiences as British-born residents in South Africa.

Researchers interested in the British in Australia have also experienced enthusiastic responses to requests for interview. Wills believed this was because 'many of them were ready to tell their stories as *British* migrants – as part of the multicultural story of Australia – but with no particular sense of their claim to now be telling the *national* story in Australia' (2010, p. 233). This desire to tell one's own story in relation to South Africa's national narrative was certainly present in our sample. It was not just that the British had been 'invisible migrants', as they had in post-war Australia (Hammerton and Thomson, 2005, p. 9), but that many felt ignored by popular and academic understandings of international migration, and misrepresented as having complicity in apartheid and perceptions of ongoing colonial privilege. For some, there was a further sense that South Africa itself was neglected and stereotyped incorrectly in the international imagination. In addition, for some of the older residents, there was also anger against the United Kingdom, which they felt discriminated against them through the freezing of their pension rights (a policy not applied to British residents in other territories, such as Spain).

There were also certain and troubling expectations of us as researchers: that we automatically understood and agreed with their perspectives, that we would help publicise and end the pensions issue and even that we could help return a town bell taken by British forces during the Boer War! Over the years since the article first appeared, we have continued to receive emails from people keen to be involved. For a multiplicity of reasons, this *is* a group of transnational migrants who want their voices heard.

Migration, space and transnational identities

This book's interest in migration and transnational identities in the dynamic context of South Africa situates itself across a range of contemporary theoretical and empirical literatures. Our position in relation to these is discussed fully in Chapter 3, but here we will give a brief outline in order to contextualise the research on which this book is based. First, it draws on the broader contemporary literature on 'privileged migrants', whether due to professional, career and/or lifestyle motivations. 'Privileged' is a clearly relative term, and it refers to more than the movements of an exclusive, highly mobile and wealthy 'transnational elite' (Sklair, 2001). Rather, it is a broader concept, incorporating a range of spatial mobilities undertaken by people with diverse backgrounds. While these are primarily displacements undertaken voluntarily by relatively affluent, middle-class and largely professional people who have the necessary resources – money, time and credentials – to decide to live in a country other than that of their birth (Amit, 2011), the class and occupational backgrounds of privileged migrants are by no means fixed. In certain contexts, such as Australia and South Africa in the 1960s and 1970s, (white) working-class people were also welcomed with attractive work opportunities and promises of social and economic mobility (Hammerton and Thomson, 2005; Elder, 2007). In this way, South Africa has, at certain stages in its recent history, gladly admitted white British migrants to fulfil both manual and non-manual occupations. Through this migration policy, a diverse group were brought together to enjoy a new, advantaged lifestyle (Peberdy, 2008).

While it is often difficult to disentangle the exact reasons that push such people to migrate, there is a growing body of work that aims to interrogate the expectations, aspirations and experiences of a group that has the agency and power to choose to leave their established homes and lives for a new spatial context (Leonard, 2010; Fechter and Walsh, 2012). The aim here is to provide comparative detail to the broad church of international migration studies, encompassing as it does the displacements of refugees, asylum seekers, undocumented 'illegals', retired sun-worshippers, gap year and foreign exchange students, and unskilled, semi-skilled and highly skilled labour.

International migration of all these types is intrinsic to global capitalism, yet the fractured politics of national borders and the multifarious demands of multinational corporations, labour markets and transnational finance mean that the social, economic and cultural capital of this global traffic is multiply striated (Braziel, 2008). In order to understand the granularity of these differences, we need to know about the lives and experiences of all migrants – from those more privileged at the top of the spectrum to those at the lower end. As Avtar Brah argues, 'the question is not simply about who travels, but when, how and under what circumstances?' (1996, p. 182). Much of the existing research suggests that, for the former group, geographical shifts are usually imagined to be part of a transformative quest to improve their quality of life – within their work and careers (They are often referred to as 'professional migrants'), through environmental factors such as better weather, food, culture and accommodation ('lifestyle migrants'), or a complex mixture of all of these (e.g., O'Reilly, 2000; Fechter, 2007; Coles and Fechter, 2008; Benson and O'Reilly, 2009a; Leonard, 2010; Amit, 2011; Benson, 2011; Fechter and Walsh, 2012).

Benson argues, for example, that individual migrants who relocate for lifestyle reasons 'imagine that they will be able to improve and take control of their lives...the act of migration is thus understood as part of a search for a better way of life...'(2011, p. 7). For Benson and O'Reilly (2009a), lifestyle migration is often about imagined escapes from monotonous lives and the drudgery of routines, from materialism, consumption and urban living, although resulting experience often counters these dreams. Those who relocate for work and career reasons may have more grounded motivations; indeed, while a key factor may be a transition to improved consumption opportunities and urban living, the link with the reflexive project of the self and the quest for improving the quality of life is often a common aspiration (Amit, 2002; Nowicka, 2006; Scott, 2006).

The research and context on which this book draws complicates these understandings of privileged migration. We need to be wary of erasing 'the real and substantial differences between the conditions in which particular movements across spatial borders take place' (Ahmed, 1999, p. 332) through the application of this catchall category. Through the eclectic range of 'lifestyle' and 'professional/work' migrants that we talked to in South Africa, we found that privileged migration is often not purposeful or the result of personal empowerment, nor is it always the result of unhappiness with a present lifestyle. We argue that this category of migration can also be the result of a complex range of accidental, spontaneous, serendipitous, or even more 'forced' factors that work to blur notions of motivation and choice as well as some of the dichotomous understandings on which conceptualisations of privileged and less-privileged migrants are constructed (Hatfield, 2011).

As we will show, South Africa interrupts some of the foundational assumptions of privileged migration due to its complex social and political context. Far from seeking an unambiguous, self-motivated escape to a better life, the motivations of some of our respondents – white, privileged migrants from the Global North – were highly complex and contradictory. It was true that some perceived South Africa as a landscape washed with sun and possibility and had come as part of an imaginative and even mythological quest to engage with the landscape and its distinctive pleasures (Foster, 2008). However, the decision processes of others were more diverse: some were firmly instructed that they either had to relocate to South Africa or lose their jobs; others tearfully left work and family members behind to accompany partners, parents or children, often with dire warnings ringing in their ears of what they might find; while some failed to make it to their initial country of choice and ended up in South Africa.

Stories such as these suggest that privileged migration also includes a disparate group who could be termed 'accidental migrants': those who, while still privileged – in that they usually do not have to worry about rejection by immigration policies or border controls, nor necessarily about income or accommodation – nevertheless experience some disempowerment, for a range of complex reasons that are not always of their own making. This loose category recognises the intersected relations between migration and power, and that decision-making abilities are fractured by *inter alia* gender, age and occupation to complicate the concept of 'voluntariness'.

Notions of privilege are further confused by the fact that, as Benson (2011) demonstrates, imagination does not always correspond with experience. Hoped-for utopias may, in actuality, turn out to be a far cry from initial expectations: the social, political and economic realities of everyday life can produce very different and heterotopic conditions from 'the good life' of dreams and fantasies. The reality of South Africa's racial divides, the gap between rich and poor, and the restrictions on personal freedom imposed by gated communities and heightened urban discourses of crime and violence came as an unpalatable shock to some of our respondents. Conversely, others who came to South Africa with substantial misgivings, full of the stereotypical 'knowledges' about the country that abound in the Western/Northern media headlines (Holland and Roberts, 2010), found instead 'a world where dreams are made; a world in which [they] belong' (Bhengu, 2010, p. 54). The South African context refracts the conceptualisation of 'privileged' migration still further by bringing to the fore the potential of the social, economic and cultural capital that are provided by, and attributed to, race, nationality and class. While unanticipated by some, the unearned rewards these aspects of identity can deliver are variously received as welcome or sources of ambivalence.

This book thus seeks to broaden and complicate the contemporary literature on privileged migration through the intricacies of the South African context, so 'migration' forms our first theoretical axis. We explore this more fully in Chapter 3, where we discuss the diversity of migrants and migratory experiences (O'Reilly, 2000) found in our research. Broadly speaking, we identify three main positions: first, those who have made a permanent break, moving to South Africa and settling there with no intention of returning to the United Kingdom. Some have taken out South African citizenship, and some have become thoroughly embedded by forming new family relationships with local residents and having children. Some have established new businesses that rely on local labour markets, or participate in local politics and neighbourhood activities. Also included in this group are those who emigrated as children, accompanying their parents and growing up in South Africa. While they retain their British passports, the United Kingdom is often perceived as tangential to their lives. Others in this category may retain a more separated existence, perhaps socialising only with other expatriates from their home countries and making little effort to learn any of the local languages or adopt local cultures.

Second is a more mobile group – those who return to the United Kingdom on a regular basis, some maintaining two homes and spending time in each, depending on factors such as work, weather and family commitments. These migrants may have legal status as permanent residents in South Africa but also maintain their rights in the United Kingdom. While some of these adopt a set routine, such as 'snowbirds' who spend summer in one home and winter in another (Oliver, 2011, p. 130), others may be transients, travelling easily between the two places with no set pattern for times and durations. A third group are the short-term or seasonal migrants (O'Reilly, 2000), such as those who have come on corporate- sponsored, fixed-term contracts for a couple of years, or foreign diplomats based in South Africa before moving elsewhere. While other scholars such as O'Reilly (2000) make a provision in this category for students and gap year travellers spending time abroad, or those who own holiday homes and only visit for short spells, we did not meet any of these latter migrants during our research in South Africa. We recognise, however, that this is a growing sector of migrant activity and indeed, some of our respondents, especially those in the Western Cape, considered themselves to be living in a semi-permanent holiday home, although only occasionally returning to live for a spell in the United Kingdom or Europe.

The term 'expatriate' can apply to all these types of migrant but, as Leonard has argued (2010), the expression has additional, more discriminatory connotations (see also Fechter, 2007; Fechter and Walsh, 2012). Most commonly, it is used to refer to privileged migrants from the West who, in most instances, are white. Its roots are in its application to communities such as the British in the colonies, or the Americans in 1920s Paris or Munich, but more recently it is used, not least by the migrants themselves, to describe their status as (white) skilled professionals who live and work overseas yet still hold, sometimes fervently, the (Western) citizenship of their birth. It is thus an exclusionary term, and as such is often deployed within the recent academic literature on privileged migration with this in mind: to emphasise who may not be included by virtue of their race, nationality, culture and class as well as to describe those who are. While eschewing any essentialism within this category (O'Reilly, 2000), we conceptualise the British in South Africa as 'expatriates' and the research will demonstrate our use of the term in this self-conscious sense.

It is clear then that privileged migration is an unbounded and multilayered category that includes people at all stages of the life course and from a variety of backgrounds. Further, people may shift and change between types, such as those who start out as tourists, perhaps with a holiday home, and then decide to settle permanently, or those who think they have migrated for good, only to realise they want to make frequent trips home. This slipperiness underscores the connections between privileged migration and tourism, and the ways in which, for some, migration can enable extended consumption of place, culture and landscape, performances of longed-for, yet fantastical, roles and activities, breaks from usual routines and responsibilities, further travel into areas that would not normally be affordable or do-able from home contexts, perhaps all the while retaining a 'gazing' positionality (Franklin and Crang, 2001, p. 15; see also Urry, 1995; Hall and Williams, 2002; Coles and Timothy, 2004; Urry and Larsen, 2011).

The diverse notions of 'belonging' and 'home' are brought into question through the range of migratory positions amongst the British in South Africa. Migration is often employed as a metaphor for movement and dislocation (Ahmed, 1999; King, 2012), and even conflated with nomadic conceptualisations of identity based on exile and loss of belonging and home (Chambers, 1994). However, as we discuss more fully in Chapter 3, these notions are highly complex, and feelings of belonging and home are contingent on a multiplicity of imaginative, sensory, material and spatialised factors. As we will demonstrate in this book, while migration certainly results in a reconfiguration of relationships with the place of birth and home feelings of belonging and un-belonging to both the United Kingdom and to South Africa were highly variable and conditional on a range of biographical and social factors. Many of our participants expressed simultaneous feelings of belonging and un-belonging, as different 'landscapes', both imaginative and lived, were drawn upon to construct senses of 'home' in the new migratory context as well as to position themselves with their spaces of origin, both local and national.

Indeed, the notion of positionality connects with a second broad area of literatures that we draw upon, those of transnationalism, translocalism and diaspora, which more centrally address the relations between migration, space and transnational identity-making. Given the variety of mobilities that are incorporated in this book, to what extent are subjectivities produced through nationality, race and ethnicity, gender and class changed or maintained through acts of geographical displacement from 'home' to 'away'? To what extent do these migrants cast off the grinding mores of home to escape to new lives and identities in new contexts, participate fully in civic and local relations, and establish new roots? Or do they continue to participate in the political, social and cultural lives of their countries and places of origin (Levitt, 2001), perhaps with nostalgic memories of imagined homelands? To what extent do they stick to their compatriots, other British people, to form a 'community' in the new context within which most of their social life is conducted? In other words, can and should they be conceptualised as a diaspora?

The 'transnational from below' approach is concerned with answering such questions, through a focus on how migration is experienced at the micro-level of local places, institutions and individuals (Vertovec, 2001). For, as Guarnizo and Smith argued, it is in reality 'the everyday practices of migrants that provide a structure of meaning to the acts of crossing borders' (1998, pp. 18–19), and these 'anchored in' (Smith, 2001, p. 3) practices reproduce social relations between nations. Transnationalism thus connects wider global forces with a material and grounded exploration of how migrants draw upon the multiple nations and communities of their biographies in the construction of their daily lives and identities. Translocal geographies refine the approach still further, by exploring the ways in which these national practices and relationships are grounded and maintained at the local level, through the connections made between local–local contexts. Translocalism identifies that migrants may overlap places and times in their everyday lives, both materially and symbolically, to connect the here and the there through a range of embodied and imagined daily practices, activities and movements. It is through these grounded, routine, material and embodied practices, as well as the identifications and imaginations of ordinary migrants, that nation states, local communities, and transnational connections are all mutually constituted (Basch et al., 1994; Vertovec and Cohen, 1999; Smith, 2001; Brickell and Datta, 2011). While in some instances these may be self-conscious, reflexive strategies to construct a certain sort of 'habitus': having a street party for

British neighbours in a Johannesburg suburb to celebrate the Queen's Jubilee, or putting up a Union Jack at your place of work during the 2012 Olympics; other practices may be more pre-reflexive and habitual: making a cup of Yorkshire tea at 4 o'clock, or spreading Marmite on the morning toast, reading British newspapers and watching the BBC (Bourdieu, 1984; Oliver and O'Reilly, 2010). Central to translocalism, therefore, is the need to recognise that a broad range of other spaces, places and scales intersect migration experiences beyond the national. It is an approach that aims to answer Burawoy's (2000) call for theoretically informed empirical research, which transcends the confines of a national myopia to embrace analytically 'the wider forces, connections and imaginations in a global world' (Brickell and Datta, 2011, p. 5). At the same time, it seeks to ground these 'global ethnographies' (Burawoy, 2000) in the material, symbolic and sensory spaces and places that are important during migration processes – the ordinary locales where identities and relations are actually negotiated and transformed. Such insights are particularly significant for us in this book, concerned as it is with a diversity of migrant experiences, spaces and connections. As such, space and place form the second theoretical axis of this book and are examined more fully in Chapter 4.

As indicated above, a further question presaged by a focus on the reconstructions of national and local communities and practices in new migratory locales is the extent to which such nation-based communities can be regarded as diasporas. Traditionally, this concept has been applied 'from below', to describe processes of non-voluntary, usually violent, displacement and permanent exile (Gilroy, 1997; Baumann, 2010). At its core lies a sense of longing – 'the image of a remembered home that stands at a distance both temporally and spatially' (Stock, 2010, p. 24). Whether this term should also be used to describe expatriates – privileged people who have the power of choice over their migration – has been the subject of recent theoretical debate. However, there is a growing consensus that opening up the concept to recognise the 'changing cultural practices and identities that the historical and contemporary movements and mingling of peoples has generated' (Alexander, 2010, p. 488) might be a useful move forward in helping to gain a more holistic understanding of the ways in which race, privilege and disadvantage may work in everyday practice. Knowles (2003, p. 161), for example, has suggested that repositioning the concept 'to incorporate the mobile networks and habits attendant on privilege' helps to reveal 'the other side' of the political circumstances of disadvantage. Brah (1996, p. 181) makes a similar point in her concept of

'Diaspora Space', which she describes as 'a conceptual category "inhabited" not only by those who have migrated and their descendants but equally by those who are constructed and represented as indigenous'. In other words, a key contemporary challenge for diasporas (Knott, 2010, p. 83) is to engage with the 'realities of settlement', the political contingencies, the co-constitutional relationships of diaspora space, and the location of diasporic subjectivities.

In this book, we aim to build on these more rounded and grounded conceptualisations of transnationalism, translocalism and diaspora by developing Brah's concept of diaspora space in both its conceptual and material forms. Inspirational here are the ways in which space and place have been opened up by new geographical perspectives, which explore the simultaneous social, cultural, economic, political, historical, emotional and embodied makings of place through spatial materialities, performances, processes and meanings (Lefebvre, 1991; Massey, 2005; Anderson and Harrison, 2010). These multifaceted approaches provide a useful way in to looking at 'the realities of settlement' (Knott, 2010, p. 83) and their co-constitutional qualities. Exploring the actual places and spatial practices of social diversity – residential, domestic and working environments, cultural and leisure venues, and, as Clifford terms them, the 'old localising strategies' (1994, p. 303) within these – provides a useful point of access to investigate the multiplicities and complexities of British migrant lives, identities and relations. As argued elsewhere (Leonard, 2010), space is not as a neutral backdrop; it is thoroughly implicated in the construction and performance of particular identities, social and cultural practices and social relations through its materiality, its histories and cultures (Lefebvre, 1991). We argue, for example, that whether activity happens in Bryanston or Sophiatown, in Camps Bay or Hermanus, in Ballito or Pietermaritzburg matters: it is through the lived dimensions of these distinctive places that identities, meanings and status, as well as associated embodied capacities such as experience and belonging, emotions, feelings and memories, are produced. Further, drawing on Lefebvre (1991), place enables us to integrate these affective aspects with material articulations as well as to attend to the power relations produced by and through the social production of space. In other words, place allows us to see how space is both socially produced and implicated in producing social identities and relations: how it is both the effect and cause of social life (Dyb and Halford, 2009). This incorporates both reflexive performances and pre-reflexive, taken-for-granted habits and routines (Bourdieu, 1984): all are processes of distinction, key means by which race, nationality and class are constituted, mobilised and bounded (Bennet et al., 2009).

Finally, such an engagement joins the poststructuralist-inspired move to locate, unpack and dismantle identity-making, and particularly the place of race and ethnicity within this. Of key concern here are the fluidity, contestations and ambiguities that may exist in the ways that raced identities are 'made', practised and lived (Alexander and Knowles 2005), an interest that connects with the third broad area of literature on which we draw: whiteness studies and its intersections with (feminist) post-colonialism. These offer further valuable insights into the imbrications of raced identity-making by acknowledging the importance of geographical histories – Britishness and whiteness – and that the transnational relations of British migrants cannot be understood, for example, without reference to both European and world history, and particularly the transitions from colonialism to post-colonialism (Colley, 1992: 9). Although the full applicability or the extent of the colonialism/post-colonialism transition to the South African cultural and economic context is open to question, tracing the legacies of colonial productions of whiteness and nationality as they are reconfigured in postcolonial spaces is an important dimension of conceptualising contemporary expatriates. There has been some inspiring scholarship exploring post/colonial white and indigenous relations, and the complex and sometimes contradictory place of race, gender and class within this, not least within the South African context (e.g., Gaitskell, 1983; Walker, 1991; McClintock, 1991; Hetherington, 1993; Dagut, 2000; see also Coles and Fechter 2008, Bickers 2010). The analytical framework pulling this work together is based on non-essentialised conceptualisations of whiteness and other identities, and understands that individual contexts and the specificities of particular places, spaces and times have consequences in the ways in which they offer distinctive resources to configure raced, gendered and national identities in diverse and multiple formations. A key aim here is to analyse how white people are able to utilise and rework racialised social hierarchies in and across many different places, spaces and times. Because, as Cohen argues, 'the shape and edges of British identity are... historically changing, often vague and, to a degree, malleable – an aspect of the British identity I have called a "fuzzy frontier"' (1994:20), this is a particularly apt approach for the study of British identity and belonging in a transnational context and informs the third axis of our theoretical approach, transnational identities.

The questions and debates addressed within these three bodies of literature lie at the heart of this book. It is from these that we draw the three key axes of our theoretical approach: privileged migration, space/place and transnational identities, which are used to frame our investigation: how the British in South Africa construct and maintain their ties to the nations, and the 'locales', that they come from, while at the same time establishing roots in new places of settlement (Levitt, 2010, p. 39, Brickell and Datta, 2011). Furthermore, we are interested in whether and how they participate as citizens, how they draw on their whiteness and British nationality in the construction of their identities and relations, and the extent to which, if at all, they can be considered to be diasporic. However, while we argue that South Africa offers a unique and important context to explore these theoretical and empirical questions, our interest and commitment to the project is very much more than this. We also have a distinctive political enquiry to explore because of South Africa's exceptionally dynamic, fragmented and fluid national context. In short, following Hall, we ask,

> What is the relationship between the mobilisation or performance of racialised and other forms of ethnicity and identity at the local, micro, more ethnographic level and the large thing that brought us into the field at the beginning, namely a racialised world...a world in which material and symbolic resources continue to be deeply unequally distributed? (Hall cited in Alexander, 2009, p. 474)

The context of South Africa

South Africa has a unique history of race relations, produced through periods of colonisation, racial segregation and democratisation. At the heart of this lies the system of apartheid by which the country was framed politically, socially and materially from 1948 to 1994, (Butler, 2009). As we discuss more fully in Chapter 2, even before this time, the country was far from integrated. Since the arrival of the first European migrants in the mid-seventeenth century, there had been continuous skirmishing for power. However, in the period from the 1870s onwards, three groups of people emerged as particularly significant in the battles over resources and power: the African farmers known as the San, Xhosa and Zulu, the Dutch immigrants, known as Afrikaners or 'Boers', and British imperialists (Macmillan, 1929).

The Boers were the descendants of the early Dutch colonists from the Cape who had supplied the Dutch East India Company and had later spread north and east into African land. Here they had grasped seemingly empty stretches of land that resulted from the divisions between different African peoples (Butler 2009). Meanwhile the British, who had acquired the Dutch East India Company in 1802 and taken control of the Cape Colony, had started to take possession of the coastal regions, thus also granting themselves land without the consent of its indigenous peoples.

The two white communities were already divided, but the period after 1870 was marked by a particularly dramatic disintegration of their relations. Diamonds and then gold were discovered in the Transvaal region, which is now known as Johannesburg, 'City of Gold'. This fuelled the British desire to gain control of the whole of South Africa, culminating in the Boer War of 1899–1902. After the defeat of the Afrikaners, the country was unified as a British colony through the 1910 Act of Union and became one of the colonial dominions where British settlement was actively encouraged. As a British Dominion, it shared the racial and governmental features of the British Empire: namely that whiteness and a British nationality delivered substantial social mobility, power and privilege. Indeed, it was the racialised political machinery developed at this time that laid the economic, political and institutional foundations of the later apartheid system (Beinart, 2001; Butler, 2009).

After 1910, emerging systems of racial segregation deepened through the need for migrant labour in the British-owned mines and on the British and Afrikaner farms. A flexible migrant labour system required mobility, and to this end, African access to land was squeezed by allocating 87% of land to whites and prohibiting land purchase and non-labour based tenure by Africans. Although there were some effective pockets of resistance, with some successfully buying land and establishing 'black spots' in white South Africa (Sparks, 1997), this policy, combined with a complex set of pass laws that prevented blacks from moving around the countryside to sell their labour, meant that many had little choice but to come to the cities to seek work. Here, however, spatial segregation practices were entrenched still further, as well as acting to control the influxes of the African population and preventing their entry into designated 'white' spaces.

At the same time, however, conflict within the white community intensified. Compared to the Afrikaners, many of whom were unskilled and poor, the British were prosperous, and an emerging middle class soon developed that scorned its neighbours, while the Afrikaners still resented the outcomes of the Boer War. In the 1900s, Afrikaner nationalism emerged in sharp contrast to British colonial authority and towards the other racial groups in South Africa. This political ideology was formed by, and found its expression in, a number of cultural organisations, such as the Dutch Reformed Church, the Broederbond, and Stellenbosch University. Its main political focus became the National Party (NP), which was founded in 1915. The NP developed ideologies of racial 'purity' and even more fundamental racial segregation. These racialised ideas became increasingly popular amongst the Afrikaans-speaking white population, who were associating black urbanization with fears of 'swamping' (Beinart, 2001; Butler, 2009) as well as being concerned about their own jobs and livelihoods in a time of economic hardship following the Boer War. In 1948, the National Party won an election victory under the mandate of apartheid, a system of governance that remained in place until the first universally democratic elections of 1994. As we discuss more fully in the next chapter, a key plank of their campaign had been an anti-British and anti-English-speaking white platform, and a clear strategy of clearing out English speakers from the higher echelons of the Civil Service and the Army. This was accompanied by a general gerrymandering of electoral constituencies with majority English-speaking voters to reduce their influence (Rotberg, 1987, pp. 79–83).

While the NP immediately introduced the Population Registration Act, which enforced the classification of people into four strict racial categories: White, Coloured, Indian/Asiatic and Native (later Bantu or African), it was not until the 1960s that apartheid really reached its zenith. Up until this time, the racial segregation in South Africa was arguably not so different from other parts of colonial Africa, or indeed the world. However, after South Africa declared itself a republic in 1961, apartheid entered a second phase, in which space was drawn upon invidiously as a fundamental resource for racism and discrimination. Under the new policy of 'separate development', an engineered system of 're-tribalisation', black people were forcibly removed from 'incorrect locations' to the ethnic-based developments of newly created Homelands or 'Bantustans'. In 1970, homeland citizenship was forced upon all Africans, who had to be assigned to an ethnic group according to rules of descent. By 1989, 3.5 million black Africans, Coloureds and Indians had been forcibly removed after they were judged to be of the incorrect ethnicity for their location (Thompson, 2001; Butler, 2009). The ultimate aim of the Homeland policy was to remove African access to any area other than the homelands, unless white employers needed them for labour. In 1967, the Government strengthened this position by prohibiting Africans from visiting any urban area for more than 72 hours without a special permit. Under this law, the number of African arrests rose dramatically, peaking in 1975–1976 at nearly 400,000 (Thompson, 2001).

Ultimately, however, the system was unsustainable. In the decade between 1960 and 1970, while the black population in white urban areas fell by over 200,000, it grew in the reserves by almost a million, resulting in substantial overcrowding and impoverishment (Butler, 2009). However, as the black population rose, so did their political power, making it increasingly difficult to maintain spatial control. This, together with the rising power of the predominantly, but not exclusively, black ANC, as well as the growing global antagonism to the South African regime marked by a series of sanctions and boycotts including the expulsion of South Africa from the Commonwealth, started the gradual erosion of the NP. The 1970s and 1980s witnessed a series of anti-apartheid resistances, including the boycotting of commuter buses, strikes and demonstrations against the school system. These incidents, which included the renowned Soweto Uprising in 1976, were dealt with by increasing levels of brutality by the militarized Afrikaner regime. Many ordinary black people, including schoolchildren, were caught up in the riots and deaths that followed. This provoked international condemnation and the deserting of the NP by Afrikaner intellectuals, and with the eyes of the world upon them, the Government realised that some changes would have to be made.

By the mid-1980s, some segregation laws had been eliminated, and black people were able to use a few of the lower classes of public facilities and transport. The Government was also 'turning a blind eye' (Thompson, 2001, p. 221) to black occupation of some of the white residential areas of Johannesburg, such as Hillbrow. However, the reform process had its limits: the Land and the Group Areas Acts still excluded Africans from land ownership outside the Homelands, and African communities were still being relocated. Consequently, anti-apartheid resistance was escalating, and in a desperate attempt to maintain control over the black population, the Government declared a national State of Emergency in 1986. But the writing was on the wall: things had to change. With the appointment of the more strategic F. W. de Klerk as the new president in 1989, dialogue was at last opened with the ANC, culminating in the cancellation of the state of emergency in certain provinces (although in others, such as Kwazulu-Natal, emergency regulations remained in place), the repeal of the remaining apartheid laws and, eventually, the release of the imprisoned ANC leader and activist, Nelson Mandela, in 1990. On 27 April 1994, the country held its first universal franchise democratic elections (Beinart, 2001; Sparks 1997; Thompson 2001; Butler 2009).

When Nelson Mandela was inaugurated on 10 May 1994 as South Africa's first black president, the 'rainbow nation of God' (as Archbishop

Desmond Tutu called it) was full of hope that the 'better life for all' that the ANC had promised would in time be achieved. As Mandela explained:

> The moment to bridge the chasm that divides us has come... We enter into a covenant that shall build a society in which all South Africans, both black and white, will be able to walk tall without any fear in their hearts, assured of their inalienable right to human dignity-a rainbow nation which is at last at peace with itself and the world at large... We must therefore act together as a united people for national recovery... Never, never and never again shall it be that this beautiful land will experience the oppression of one by another. (cited in Johnson, 2009, p. 3)

Having been excluded for so long, now the country was the focus of world attention, and visitors and new migrants (both legal and illegal) from all over Africa flocked in as tourists or looking for work (Johnson, 2009). In macro-economic terms, the post-apartheid South African economy returned to growth, and there is no doubt that some black people benefitted economically and socially, joining a burgeoning black middle class (Southall, 2004). However, the realities of post-apartheid South Africa, and the feasibility of its rainbow nation discourse, are highly complex, and debates rage as to the extent to which the hopes and aims have been achieved, if at all. In particular, these have been challenged from May 2008 onwards by a succession of xenophobic attacks on Zimbabwean, Congolese, Somali and Nigerian 'foreigners' in urban areas such as Johannesburg, Cape Town and Port Elizabeth (Crush, 2008). Triggered by power cuts and declining economic fortunes, spouts of violence have moved ever closer to the white residential areas. For some whites, not least the British, this has been what they had been dreading: evidence that the country 'has gone to the dogs'. Taking advantage of their privileged mobilities (Andruki, 2010), they have taken flight.

The British in South Africa

What of white British residents in South Africa over this time? What was their position in the long period of racial and spatial segregation that has so blighted South African history? While, as mentioned earlier, Macmillan's canonical history (1929) held that 'Britons' were centrally implicated in building the racial architecture of South Africa, more recent political historians argue that while the country was governed by the (Afrikaner) National Party, British immigrants and the wider English-speaking white community (largely of British and Irish descent) occupied a politically marginalised and socially ambivalent position. Indeed, Sparks contends that the central political relationship was a binary one between the Afrikaans-speaking whites and black Africans, describing British migrants merely as playing a 'curious role in a drama cast for two' (1997, p. 46). On their side, the British were sometimes accused by Afrikaans-speakers of being uncommitted to the nation, of failing to act as full citizens, and of being *soutpiel*: having one foot in South Africa, one foot in Britain and a penis dangling in the Atlantic! However, the declaration of the republic in 1961, and South Africa's withdrawal from the Commonwealth, marked the beginning of a rapprochement between the National Party government and English-speaking whites. The National Party, having now achieved full independence from Britain, started to move away from its ethnic nationalist platform to appeal to a more diverse group of whites in their constituency, including English-speakers. South Africa's rapid economic growth in the 1960s and 1970s coincided with the reintroduction of the assisted passage scheme for skilled white migrants and the active recruitment of certain professions and skills from the United Kingdom by the South African government. At the same time, Britain in the 1970s was in the midst of economic recession: 'the sick man of Europe' (Pearce and Stewart, 1992 cited in O'Reilly, 2000; 33). Unemployment was rising, and in contrast, while not holding any significant political power, British citizens who settled in the country were rewarded significantly in terms of lifestyle and social and economic status: whether professionally skilled or manual workers, their race and nationality guaranteed them middle-class ascription and good remuneration. The price of this life was, for many, 'to live a life of more or less large-scale, if never perfect, denial' (Goldberg, 2009, p. 521). However, unpalatable political events such as the 1976 Soweto Uprising and the declaration of the national State of Emergency in 1986 meant that denial was increasingly impossible, and white emigration rose dramatically over this period.

Since 1994, and the shift from an authoritarian white minority regime to a multi-racial democracy, South Africa has come to be viewed more positively by the outside world. Its full readmittance to international flows of trade, finance and cultural exchange has been accompanied with significant increases in British tourism, second home ownership and retirement migration to the country, along with continued professional and other forms of labour migration. Between 2005 and 2009,

South Africa was the seventh most popular destination for British emigrating retirees, and now has the eighth largest British-born community in permanent residence (Finch et al., 2010). However, many argue that the divisions within the country remain, not only between blacks and whites, but also within and between the white 'community'. In particular, English speakers have continued to reveal differing positions since 1994; interestingly, 'both conservative and liberal English-speaking South Africans seem wary of accepting the new dispensation and are accused by Africans of being less prepared to adapt than are Afrikaners' (Lambert, 2009, p. 611). This differentiation within the white communities occurs amidst the wider crisis in white identities after apartheid, as there is now 'an acute sense of loss of the familiar, loss of certainty, loss of comfort, loss of privilege, loss of well known roles...a delusional home now collapsed' (Steyn, 2001, p. 150). Although the crisis of whiteness has led to significant white emigration from South Africa, it is not necessarily accompanied by a loss of discursive confidence or insistence that South African whites have no right to live in and define the country (Johnson, 2009). Indeed, Steyn and Foster argue that 'In this new context, the central question for whiteness, as the orientation which takes its privilege as normal and appropriate, can be put simply: how to maintain its advantages in a situation in which black people have legally and legitimately achieved political power?' (2008, p. 26). While this question has received considerable academic attention in relation to the Afrikaner community (Steyn, 2001; Davies, 2009), to date there has been little focus on other whites, such as the British. It is this gap that our research aims to fill.

The research

It was against this exceptionally dynamic political and social context, therefore, that our research was planned. As two researchers who were both familiar and fascinated with the country, and who fully support the ideals contained in the vision of the post-1994 South African nation, we were keen to explore how other British residents conceptualised these. What is the level of British engagement with and participation in the new ideologies of post-apartheid South Africa? We were keen to investigate this through ethnographic research with a broad variety of British-born residents, in order to explore their lives and experiences and the extent and manner to which they were accommodating themselves to the changing political and social regime. In particular, we aimed to look at how the British positioned themselves within South Africa in discursive and embodied terms. First, how, in their talk, did they conceptualise their attitudes and norms? How did they describe themselves, their lives and their social relationships and the extent of their civic and political engagement? What did they think about the social structures within South Africa – had the intersections of race, nationality and class changed? Had their own performances and relations of race and nationality changed? What did they think about the United Kingdom and its changing multicultural texture? Did they (still) 'feel' British? Or South African? Or, to borrow the now much-outdated Afrikaans' term, *soutpiel*: neither of these? And what did any such 'feeling' mean to them in practice? Here, then, we are drawing on Foucauldian approaches to language and discourse, which views these as social practices: 'a social construction of reality from a particular perspective, which draw upon a form of privileged knowledge or social and ideological practice' (Baxter, 2010, p. 14, Foucault, 1972, p. 49).

Second, we were also interested in their embodied performances and dispositions – where and how they lived, travelled, worked, shopped and spent their leisure time. Which spaces and places did they inhabit? Where do they feel most comfortable? Were there spaces to be avoided? Who did they work and/or socialise with, and had this changed? What were their daily routines and practices, their cultural tastes, and activities in both material and imaginative forms? And how did race, nationality, class and gender inflect these? Here we are drawing on Bourdieusian approaches to think about social practices in relational terms, and how cultural and social capital are linked to fields and the formation of social groups, as well as the everyday iterations of habitus (Bennet et al 2009, Bourdieu 1984, Miller 1998). We are also inspired by Lefebvrian approaches to space, which recognise that it is both a physical and embodied, phenomenological experience as well as socially constructed through discourse, the imagination and the material. These theoretical underpinnings are discussed more fully in Chapter 3.

Our research was primarily based in the cities and surrounding countryside of Johannesburg, Cape Town and Pietermaritzburg near Durban, three key sites of British dwelling, and we took a multi-method, ethnographic and biographical approach in order to gain 'thick' data of British lives and experiences (Geertz, 1973). This included visual methods and unstructured interviews, but also, in many cases, mobile methods; as a key aim was to explore the spatial attachment to place, and how people draw on space and place in the production of their identities, everyday practices, and senses of social networks, the 'mobile interview' was chosen in addition to more conventional, static, typically room-based interviews conducted in hotels, homes and workplaces (Clark and Emmel, 2010). Thus, during the significant amounts of time we both spent in our research contexts during the empirical stage between 2010 and 2012, we accompanied some of our participants as they went about their daily lives, joining in on their drives around the city, going shopping, collecting children from school, and spending time in various work contexts, as well as participating in leisure pursuits such as walks through gated communities, horseback rides, and even safaris through privately owned game parks. We attended social occasions at the invitation of our participants, as well as functions organised by both local businesses and multinational corporations: these ranged from casual *braais* [barbecues] and informal dinners in people's houses, to meals in restaurants, garden parties, office parties and even diplomatic functions.

During this time, over 60 interviews were collected from a mixture of long-term residents who had lived in the country since the 1940s, some beneficiaries of the 'Assisted Passage' scheme of the 1960s and 1970s, others who had arrived later, including after 1994, and some who had only been in residence for a year or so. Interviewees were a combination of self-selected people who had responded to our newspaper article about the research as well as participants identified through our personal contacts and the snowball method. In spite of the fact that it is widely sold in newsagents across South Africa, we were aware that an article in *The Telegraph Weekly World Edition* – a weekly newspaper aimed at British expatriates – might attract a particular demographic. Consequently, we were concerned to widen our sample to include people who may not have initially thought to offer themselves for the research project. Although by no means claiming that our final sample of participants is in any way 'representative' of British people in South Africa – which, as we have discussed, is in itself an arguable category, simultaneously both embraced and denied – we did seek a 'multiplicity of cultural voices' (Prasad, 2005, p. 90). Our aim was not to generalise, but to generate an intensive examination of a range of 'British' residents in order to develop theoretical understanding of their positions (Bryman, 2001). We used our contacts to attempt to access women and men of varying ages and from all social and occupational backgrounds, working and middle class, and from across the regions and countries of the United Kingdom. Further, as the concept of space was of particular interest, variety was sought in the places in which people lived and worked, as well as the connections they held with the United Kingdom.

The interviews followed a loose structure, but we were particularly interested in when and why our participants had migrated to South Africa, their memories of their thoughts and feelings on first arrival, how their lives had unfolded, their responses and views on South African life and politics during and after apartheid, and their thoughts and plans for the future. As we were also interested in issues of nationality and identity, enquiries about their relationship to the United Kingdom and feelings of national identity were also included. As well as these transnational questions, our interest in place and space meant that we followed these up with questions about their more local spatial relations and identifications. In many cases, we had to talk very little, as people were keen to give their stories, and we were interested in their selection of themes and topics that they felt relevant to our research.

Once collected, the interviews were transcribed and submitted to thematic analysis, wherein we searched for all the places where our key concepts were evident in our participants' narratives. We were particularly interested in the language they used and the differences that existed among our participants to refer to our key themes and particular events such as apartheid and its demise. Further, for each participant, we approached their whole transcript as a biographical account, or life story, seeing that their talk about their lives and key episodes within these reveals ways in which they construct their identities in the past, present and future, both to the listener and themselves (Halford and Leonard, 2006).

Conducting the research was a privilege: it is always fascinating and, at the same time, humbling to be allowed into people's lives, and we are very grateful to all our participants for their time, hospitality, honesty and clarity. While we both entered the project through a preexisting acquaintance with South Africa, the research process opened our eyes to new levels of nuance and complexity, which at times were inspirational, insightful, challenging and sobering. Our approach to the analysis is to acknowledge fully our role in the research process. To this end, we position ourselves openly within the presentation and discussion of the research, and its analysis is of course solely our interpretation of our findings and experiences.

Structure of the Book

The experiences, views and aspirations of the British migrants we spent time with unfold through the various chapters of the book as we draw upon our ethnographic material to present our arguments, analysis and interpretations. From the start, our aim is to intertwine the empirical data with supposedly more 'abstract' discussion, in order to underscore the ways in which history, politics and social structures constantly animate at the micro-level of daily life. We thus commence, in the next chapter, with an exploration of the historical dynamics of British migration to South Africa. We discuss the evolution of British colonial relations with South Africa, South Africa's development as a white settler state and the imperatives and constraints of apartheid from 1948 to 1994. The chapter documents apartheid and post-apartheid migration policies, and the extent of white migration and British immigration to the Republic, as well as more recent pan-African migration policies, some of which have led to outbursts of xenophobic violence, to examine the complexities of the political and racialised context. The chapter argues that while the history of immigration to South Africa reveals that the prospect, status and presence of British immigrants has always been a politically controversial and potentially socially divisive force, the British have also formed a key dynamic in the socio-politics of South African nationhood.

Processes of migration are also highly complex, and Chapter 3 draws on current developments in transnational migration research to establish how we may understand these theoretically and conceptually. We argue that migration needs to be understood as a multifaceted process operating at multiple scales: while new identities may be constructed through migration within the new local and national contexts, they are also produced through the relationships that often continue to exist at home, again at both local and national levels. This is an approach that is thus grounded in the local and very specific contexts of daily lives, while simultaneously acknowledging global and transnational networks and relations. The emphasis is on the material, social and spatial practices of men and women and the ways in which they make connections across and between the societies of home and away. How these practices are constitutive of identity, and the roles that race, gender and class play in this, is one of the key foci of the book. The chapter draws on and reviews contemporary literature in this area, while at the same time arguing that the South African context complicates existing theory to make a significantly new contribution to our conceptual understandings of privileged migration. Not neatly contained within either the 'lifestyle' or 'labour' migration approaches, British migration to South Africa is revealed to be far less strategic, but a complex mixture of wishes, fantasies, whims, accidents, indecisions, changes of mind and even reluctance. In addition, and again in contrast to the findings of other research, migrants to South Africa are therefore often not concerned to make a complete break with 'bad Britain' (O'Reilly, 2000), but can retain a complicated and even diasporic relationship with their homeland. Further, race, and more specifically, whiteness, is such an intrinsic and significant aspect of the migration experience within the South African context that it cannot be the invisible factor that it is in much of the existing literature on British migration.

These chapters form the backdrop to the chapters that then follow. Chapter 4 builds on the historical and political analysis in Chapter 2 to consider more specifically the ways in which space – the physical landscape of South Africa – has long been drawn upon to operationalise racial segregation. We introduce the highly diverse contexts of Cape Town, Johannesburg and Pietermaritzburg, within which our respondents lived, and show how five key tropes dominated their narratives about space and place. For the British, South Africa is at once a space of desire and anxiety: a place of spectacular consumption, to be encountered and gazed at for the uniqueness of its landscape, animals and peoples; a space of distinction, by which 'race', class and nationality are constructed and status sought; a place of fear, in which mobilities are restricted both imaginatively and physically; a space of connection, by which local and transnational links are established; and a space of change, by which, in the present moment, their hopes or fear of and for the 'new South Africa' are imagined and managed. It was these five tropes that influenced the ways in which they engaged and identified with the spaces and places of South Africa in both embodied and imaginative terms. They reveal how many British residents juggle a simultaneous sense of belonging and un-belonging, and it is these complex attachments that form the focus of Chapters 5 and 6. Dividing these emotions over two chapters was purely a heuristic device, however, and allocating our empirical evidence between the chapters often proved to be extremely challenging; such was the ambivalence and simultaneity of senses of un/belonging to both South Africa and the United Kingdom. We argue that belonging is a shifting and contingent state, never fully expressed, and frequently contradictory, coexisting with feelings of alienation. To achieve a sense of belonging to South Africa took work, and processes of adaptation took time and were rarely fully achieved. Chapter 7 turns to consider more directly British people's responses to the dynamic politics and changing society of South Africa. The transition from an apartheid state to a post-apartheid democracy acted as a tipping point in many people's narratives, which were consequently framed through a 'before/after' temporality, whereby life 'now' was compared to the past, either from experience or imagination. However, narratives about the political, social and economic changes were not contained within South Africa alone: they usually intersected with what was perceived to be happening in the United Kingdom. This meant that attitudes towards, and decisions about, continuity and change within South Africa were often conceptualised in relation to questions of continuity and change at 'home'.

The conclusion draws together the various themes discussed in the book and revisits the central questions introduced in Chapter 1. We analyse whether the identity of 'British' does have traction in South Africa, the extent and manner to which this identity is drawn upon as a frame by which to understand daily life there, and the way in which this may mediate senses of belonging and citizenship. We argue that our interviews with our sample of British-born residents in South Africa suggest that, while the subject positions of these migrants is in flux in the dynamic contemporary context, discourses and embodied performances of Britishness continue to offer them important resources for identity-making. With the exception of Claudia, with whose challenge we opened this chapter, for all our respondents being 'British in South Africa' was an identification that was not only meaningful, but ongoing.

2
The Historical, Political and Social Dynamics of British Migration to South Africa

> Immigration is the call. We want men and women. We want our population to increase in leaps and bounds. Let us once more open our doors – we want to make hay while the sun shines...We can get thousands – hundreds of thousands – millions of them.
> — General Jan Smuts, MP and Prime Minister, speaking to the Transvaal United Party, 1946; cited in Peberdy, 2009: 85

> Never was a country so different from what it was represented, for most writers have given it the character of a fertile country, but except in small spots, it is very much the contrary.
> — Lieutenant Francis 1821, Cape Colony cited in Edwards 1934: 79

At the age of 88, Peter sits in his immaculately ordered home in a retirement village just outside of Cape Town. Peter recalls that, shortly after the Second World War, he was offered the choice between teaching positions at an Anglican seminary in Wales or in Grahamstown, South Africa. Financial support from the South African Governor General's Fund and the desire to try something 'new' and escape the harsh conditions of the British winter of 1946–1947 persuaded him and his wife to choose South Africa. They arrived four months before the victory of the National Party in 1948.

As Peter reflects on his life spent as an Anglican priest and professor of theology in South Africa, the realities of the country's politics and society intersect his narrative:

> I've had a very interesting time in South Africa ... the end of the apartheid was quite right, and there is no doubt that there were many times, many occasions where I thought that we must make every effort to get out of here, especially after Sharpeville [the Sharpeville massacre 1960] and what followed even with the creation of the Republic – in 1960, was it? Yes. I was in Queenstown, and there was a lot of trouble there, and so one way or another, we kept on staying.

Peter was made aware of political tensions between English-speaking whites and Afrikaans-speaking whites in multiple ways: in his debates with colleagues and students; in the successive waves of British emigration from the country following political shocks; in his involvement in protests over the death of liberation struggle activist Steve Biko in 1977; and in the dilemma his family faced when his sons were conscripted into the apartheid-era South African Defence Force. When Daniel asked him if he thought South Africa's history could have been different, Peter finds a well-worn history book and talks of a noted Cape Colony (and British-born) politician: 'John X. Merriman: in 1914 he wrote, he was a member of parliament at the time, "I appeal to this House on grounds of fair play to give every man a chance irrespective of colour and irrespective of race. The race that tries to keep itself up by artificial props is doomed." Remarkable, 1914, a hundred years ago!'

The Anglican Church in South Africa was in the vanguard of moral and political criticisms of apartheid, so Peter's life was bound to be drawn into the political struggles of the country. Even so, his framing of his life story in relation to the fraught nature of South African history was not unusual; this was a universal feature that pulled together the interviews we conducted.

British migration to South Africa has a long but troubled history. Deeply politicised throughout the nineteenth and twentieth centuries, the encouragement (and discouragement) of British settlers was a tenet of both pro-imperial and Afrikaner Nationalist leaders. South Africa was one of the United Kingdom's first 'colonies of settlement' (Cohen 1994: 7) and as a Dominion, it should have seen the same mass settlement that occurred in Canada, Australia and New Zealand throughout the twentieth century. However, South Africa's history of division and conflict among white settlers, and the greater numerical and militant strength of the indigenous population, made British hegemony considerably more fragile and ultimately unsuccessful. Indeed, as Dubow notes, South Africa 'was the least thoroughly Anglicised and undoubtedly the most troublesome of all the "white" Dominions' (2009: 4). Studies undertaken of other significant migration flows from the United Kingdom have contextualised and related these population flows with the specific history of the relations between the UK and the country of destination (Cohen 1994; Drake and Collard 2008; Leonard 2010; O'Reilly 2000). This chapter will develop this approach and explore the historical dynamics of British migration to South Africa, contextualising these migrations in relation to British colonial relations with South Africa, South Africa's evolution as a white settler state, and the imperatives and constraints of apartheid from 1948 until 1994. In post-apartheid South Africa, policies have increasingly restricted UK immigration, although British people continue to migrate to the country.

The history of British settlement in South Africa

In the fifteenth century, the Portuguese are likely to have been the first Europeans to have set foot on what would become South African soil. Bartholomeu Dias named the southwestern tip of Africa 'the Cape of Storms', but King John II of Portugal renamed it, more optimistically, as 'The Cape of Good Hope'. In 1578, Sir Frances Drake was the first recorded British explorer to catch sight of the area. Like many subsequent European visitors and settlers, the striking physical beauty of the region captivated him. Drake wrote that 'This Cape is the most stately thing, and the fairest Cape we ever saw in the whole circumference of the earth' (cited in Stone 1973: 91). In 1652, Jan van Riebeck colonised the Cape area for the Dutch East India Company (the *Vereenigde Oost-IndischeCompagnie* (VOC)). The primary purpose of this settlement was to provide a safe coastal port and refreshment station between the Netherlands and its colonies in the Dutch East Indies. Cape Town gradually expanded, resulting in a number of violent conflicts with the indigenous Khoikhoi population as the VOC sought to increase its hold over the region. In the seventeenth century, French Huguenots fleeing religious persecution from the Catholics joined the Dutch settlers. Economic factors, war and corruption led to the decline of the VOC throughout the eighteenth century. This decline largely isolated the Cape, but it was the Napoleonic War that drew the British into the area, which they occupied in 1795, then sought to formalise and strengthen their control. The Cape was finally ceded to the United Kingdom in the Treaty of Paris in 1814.

In 1820, South Africa's status as a settler colony was confirmed with the arrival of 5000 British settlers in the Eastern Cape (Stone 1973: 92). At this time, the total white population stood at 42,700 people (Peberdy 2009: 11). The settlement scheme was prompted by the withdrawal of British garrisons at the end of the Napoleonic War: the Governor, Lord Charles Somerset, was concerned that this jeopardised control of the Cape's eastern 'frontier' along the Fish River, where there had already been armed conflict with the indigenous Xhosa population. Somerset believed that a human 'buffer' of British settlers at the Albany region of the frontier would secure the colony (Edwards 1934: 29–30, also Lester 2001). The British government had some strategic interest in Cape Town as a port en route to India, and there was also a growing belief that emigration was a means for ensuring domestic labour supply, dealing with unemployment (which was very high following the Napoleonic War) and, by implication, reducing the threat of political radicalism.

Somerset persuaded the British government to grant land and resettlement grants to assist passage to the Cape and then, in turn, began an artful and highly disingenuous campaign to lure British settlers to the colony. Making no reference to the strategic plan of creating a human buffer zone, Somerset's 'fertile imagination conjured up a picture of a land flowing with milk and honey' (Edwards 1934: 31). The scheme was consequently heavily oversubscribed, and ships left London, Liverpool, Portsmouth and Cork. The 1820 settlers were predominantly urban artisans with little experience of farming, and the Albany region was largely characterised by infertile land; indeed, the area had been termed the *Zuurveld* (sour land) by Boer farmers in the eighteenth century. In addition, the settlers were subject to frequent attacks from the black Xhosa population. Conditions of extreme deprivation and increasing starvation developed and 'it took only a matter of months for the 1820 settlers in the Eastern Cape to complain that they had been abandoned by a cynical British government' (Dubow 2009: 18).

Over the following months and years, the British settlers largely abandoned the frontier farms and converged on the town of Grahamstown in the Eastern Cape. Here, their hostility to Lord Charles Somerset, and to the British government more generally, led to the formation of a critical press and an emerging political class in South Africa. The conditions of the settlers was also taken up by *The Times* newspaper in London and caused scandal in parliament. Essentially, the settlement scheme to South Africa as a bridgehead for mass settlement was a failure, but the Cape was secured as a colony, and the history of the '1820 Settlers' would continue to be used as a symbolic justification for the Britishness of the Cape (and South Africa) throughout the nineteenth and twentieth centuries.

The other region of southern Africa that the United Kingdom colonised and defined in the nineteenth century was Natal, along the eastern Indian Ocean coast. The first permanent settlement of Natal was in 1824, and the United Kingdom annexed the region as a colony in 1843. In 1846, an assisted emigration scheme was introduced and, by the end of the 1850s, 10,000 British immigrants had arrived in Natal (Stone 1973: 37). Unlike in the Cape Colony, British immigrants outnumbered Boers in Natal, and this led to a distinctive colonial identity. As Lambert notes, 'alone among South Africa's British communities they used their colonial name, Natalians, to distinguish themselves. During the imperial years they evolved a distinctive, even idiosyncratic, British community, a South African Ulster and the "last outpost of Empire"' (1990: 150). Natalian society in the nineteenth century was noted for its English bourgeois predilection for status and hierarchy, and significant urban centres in Durban and Pietermaritzburg were developed (Stone 1973: 107–108).

The discovery of diamonds at Hopetown (in what is now the Northern Cape) in 1867, and then subsequently of gold on the Witwatersrand in 1886, provoked the most significant influx of immigrants from the United Kingdom (and elsewhere). Between 1873 and 1883, there were 22,300 assisted migrants from the United Kingdom, many of whom were specifically attracted by the gold and diamond 'rush' and were instrumental in developing Johannesburg as a city (Stone 1973:114). However, the fact that men dramatically outnumbered women concerned the British Government, anxious about the long-term sustainability of British presence. In 1862, the Female Middle-Class Emigration Society was established to create a flow of unmarried migrant women to the colony, with the hope that they would, as prospective 'imperial mothers', 'play an essential part in the reproduction of the white labour force and the production of a British "race" majority' (Van Helten and Williams 1983: 18). Between 1901 and 1910, over 4000 single women left the United Kingdom for South Africa, many destined for domestic service in the Johannesburg area. Indeed, no other empire state attracted single women through an assisted emigration scheme of such a large scale (Van Helten and Williams 1983).[1] As a result of these combined factors, South Africa's white population tripled between 1850 and 1891 to reach approximately 620,000 people, and by 1911, the white population stood at 1.2 million people (Peberdy 2009: 11). British settlement in what would become South Africa was thus a somewhat uneven process across the 1800s, but by the end of the century, the Cape Colony and Natal had developed significant British communities and had evolved a distinctive British colonial identity (Lambert 2010).

From the outset, the circumstances of British settlement in South Africa created tensions between the settlers and the indigenous black population on the one hand, and between the settlers and the British government on the other. Yet it was the political and social pressures within the white communities, between the British and the Boers, that were to define the development of South Africa and make British immigration contentious at policy and symbolic levels. Relations between the British and the Boers were tense from the beginning. A letter from one of the 1820 settlers to the *South African Journal* newspaper in 1823 made clear that an advantage of mass British immigration to the colony was the 'engulfing of the British upon the Dutch population', who the correspondent considered to be 'more apathetic and lucre-loving' compared to the 'free spirit which Englishmen inhale' (cited in Edwards 1934: 90–91, also Lester 2001: 15–16). Partly in response to an 'Anglicisation policy' adopted by the British, the Boers embarked on the 'Great Trek' in the 1830s out of the Cape Colony into the interior of what would later be defined as South Africa, Zimbabwe and Mozambique. As a result of the 'Great Trek', the Boer Republics of the Orange Free State and the South African Republic (informally called the Transvaal) were formed. The gold and diamond rush of immigration from the 1860s to 1880s had thus predominantly been into the Boer-controlled Transvaal region (RSA 1989: 68). As John Stone writes, 'From the 1870s onwards the immigrants had become pawns in the power struggle between Briton and Boer. The military conquest of the Bantu had temporarily eliminated the majority of South Africans from the chessboard of political conflict, leaving the ground clear for a direct confrontation between the two white cultural groups' (1973: 114–115).

The 'Boer Wars' between the United Kingdom and the Boer republics in 1880–1881 and 1899–1902 were essentially fought for control over South Africa's mineral resources and to strengthen the British Empire. The United Kingdom's eventual victory was a source of deep humiliation and bitterness for most of the Afrikaner population, who were still the majority of the white population.

The formation of the Union of South Africa in 1910 united the two British colonies and the three Afrikaner Republics as a Dominion of the British Empire. The lead-up to the formation of the Union had seen colonial administrator Lord Milner pursue an aggressive Anglicisation policy. This policy sought to place South Africa firmly in the British imperial project and included the promotion of the English language, culture and law in education, religion and all areas of national life; another key tenet was to encourage mass British immigration (Fedorowich 1991). Milner stated that 'If, in ten years hence, there are three men of British race to two of Dutch, the country will be safe and prosperous. If there are three Dutch to two British we shall have perpetual difficulty' (cited in Stone 1973: 120). However, Milner's specific desire to encourage British soldiers who had fought in the Boer Wars to settle in South Africa was not particularly successful (Perberdy 2009: 35). The encouragement of British immigration by the Union government and the other aspects of Anglicisation were condemned as imperialist by the cabinet minister General J. B. M. Hertzog, who said in 1912 that South Africa 'had reached national manhood... South Africans and not strangers should run the country' (cited in Peberdy 2009: 37). Hertzog, who was dismissed from the Cabinet, formed the National Party, which quickly became the political focus for Afrikaner nationalism and was staunchly critical of the United Kingdom and British influence in South Africa.

During World War One, British immigration fell from an annual total of around 10,000 to just 1500 (Stone 1973: 122). In the aftermath of the war, the Dominions Office established a settlement department to encourage and assist British emigration to the Dominions, and in 1922 the Empire Settlement Act established a fund to assist British emigration. One of the policies was the free passage offered to ex-servicemen from the United Kingdom to the empire. The British government considered this emigration as a means to distribute the British population across the empire, to relieve unemployment at home and to develop imperial markets (Mlambo 1998: 135). What was striking was that southern Africa had some of the smallest numbers of immigrants under this scheme. The overseas settlement committee of the Dominions Office administered 495,242 British emigrants between 1922 and 1935: 25% went to Canada, 34% to Australia, 9% to New Zealand and only 0.2% to South Africa and Rhodesia (Mlambo 1998: 139). There were some South African-led initiatives to encourage British immigration during the interwar period. In 1920, on the anniversary of the first British settlers, the 1820 Memorial Settlers Association was formed in Grahamstown and London, with the aim to encourage and assist British immigration. Between 1920 and 1960, the association assisted over 100,000 British immigrants with financial support and/or advice (Garson 1976: 19). However, although British immigration was considered politically important as a counter balance to Afrikaner influence by the imperial authorities, mass migration failed to materialise.

In the 1920s, the growth of Afrikaner nationalism and the increasing influence of the National Party (which first won office under General Hertzog in 1924) led to the increased regulation of immigration, particularly along racial and religious lines. In 1921, an immigration act was passed that ensured Indians would be prohibited from immigrating to South Africa (Stone 1973: 122). The political debates about immigration, and the increasing definition and restrictions on who was desirable and undesirable as an immigrant, reveal the ethnic politics of both the British and Afrikaner authorities. The National Party had identified immigration policy as an important means to keep the white population 'pure' and a defence against British imperialism. Influenced by eugenics and Nazism, the South African government adopted anti-Semitic and increasingly selective immigration policies. The Quota Act was passed in 1930 and the Aliens Act in 1937 in order to regulate and restrict the immigration of Jews from Europe, along with other immigrants considered diseased or degenerate (Peberdy 2009: 76). There had been Jewish immigrants among the 1820 settlers, and by 1880 there were 4000 Jewish immigrants in South Africa. Successive pogroms in Eastern Europe increased the Jewish population to 50,000 people by 1911 (3.7% of the white population) (Peberdy 2009: 57). The Quota Act and Aliens Act ensured Jewish immigration was significantly reduced. South Africa, governed by the Anglophile General Jan Smuts' United Party, entered the Second World War in support of the United Kingdom, but the country did not adopt compulsory conscription because of Afrikaner opposition to the war, and indeed, many National Party leaders spent the war in internment camps because of their close links and open support for Nazi Germany.

During the war, South Africa became strategically important to Allied forces, and over 6 million Allied troops were either stationed in, or visited, the country. The country's climate, munificence and absence of rationing were a revelation for many of the British servicemen based there, a considerable number of whom wished to settle there more permanently after the war (Smith, forthcoming). In 1945, South Africa was one of the ten richest countries in the world with an economic growth rate higher than the United Kingdom's (Peberdy 2009: 89). As the appeal of the prime minister, Jan Smuts, at the outset of this chapter makes clear, the South African government once again, in rhetorical terms at least, sought to encourage mass British migration to the country. Smuts considered immigration to be a priority to sustain economic growth, to maintain and strengthen ties with the United Kingdom and the Commonwealth, and to provide security by increasing the numbers of the white population in relation to the black population. The government entered into an arrangement with the Union Castle Line ships to transport the new wave of British settlers (Smith 2013). This policy was strongly opposed by the National Party, however. In parliament, the party's leader, Dr D. F. Malan, tabled a motion calling the scheme 'imprudent in concept and disastrous in its consequences', and more broadly, the party believed mass British immigration was designed to 'plough the Afrikaner under' (cited in Stone 1973: 131; Peberdy 2009: 91). However, in spite of this, the scheme was an initial success, and in the three years after the war, more than 20% of all British emigrants moved to South Africa and Rhodesia (Smith 2013). By 1947, 87% of the 25,000 immigrants to South Africa were British, with the Union Castle Line having a considerable backlog of applicants (Stone 1973: 133).

The narrow election victory of Malan and the National Party in 1948 tightened immigration policy for over a decade, as 'the National Party saw immigration as a threat to its national aspirations, its vision of a (white) South African national identity and possibly even the implementation of apartheid' (Peberdy 2009: 59). The contract with Union Castle Line was cancelled, and preferential treatment for British immigrants was ended. The British were now to be subject to the same health, occupation and political affiliation scrutiny as other white migrants (Peberdy 2009: 100). As exemplified by Claudia's story in chapter 1, the new South African Citizenship Act of 1949 removed the 'Britishness' of South African citizenship and meant that British residents were no longer automatically naturalised, but subject to a six-year residency requirement along with other criteria (Peberdy 2009: 101).

Smith argues that the desire to restrict British immigration was not initiated by the National Party, but was actually considered by the Smuts government (2013: 133–134). In contrast to Smuts, the Nationalist's rhetoric was hostile towards the British and the notion of British immigration, but the fear of creating a 'poor white' problem and threatening racial privilege by allowing mass immigration was a policy consideration for both Smuts and Malan (Smith 2013: 155–158). In the broader context, Australia had adopted an assisted passage scheme in 1947 and Canada in 1952, while Rhodesia also sought to encourage British immigrants. It is hardly surprising, then, that British immigration dropped sharply in 1949, and emigrants were tempted in greater numbers to other Commonwealth countries during the 1950s, yet it is still the case that British migration to South Africa was higher in the 1950s than it had been in the interwar years (Smith 2013: 156–157).

Republic and immigration

As apartheid legislation was implemented – regulating and excluding black labour and preventing the free movement and settlement of black South Africans, with an ultimate aim of removing South African citizenship from all black Africans – the need to increase the amount of skilled white labour increased. In 1958, the Viljoen Commission into South African industry reported that 25,000 immigrants were needed annually if economic growth were to be sustained. The government established the South African Immigration Organisation (Samorgan) to encourage and administer immigration, but its focus was on the Netherlands and Germany, not the United Kingdom (Peberdy 2009: 112–113). Decolonisation across Africa and a desire to prevent any reduction or compromise on apartheid legislation increased the pressures for a change in immigration policy, but it was the declaration as a republic and its exit from the Commonwealth in 1960 – which Prime Minister Dr H. F. Verwoerd felt were the seminal and triumphant moments in South Africa's history that lead to a profound change in government attitudes towards British immigrants. Verwoerd considered these the ultimate achievement of Afrikaner independence from British colonialism. Having largely removed English speakers from the ranks of the state bureaucracy and military, gerrymandered the electoral system, and effectively broken the United Party as a threat, the National Party was firmly entrenched in office.

Following becoming a Republic, Verwoerd believed that English-speaking whites could be assimilated with Afrikaners and that British immigrants no longer posed a national threat (Peberdy 2009: 110). Immigration was also now important because the South African economy was growing rapidly, with growth rates averaging 6% and 8% between 1964 and 1972 (Peberdy 2009: 114). If racial job reservation were to continue, white immigration was essential. The new (English-speaking) minister for immigration, A. E. Trollip, expressed the change in South African immigration policy clearly: 'The choice is simple: immigration or the disintegration of the South African economy' (cited Peberdy 2009: 114). In 1961, South Africa once again introduced a generous assisted passage scheme for immigration, but this time it was focused primarily on the recruitment of British immigrants.

In 1961, the South African government set an annual target of attracting 30,000 white immigrants a year. Immigration rose from 9,789 white people in 1960 to 48,048 people in 1966 (Peberdy 2009: 119). The assisted passage scheme paid approximately 80% of the travel costs, gave a large loan per immigrant (which in 1966 was replaced by a grant), guaranteed free accommodation for a limited period upon arrival and had no minimum residency requirements. These terms were more generous than Australia and Canada's assisted passage scheme at the time. In Stone's sample of British immigrants, 58% replied that the assisted passage scheme was a significant reason for choosing South Africa over other destinations (1973: 163). As well as the immigration office in South Africa House on Trafalgar Square in London, Samorgan opened immigration offices on Cockspur Street in London (in the same building as the 1820 Settlers Memorial Association offices) and in Manchester, Birmingham, Glasgow, Sheffield and Newcastle (IDAF 1975: 10). In 1965, the 1820 Settlers Memorial Association conducted a survey of the British immigrants it had assisted and concluded the primary factors for choosing South Africa were 'greater opportunities: the expectation of a better standard of living and a brighter future for children in a vigorous young country... with climate and taxation as highly important secondary considerations' (cited in Stone 1973: 141). In the years before the assisted passage scheme (1946–1961), 115,394 British emigrants settled in the country and at the height of white immigration (1961–1977) 243,000 British-born citizens settled there (RSA 1989:101). Between the 1960s and 1975, South Africa gained between 20,000 and 35,000 immigrants a year, which accounted for no less than 46% of white population growth (RSA 1989: 85). Of all white immigrant nationalities, British immigrants were consistently and by far the largest community, comprising between 45.6% and 30.2% of annual immigrant arrivals between 1946 and 1987. Similarly, the UK was also the leading destination for emigration between these years (RSA 1989: 101). British-born 'colonial refugees' from elsewhere in Africa and particularly from Rhodesia towards the end of the Rhodesian civil war and the transition to black majority rule and the construction of Zimbabwe resulted in the majority of the white Rhodesian population (many of whom were British-born citizens and all of whom were entitled to British citizenship) migrating to South Africa from the late 1970s (Frederickse 1986). However, despite the generosity of the scheme, and the efforts South Africa made to attract British migrants, of all the emigrants to leave the United Kingdom in 1964, only 5% went to South Africa, and this only rose to 10% in 1972. Of the two million emigrants who left the United Kingdom between 1964 and 1972, South Africa's share was 147,000 compared with Australia's 724,000 and Canada's 328,000 (IDAF 1975: 7); although for a short period in the early 1970s, South Africa overtook Australia and Canada (IDAF 1975: 7). This could be explained by the increasing instability and turmoil within South Africa, which had started to be reported in the media in the United Kingdom by the 1960s. Political events in South Africa such as the Soweto Uprising in 1976 and the declaration of successive States of Emergency from 1985 onwards were widely covered globally and contributed to net white emigration, particularly in 1977 and from 1986 onwards (RSA 1989: 98). With the fluctuations in white immigration and the South African state's growing vilification by the Western world, it became increasingly opportunistic, attracting Polish and Taiwanese who, as we discuss further below, were classified as 'white' (Frederikse 1986; Peberdy 2009: 125). Thus, as throughout its history, South Africa's attempts to attract British immigrants met with mixed success, and also continued to be beset by political controversy and broader official reluctance to allow mass immigration.

Shades of white immigrants

Race was an important qualification for entry, and although immigrants' whiteness was essential, the South African state continued to be vexed about the differences between 'appropriate' and 'inappropriate' white immigrants. Prospective immigrants had to confirm they were white in writing as well as providing a 'very clear' photograph of themselves; their race would then be confirmed in the initial interview conducted by immigration officials and when they arrived in South Africa (IDAF 1975: 2). Daniel's mother, travelling out on the Union Castle Line in 1970, remembers being told by one of the crew (presumably in jest) to beware of too much sunbathing, as 'They won't let you in if you are too dark!'

Despite the clear need to the state to encourage mass white immigration if apartheid governance were to be sustained, immigration policy remained both selective and a contentious political and social issue. As Peberdy notes, 'Although white immigration was desirable, individual white immigrants might not be' (2009: 34). Only those with technical, professional or managerial skills were eligible for the assisted passage grants; atheists were refused entry, as were communists, anyone with a criminal record and those who had had children outside of marriage (Peberdy 2009: 129; IDAF 1975: 3).

In 1967 and 1968, the rank and file of the National Party expressed their hostility to the government's immigration policy. Stone summarises many of the concerns expressed about 'immigrants acquiring key positions; whether they would become naturalised and, if so, whether they would vote for the National Party; whether they would associate themselves with the Afrikaans churches; and what measures were being taken to prohibit or reduce the entry of Roman Catholics' (1973: 28). In particular, alarm was expressed by the extent of immigration from southern Europe. This had been particularly significant from Portugal (and from its colonies of Angola and Mozambique) since the Second World War. Southern Europeans' Catholicism and their propensity to have darker skin, as opposed to Protestant and 'whiter' northern Europeans, were the primary focus of National Party activists' alarm. At the 1967 Transvaal National Party Congress, one delegate remarked 'Roman Catholics are an even bigger danger to us than the communists, because at least one can lock up a communist'; while another exclaimed, 'Coloured people cannot marry my daughter when she is 21, a Portuguese can!' (cited in IDAF 1975: 2). The minister for immigration restated the choice of encouraging white immigration or endangering job reservation and white rule, but in the same year, stricter controls were placed on immigrants from southern Europe. Applicants from Italy or Portugal with more than three children had to be referred to officials in Pretoria and, in certain periods, officers were told to refuse applications from Madeira and Cyprus (Peberdy 2009: 126; Stone 1973: 28).

As will be discussed in the following chapters, many of the British immigrants we spoke to recounted stories of the difficult encounters they had with Afrikaner culture and their sense of alienation and even discrimination from Afrikaans-speaking white people. The declaration of a republic and the triumph of the National Party had not entirely assuaged deeper social and political divisions about the British and English-speaking whites. Afrikaner nationalism could also not resolve the dilemma of the need to be a settler state in broad terms if white minority rule were to survive, and the religious and ethnic hostility to whites from other religions, cultures and linguistic groups.

The politics of migrating to South Africa

The politics of emigration to South Africa became increasingly apparent as the 1960s progressed. The Sharpeville massacre of 1960, where 69 black demonstrators were shot dead by the South African police, provoked international condemnation and forced South Africa's exit from the Commonwealth in 1961. In the United Kingdom, the Boycott Movement was founded in 1959 by a group of South African political exiles; this was renamed the Anti-Apartheid Movement in 1960. The Anti-Apartheid Movement held ongoing protests outside of South Africa House and focused on a number of issues, such as calling for economic sanctions against South Africa, ending sporting and academic links and boycotting the purchase of South African products and services (Gurney 2000; Klein 2007). By the early 1970s, the UK Labour Party conference and the National Union of Students had passed resolutions to call for restrictions and disincentives for British emigration to South Africa. The British Medical Association, Equity and the Trade Union Congress had taken steps to prevent the encouragement and assistance of emigration by their members to South Africa. In 1975, the International Defence Aid Fund for Southern Africa (IDAF – a London based anti-apartheid organisation) published a review of British emigration to South Africa and its role in sustaining apartheid. It concluded, 'Every white immigrant to South Africa is taking away a potential job from an African or other black person, and simultaneously reinforcing the numerical strength and the psychological and political dominance of the ruling white minority' (1975: 1).

Despite the growth in political activism and hostility towards apartheid in British society, the United Kingdom's diplomatic and trade relations with South Africa were essentially friendly. Furthermore, South Africa benefitted from the same generous exchange allowances as Dominion countries, which also aided emigration. The United Kingdom's strong trade relations with South Africa led to British (and South African) businesses fuelling emigration further by recruiting staff for their South African branches. Although certain organisations had publicly opposed and taken steps to prevent emigration, others, such as the Association of Commonwealth Universities and the professional associations of engineering, dental and architects, had links with their South African equivalents or continued to assist South African authorities in recruiting British migrants. The continuing presence of the British Council in South Africa also aided the sense that South Africa was part of a broader 'white way of life' and could therefore create the 'stimulus or opportunity to emigrate' (IDAF 1975: 13). As the International Defence Aid Fund wryly noted (and as we found in our research) the prominent position of South Africa House on Trafalgar Square and its close proximity to the High Commissions of Canada, Australia and New Zealand, attracted 'passersby' who could walk in, look at the promotional literature and decide to emigrate to South Africa 'almost by accident' (IDAF 1975: 61). The South African government, Samorgan and the 1820 Settlers Memorial Association all became increasingly opportunistic in recruiting British immigrants; for example, when the Hawker Siddeley aircraft factory in Plymouth announced redundancies, the South African Atlas Aircraft company sent a recruiting team to Plymouth. Specific teams were also sent to recruit engineers, bus drivers or post office employees (IDAF 1975: 12).

Given the complex socio-political dynamics in South Africa concerning British immigration, the country's appeal to potential British immigrants was different from other former British colonies that also sought British migrants. In the post-war era, the 'old Commonwealth' countries all vied for British immigrants. In the 1950s, while South Africa had effectively discouraged British migration, Australia and Canada considered mass migration from the United Kingdom as not only essential for economic growth, but as politically and socially important for their Anglo-Saxon nation-building project (Hammerton and Thomson 2005: Jupp 2004; Wills 2009; Wills 2005; Wills and Darian-Smith 2004). The Australian government's 'bring out a Briton' immigration campaign drew from the government's framing of Australian society as being essentially British in political, social and moral terms (Hammerton and Thomson 2005: 9; Wills and Darian-Smith 2004: 4; Wills 2004). British immigration was seen as constituting and securing Australian national identity and, like South Africa, the country operated a 'whites-only' immigration policy that was in force until 1970 (Jupp 2004: 150; Wills 2004: 351). The increasing evidence of 'return' migration, by approximately 40%, of British and other white immigrants provoked considerable concern and political debate in the country (Hammerton and Thomson 2005: 264, 275–282; Jupp 2004: 144–145). South Africa, by contrast, did not officially seek to present itself as 'essentially British', although certain organisations, such as the 1820 Settlers Memorial Association and certain regions of the country, such as Natal, did do this.[2] The 1820 Settlers Memorial Association, for example, sought to project an image of the country as a hospitable one for the British, and offer 'a more personal, unofficial interest' in assisting emigration as well as supporting newly arrived British immigrants integrate and settle once in the country (IDAF 1975: 11). The organisation offered social contacts with other white South Africans, specific women's groups to help avoid isolation and support with cooking 'new cuts of meat and vegetables', and discounts on return air travel to visit family and friends (IDAF 1975: 11). The association's publication, 'This is South Africa', began by stating that South Africa 'is known for its political and economic stability in a continent of continual change: it is unequivocally anti-communist in outlook and policy and as such is a bulwark of Western civilisation in Africa' (cited in IDAF 1975: 11). The Association's 'British' presentation of South Africa belied the ongoing political and social realities of the time, but its obscuring of apartheid and associated unrest and the representation of the country as Western, capitalist and 'civilized', was more in tune with the official appeals to immigrants. This familiar socio-political environment was the backdrop for the primary attraction of the country to British people, bolstered further by promises of wealth, leisure, good weather and personal fulfilment (IDAF 1975: 11)

South Africa was thus presented as a white, Western country where lifestyle aspirations could be fulfilled. According to an advertisement placed by South Africa House in *The Sun* newspaper in 1973, South Africa was a place 'where skilled men like you can and will find that elusive pot of gold ... high salaries, lower cost of living, good educational facilities for all, sports amenities, social life and the proverbial summer without end' (cited in IDAF 1973: 11). In 1971, Barclays Bank, which at that time was the largest bank in South Africa, published a guide for British people about emigrating and living in the republic. The Barclays guide's first sentence was 'South Africa probably has the highest annual average number of hours of sunshine in the world' (1971: 1). The description of South Africa's politics and society as a 'parliamentary democracy' (1971: 28) where job reservation was applied 'not only to keep wages stable but also to assist in creating separate non-white industries ... in order to build up non-white areas as separate economically viable units' (1971: 12) replicated exactly the National Party government's description of the country. The guide explained life for the 'average' white South African to its British readers:

'Most South Africans rise early, work hard from eight or eight-thirty to about five, spend their evenings more at home than out and play sport or relax in other ways at weekends. They frequently entertain at home, dine out and dance fairly often, read a fair amount and some of them go fishing, swimming and camping when they have the time. Drive-in cinemas are popular' (Barclays Bank 1971: 27).

These lifestyle appeals mirrored attempts by Rhodesia, South Africa's neighbour, to lure British immigrants with 'the promise of easy living and material gain in return for settlement' (Brownell 2008: 592). Essentially, South Africa offered white British settlers the lifestyle benefits of apartheid, such as increased wages, large houses, and domestic help, along with the physical and psychological benefits of endless sunshine in a large, spacious country, considered by many to be beautiful.

This picture of South Africa was increasingly contested as the 1970s progressed, however. An opponent of apartheid, the Reverend French-Beytagh, wrote in the *Evening Standard* that the 'other side of sunny South Africa' included violence, fear, the reality of compulsory military service for all white men, 'and last, but not least, its lack of television, bingo and other amusements enjoyed by the British public' [Television was only introduced to South Africa in 1975] (cited in IDAF 1973: 15). Furthermore the *'braaivleis* [barbecues], rugby, sunny skies and Chevrolet'[3] lifestyle that a South African advertisement expressed in the 1970s was only appealing should that socioeconomic situation be sustained. Political tensions and economic recession threatened to undermine the basic premises of apartheid South Africa's appeals to the British.

In Rhodesia, this is precisely what occurred. As Brownell notes, Rhodesia's white population was 'one of the most unstable and demographically fragile ruling ethnic castes in any polity anywhere in the world' (2008: 592), largely because white immigrants were primarily there for material and lifestyle gain and left when international isolation and civil war broke out. White emigration became a major factor in the Rhodesian regime's collapse (Brownell 2008; Mlambo 1998).

South Africa's ambivalence about immigrants, premised on its bifurcated ethnic and linguistic identity, along with its racist, authoritarian and increasingly militarised form of government, meant that an appeal to lifestyle and material gain was its most consistently articulated message during the 1960s until the 1980s. The growing international hostility towards the republic, the economic recession of the 1970s, and political and social chaos in the 1980s did much to undermine levels of immigration and encouraged outward emigration. Nevertheless, as Britain itself was also beset by economic recession, worker unrest and mixed reactions to immigration from the Commonwealth countries, British immigration formed the single largest proportion of inward migration across the period, and British people constituted a significant and noticeable part of white South African society.

Post-apartheid dynamics

Catherine sits on the balcony of her spacious home in Hermanus in the Western Cape. As she looks out to sea, sipping a glass of wine, she explains why she returned to the UK in 1985, after having lived in South Africa since the late 1960s:

> I was very, very concerned about the politics in this country. Very concerned. I had small children, and at that stage, I remember it so clearly, riots were going on and bits and pieces. And something came over the radio or the television, there's going to be – the state president is going to make an announcement or something. I said to John [Catherine's husband], 'There's going to be a State of Emergency',

and there was. I don't even know where I got it from, because I'm not particularly – I'm not politically canny, and I don't know where I sucked that from. I just had that feeling. And I thought, 'Whoa, if it was just me, that's fine, I'll fight my own battles and I'll take my own chances.' But things, you know, there had been riots, and my late husband had been almost caught up in a township because he was working in a township...And I just thought, for the children, this is not right. I don't have the right to subject them to this sort of danger. And it was dangerous.

Catherine wanted her children to be educated in the United Kingdom but never settled back to British life. She moved to France and then returned to South Africa in the 1990s. Catherine was far from alone in leaving South Africa in the 1980s because of concerns about the changing political situation and fears about the future. As discussed above, there was substantial net white emigration from 1986 onwards. From the early 1980s, European migration to the country had become increasingly on a temporary, rather than permanent, settlement basis. Changes to the Citizenship Act in 1984 compelled white immigrant males between the ages of 15 to 25 to register for compulsory military service in the South African Defence Force in return for citizenship; failure to register could lead to the cancellation of residency rights (Conway 2012: 76–79). A report by the European Parliament surmised that the Act itself led to an immediate 25% drop in immigration and a 20% increase in emigration (cited in Conway 2012: 85).

The transition from minority rule to non-racial democracy began in 1990 and culminated in full, non-racial, democratic elections in 1994. The transition process brought South Africa close to civil war, and both during and after it, a significant proportion of white South Africans have emigrated from the republic. Indeed, the South African Institute of Race Relations reported that the white population had shrunk by over 16% between 1995 and 2005, primarily because up to one million whites had emigrated since 1994 (SAIRR 2006). The United Kingdom has been the paramount destination for these migrants, because of the large British-born population and citizens entitled to British passports for ancestral reasons. The Commonwealth visa scheme (which was revoked in 2009) enabled South Africans under the age of 25 to spend two years working in the UK, which this was another means for population flows to exist between the two countries. South Africa's assisted passage scheme ended in 1991. In the same year, the Aliens Control Act replaced all previous immigration rules and rigidly defined terms of exclusion for prospective immigrants. In 2002, new regulations were introduced that 'have built higher and stronger barriers to entry for legal immigrants' (Peberdy 2009: 147). In theory, it is possible for migrants with 'exceptional skills' to immigrate to the country, but the rules and procedures are cumbersome (Peberdy 2009: 147).

Despite these barriers to migration, in 2011, the six leading non-African countries for issuing permanent residence visas for South Africa were China, India, Pakistan and UK (STATSA 2012a: 38). The UK had the fourth highest temporary residence permits issued (STATSA 2012a: 26), and South African tourism has consistently grown by 10% each year after 1994 (RSA 2008: 252). British visitors form the largest group of non-African tourists, constituting 21.5% of non-African visitors in 2008 (some 493,235 people) (RSA 2009). However, in the economic recession, British visitor numbers have fallen back to 438,023 in 2012 (17.5% of the total non-African visitors), while still remaining the largest national group outside of Africa (STATSA 2012b; STATSA 2013a).

Although the post-apartheid government has not encouraged British settlers as governments did in the past, South Africa's 'scarce skills visa' and especially its 'retirement visa' scheme have encouraged a new generation of British migrants to relocate to the Republic. The retirement visa allows for continuous residence in the republic for up to 48 months at a time and requires such migrants to demonstrate that they have a monthly income of R20,000 per month (which can include projected rental earnings from the retirees 'home' property). It is therefore relatively easy for middle-class British immigrants to acquire a retirement visa. South Africa is the seventh most popular destination for British retired emigrants (Finch et al. 2010: 37).

Further, the country's reintegration into the global economy after 1994 has deepened the presence of multinational companies in the republic, allowing for continued professional migration, particularly from the West (Leonard 2013; STATSA 2013a). However, the most significant migration flows into South Africa after 1994 have been from other sub-Saharan African countries: in particular, between one and five million Zimbabwean immigrants, both documented and undocumented (illegal) have come to South Africa in response to the political and economic turmoil in Zimbabwe (Adepoju 2002). The increased levels of pan-African migration have led to ongoing outbreaks of xenophobic violence in 1994, 1995 and most extensively in 2008, when 65 black African immigrants were killed (Peberdy 2009: 138; Crush 2008; Landau and Freemantle 2010; Neocosmos 2010). South Africa thus remains a country where immigration is defined in particular and exclusionary terms, and British immigrants exist in a dynamic and, at times, tense political and social context.

Conclusion

In 1973, John Stone wrote that a British immigrant in South Africa 'is not confronted by a solid host society in which he is immediately recognised as an outsider and a stranger; the most probable result of the internal cleavages within South African society is to ease the immigrant's entry and accelerate his integration. He is most likely to be regarded as a new recruit, a potential ally in an insecure environment' (Stone 1973: 29).

In the face of this bold claim, however, our review of the history of immigration to South Africa has shown the prospect, status and presence of British immigrants has always been politically controversial and potentially socially divisive. As Perberdy notes, immigration policy is central to state identity and nationhood: 'Who a state chooses to allow in – or keep out – is influenced by the way the state constructs and represents itself, the territory it controls and how it perceives the people who inhabit it' (2009: 20). Efforts to encourage mass settlement in South Africa by British people have never come to fruition because of these socio-political dynamics. Nevertheless, British immigrants were the most consistently significant group of white migrants for much of the twentieth century, and their presence became a key tenet of late apartheid governance. The post-apartheid era has seen significant emigration by the white community and a drop in numerical terms of British permanent settlement. Other forms of migration, such as tourism and retirement to South Africa, have significantly increased, however, and it has become a leading destination for British people in these terms. These categories are not mutually exclusive and tourism can lead to more permanent forms of migration, as we will demonstrate in the case studies to follow.

South Africa's re-admittance to the global economy after its late-apartheid isolation has led to a new flow of professional and labour migration to the country. Above all, and as the following chapter turns to discuss, British migrants' presence in South Africa has always formed a key dynamic in the socio-politics of South African nationhood. Although this presence no longer dominates debate and tensions around immigration and nationhood in contemporary South Africa, British residents' whiteness and their continuing existence in the country as permanent residents, businesspeople and tourists continue to inform the complexities of its social dynamics.

3
Transnational and Translocal Identities: Settling in South Africa

Steve came to South Africa in 1981. A working-class man from the northeast of England, he had completed his apprenticeship as a builder in the mid-1970s, at a time when the United Kingdom was in the depths of recession, and work was hard to find: 'And I just thought, "No! I've got to move on!"' Just as in the popular British TV series *Auf Wiedersehen, Pet!*, which featured a group of Geordie[1] brickies[2] who travel to Europe to find work, Steve migrated to Germany, then to Holland, and on to the Middle East in search of employment. After making a sum of money, he returned to the UK, and then received an invitation from an old workmate – 'in those days it was a telegram!' – that said, 'There's a job going in South Africa – do you fancy it?' He took the train down to London to take a 'skills test' and a medical exam, followed by a course 'you had to do in those days to get into South Africa', and 'two weeks later I was on the aeroplane!'

After a couple of nights in Johannesburg, Steve was sent on to Welkom, to a construction site 'in the middle of nowhere'. 'Next thing I know I'm the foreman, [then] I'm the general foreman...' He met a local girl, an Italian whose parents came out in the 1950s; they married and later moved to Johannesburg, where Steve is now a wealthy man, owning an extremely profitable construction business that builds large houses in the northern suburbs.

Jill and John have lived in the suburbs of Pietermaritzburg for just five years. Now in their late 60s, they have not been married long: both had been through divorces, and John particularly had lost a lot of money as a result. He was also 'totally fed up with the Labour government', so they made plans to move to France, where John's sister lived. Over a cup of tea in their living room, John explains: 'So we bought some [French language] tapes, and I listened and I listened and I listened...and I thought...this isn't going to happen! I haven't got an ear, you see, for language!' John's son was married to a white South African woman, and they had settled near her family. John says, 'I was talking to my son, and he said "Come to South Africa!"' John rationalises this as an economic decision: borrowing money in the UK was expensive with interest rates in the UK at 10% or more. 'Now the only problem we have is getting the Department of...what do they call it?' Jill interjects: 'Home Affairs!' 'Home Affairs...to pull their finger out and give us our Permanent Residence!'

Jill and John now live in a small close with several other British couples nearby. They run in and out of each other's gardens for chats and cups of tea, and Pauline's visit has obviously been the subject of some excitement – they all want to be interviewed and talk about 'Great Britain'.

Lottie, in her late 20s, has lived in Johannesburg for only eighteen months. She arrives slightly flustered to meet Pauline, explaining she had just come out of hospital but so much wanted to do the interview that she had come straight to Mandela Square rather than go home. She tells the story of how she came out with her husband, a banker: 'I had just finished having my kitchen all redone, and this job came up!' They decided to take it as 'it's a bit boring being in London all our lives!' Lottie had had to give up her job as a nurse, and now doesn't work: 'I'd probably have to do some more training, as they do things differently here...also I'm not local, and you've got all the whole BEE [Black Economic Empowerment] thing as well!' She arrived knowing nobody, although she had been given two phone numbers by friends in the UK, 'and they literally were my lifelines! They were brilliant, they were really good actually!'

Lottie has slowly started to adjust although, as she explains, she leads a rather lonely life in her luxurious house in a gated community in the northern suburbs. She suffers from occasional bouts of homesickness: 'I had one meltdown last year – nothing was working, the Internet connection had gone down. I said, "Nothing in this country works!"' However mostly she thinks, 'Well, get on with it and see the country, and obviously for him it's fine, because work's work, in a way!'

Rose and her partner Robert have lived in Johannesburg for five years, although Robert had previously lived in the Eastern Cape for nine years during the 1980s, working as an engineer on a range of infrastructure projects. As Rose drives Pauline round the northern suburbs of Johannesburg, showing her where she lives and shops – Four Ways, Bryanston and out towards Randburg – she is quite clear: she did not want to come to South Africa, and she does not want to be here now. She had a great job in London, and she and Robert were renovating a house there. In addition, she had not only been recovering from a serious illness herself but was also nursing her elderly mother. All in all, she felt she had a lot to lose through migration. However, Robert had been made an offer he felt he could not refuse: to head up the South Africa branch of a major multinational corporation. This was a big career step for Robert, who had been chosen because of his knowledge of the region. Rose therefore reluctantly agreed that they would move and is now making the best she can of their new lives. She does voluntary work in a nursery in a township just outside Johannesburg and also works hard fundraising for the nursery through Robert's company because, as she explains, 'It's important that we don't just take – we must put something back as well.' Rose and Robert come back to the UK frequently – sometimes as often as once a month. Getting a dog in Johannesburg has been an important way of becoming more settled there and trying to turn their house into 'home'.

Norman and his South African wife June came to see Pauline in her office at Southampton University. They were back in the UK for one of their regular stints in a nearby coastal city where they own a flat in which they stay for several months each year. Having seen our article in the *Telegraph Online*, Norman very much wanted to 'put us straight' about what is 'really happening' in South Africa. Now in his 70s, Norman had been a management consultant who was headhunted for a senior position in a major South African business in the 1970s. As he explains, 'So my reason for going to South Africa was purely and simply monetary-like!' Later, with June's help, he diversified into farming and horse breeding, but continued to return to the UK regularly, especially once his grown-up son decided that England was where he wished to settle. Norman is now getting to the point where he thinks he may come back for good, because 'when an Englishman – my family are multi- generations, you know – gets to an age, you think you should die in your own country'.

> What defines migrants is that most are looking for a place to stop and settle down, at least for a while. (King 2012: 136)

These stories, a small selection of the rich range of migration biographies we collected about South Africa, show how movement from one place to another, whether for a long-term change of permanent residence, a short-term contract, or retirement, may be instigated by a multiple and contingent range of factors. Lack of employment opportunities or insufficient income within the home context, better work opportunities or the chance to make more money in the destination context, family connections, or a holiday romance with either the people or the landscape of South Africa are, as we will show, just a few of the many drivers we found. Further, the stories also reveal the diverse and complex impact movement has on the migrant, affecting identity, the body, emotions and the senses as well as social, spatial and temporal relations and practices. Given the destabilisation caused by displacement, why do people migrate in the first place? Questions about the causes of *mobility* are clearly of considerable academic interest, and ones we explore in this book. However, questions of *stability* are equally important: how do people manage the more unsettling experiences of mobility after dislocation?

As our stories show, these questions are not only of interest in terms of those at the top and bottom of global social structures, where most of the academic literature has traditionally been focussed (Clarke 2005): either on studies of globe-trotting chief executives (e.g., Ong 1999; Mickelthwait and Wooldridge 2001; Sklair 2010) or developing world 'immigrants' (e.g. Levitt 2001; King et al. 2005). As Conradson and Latham point out, there are also highly significant forms of 'middling' migration: middle-class professionals, middle-aged lifestyle-shifters, gap-year travellers, older retirees – people who might be 'privileged' in that they are predominantly well educated and comfortably off, but who are, nonetheless, 'very much of the middle' (2005: 229). In recent years, considering migration in terms of 'the middle' has contributed to the ongoing development of a rich body of research that aims to challenge the conceptualisation of 'privileged migration' as an elite and ubiquitously advantaged 'transnationalist capitalist class' (Sklair 2001; Amit 2011). The narrative of a hyper-mobile professional group that travels the world, disembedded from place and any grounded sense of belonging, has thus been confronted with the recognition that migration needs to be 'increasingly sensitive to the diversity of individual experiences in different times and different places' (Graham 2000: 268). Taking a more nuanced and intersectional approach helps to reveal not only the 'ordinariness' of many transnational activities but also the emplaced and embodied nature of much transnational movement. Together with the developing 'cultural turn' in migration studies (Blunt 2007), this literature has helped to shift interest from a macrolevel economic and demographic lens towards the cultural and spatial processes involved in displacement and emplacement at the micro-level of individuals, families and communities positioned at different points within broader social structures.

The research in this book situates itself within this contemporary literature on 'middling' privileged migration, transnationalism, space and place. As stated above, we are interested first, in why British people have migrated to South Africa, a country that, as we have shown in Chapter 2, has long occupied a somewhat ambivalent and complex position within British social and political imaginings. Given that South Africa is not such a clear and unambiguous 'lifestyle' choice as, for example, France, Spain or Florida (Sriskandarajah and Drew 2006; Benson and O'Reilly 2009a), nor, for a significant part of its recent political and economic history, a global centre of transnational business activity attracting significant numbers of highly skilled international migrants such as New York, Hong Kong or Geneva, (Beaverstock 2002; Sassen 2002), what are the causes of British migration there? Our argument here is that British migration to South Africa serves to complicate dominant understandings of privileged migration, wherein migrants are conceptualised as purposeful agents for whom migration is an integral part of an individual's reflexive project of the self (Giddens 1991; Oliver and O'Reilly 2010). As we explain in this chapter, we conceptualise British migration to South Africa as more complex, often resulting from a multiplicity of causes that conjoin to bring British subjects to South Africa. For many of our respondents, it appeared that the event may very easily not have happened at all, or that it may have happened in a different way if conditions had been slightly different (Foucault 1972). However, while migration stories may be framed through a highly differentiated range of sub-discourses, we also recognise that these operate within the overarching and powerful, yet often silenced, discourse of white British entitlement to migrate (Foucault 1980). Due to their possession of both embodied and objectified capital, these migrants had a range of privileged options and, if one did not quite work out, they could simply default to another (Bourdieu 1986).

Second, we are keen to explore how British migrants comport themselves after migration and during settlement to achieve some sort of stability and sense of belonging. Integral to our approach here will be an engagement with the corporeal materialities of migration: in other words, we see that it is in the ways in which people conduct and construct their everyday lives that the social politics of identity-, home- and citizenship-making are achieved. Incorporated into the mundane routines, daily journeys and everyday interactions that constitute migratory lifeworlds are differences that span nationality/regionality, race and ethnicity, gender, class and age. The ways these differences are then negotiated, embodied and grounded lead to the construction and performance of identities, social relations, senses of belonging and citizenship with and within the new migratory context (Knowles 2003). As we go on to explain, our approach here is inspired by recent developments in transnationalism and translocalism, which focus on the ways migrants' lives and experiences are forged through the interconnected spaces of their biographies (Basch et al. 1994).

While these concerns have been explored within the broader migration literature in a wide range of locations and contexts, in studies of privileged migration, particularly those of the British abroad, there has been a tendency to narrow the focus to consider (often separately) issues of nationality, gender, class and age (e.g., King et al. 2000; O'Reilly 2000; Oliver and O'Reilly 2010; Benson 2011; Coles and Fechter 2008). Issues of race and racism are often downplayed, perceived as either irrelevant or immaterial, and 'whiteness' and its place in the making of identity and difference has received even less attention (Leonard 2010; Fechter and Walsh 2012). In O'Reilly's study of the British in Spain, she observed that in all her time in her field, she 'never once heard the terms race, racism or racist used by the British towards the Spanish' (2000: 101).

This could not be further from the case in the distinctive and complex context of South Africa. We both talked to respondents who spoke of little else. For this reason, the theoretical framework adopted in this book must take race and race-making into account, as well as the connections between whiteness and racism (Back and Solomos 2000). To this end, we also bring to our analysis insights and approaches from race and ethnic studies, and the ways that race intersects with gender and whiteness studies.

Coming to South Africa

Ruth, now retired and in her early 70s, came to South Africa in 1969. Working as a secretary in Geneva, she had found her social life somewhat lacking and thought she 'would explore a bit... so I got a visa to the States... and then got cold feet!' On holiday in Europe, she met a South African man and, as she explains to Pauline, 'to a large extent, it was romance that brought me here'. However, she also had some school friends working in Cape Town 'because a lot of British people of my age were travelling at the same time... the world was our oyster you would say!' An aunt who was living in, as it was then, Salisbury, Rhodesia (now Harare, Zimbabwe) also encouraged her to come, so, 'quite suddenly, because there was romance involved, I decided to come, come to South Africa! My parents were horrified!' Although she herself was largely ignorant of South African politics, her father knew the situation rather better and was very much against her move. However, as we discussed in Chapter 2, the 'assisted passage' scheme of the 1960s was available to Ruth and as such her application for subsidised immigration was not only immediately accepted but accompanied by substantial additional attractions: 'A certain amount of luggage, they helped me find work, they helped me find accommodation – this is the South African government, of course – and paid for me to have Afrikaans lessons. In those days, for English-speaking people, I was a secretary, jobs were very easy to find.'

Paul is in his early 40s and works in IT. In 1998, five years after leaving university, he was 'getting a little bit tired of London...bit claustrophobic and just so many people!' One of his colleagues at work, a South African, decided to return to Johannesburg to start up a branch office of the company they both worked for. One day 'he sent me an email and asked me if I wanted to come over'. At first, he was 'very sceptical....South Africa didn't have the greatest reputation...Johannesburg didn't have the greatest reputation!' In the end, he decided 'Oh! I'll give it a year to see what it's like.' His flight paid for, he went to visit the offices in Johannesburg's 'CBD' (Central Business District). As we will describe more fully in the next chapter there was a great deal of 'white flight' from this area in the 1980s and 1990s, as businesses migrated to the newer attractions of Randburg and Sandton. Paul remembers, 'I think my first sight was looking out of the window, and there was a riot going on in the street. They were the times when the school kids were rioting because they didn't have any textbooks. The textbooks hadn't been delivered to the schools, so they were running through the streets....'

Seeing that the induction wasn't going too well, Paul's colleague 'sent me off to Cape Town for a week!' Eventually, although very confused – 'I wasn't sure what to do!' – he decided to 'give it a go...it was only for a year!' 12 years later, he still lives in Johannesburg, with a South African wife and two young children. 'There we go,' he says. 'Married, settled down, loving it! So, I think...the best thing I've ever done in my life!'

Karl made time in his busy schedule to meet Daniel for coffee in Cape Town's Rhodes Mandela Place, a newly built upmarket complex including a luxury hotel, executive apartments and offices. It was an apt location to meet because Karl has played a significant role in developing and selling such developments, and he was keen to emphasise his role in gentrifying Cape Town's city centre over the past decade. This was not an achievement Karl could have foreseen when he first visited the city while on holiday for two weeks in 1999. Karl had lived in London for seven years and enjoyed his life there as a young professional: 'It was the first time I'd really travelled any distance; I hadn't really travelled much at all', but he 'fell in love with Cape Town' and booked another holiday for six weeks later as soon as he returned. Over the next three years, every holiday was spent in Cape Town: 'I came backwards and forwards, backwards and forwards... just to sit on the beach and kind of be a tourist.' Karl bought a small studio apartment in the Gardens suburb at the foot of Table Mountain and started to ponder a permanent move to South Africa. 'It wasn't an easy, quick decision to make,' he recalled. 'It was a gradual realisation that it was possible to take a risk, and the risk I took was to quit London and literally to resign from a perfectly good senior management post in the National Health Service.' Karl sold his flat in London and 'literally left everything behind and got on a plane with a couple of suitcases'. He bought a house and set about renovating it into a guesthouse, but things didn't go to plan, 'probably because I hadn't kind of put too much thought into it', he explained, 'but it was also fun'. He saw an advert to become an estate agent, applied, and within two years had been headhunted to help establish his current company and, with Cape Town's buoyant property market, things quickly took off.

Barry had nearly finished apprenticeship to be a boilermaker, and his wife Jane was a hairdresser in the northeast of England. As with many couples in the 1960s, they were attracted by the generous emigration schemes offered by former British Dominions and wanted 'a better future' for themselves and any children they might have. Some of Barry's friends on the apprenticeship had gone to Canada so, as he explained, 'Canada was really the first option.' However, he started to have doubts after 'listening to and getting photographs back from Canada and watching my mates dig themselves out of two foot of snow and stuff didn't really appeal to me either. So I think that's what swayed the decision to come out to Africa.'

Barry's brother lived and worked in Rhodesia, but it was actually the South African Immigration Organisation (Samorgan) that successfully tempted Barry with free passage, a settlement grant and a permanent job in an iron and steel works in Pretoria. When Barry's brother found out, 'he wasn't too happy about it' and warned Barry that Pretoria was predominantly Afrikaans-speaking, and 'he didn't think it was going to help us settle to be put into that situation.' So Barry and Jane spoke to Samorgan, and with the additional help of Barry's brother, Barry found a job in an iron and steel works in Benoni, outside Johannesburg. Having never boarded an aeroplane or a ship, they took one look at the 'tiny' cabin Barry's brother and sister-in-law had booked on their Union Castle line voyage to South Africa and opted for the 22-hour journey by aeroplane instead.

Barry and Jane now live close to their two children and their families in Cape Town. Life has not always been easy for them, and in recent years there have been financial, as well as personal, problems. Yet as they prepared a braai (barbecue) for Daniel, they insisted South Africa had been 'good to us'.

Susan, in her 70s, sat in the shaded heat of her garden in a gated community outside of Cape Town and reflected on her decision to move to South Africa back in 1964. Susan had returned to the United Kingdom after spending four years living with her sister in what was then Nyasaland (now Malawi). She recalled sharing a flat in London with a group of friends: 'It was January and, well, we were actually thinking of going to Australia because we had a friend – one of our flatmates was living in Australia, and she had been talking, you know, about Australia and the idea of the sunshine and all this sort of thing.' Susan went to Australia House to take up the 'ten pound Pom'[3] emigration scheme. To her dismay, there was an 18-month waiting list. 'So then we then we said, "Well, what about South Africa?" So I said, "Yeah, that also appeals to me."' Susan walked the short distance along the Strand from Australia House to South Africa House and was told 'we could have gone, literally, straight away'. Susan laughed as she recalled this whimsical decision, and when asked by her employer in London what she planned to do in South Africa, she replied 'I really don't know.' Fortunately, they offered to transfer her job as a cosmetic sales representative to their South African office. The plan was to stay a couple of years and return, or travel onto Hong Kong, where Susan's cousin lived. When the time came, Susan booked her return passage on the Union Castle line, but she met a fellow British expatriate in the final weeks, fell in love, cancelled the return, and eventually married and started a family in Johannesburg.

Stories of wishes, whims, accidents, indecisions, changes of mind and even reluctance as migrations were 'forced' by partners' career moves pepper our respondents' accounts of why and how they came to be in South Africa. For the white British, it would seem South Africa is not always a first choice, its attractions interplaying with ambivalence, ignorance, suspicion and even antagonism. In this ambiguity as a destination of privileged migration, South Africa thus brings a challenge to the literature on the subject, much of which emphasises strategic and judicious decision-making. Many migrants to, for example, Spain, France, Singapore or Jakarta and so forth are clearly able to rationalise why they migrated (e.g. Oliver and O'Reilly 2010; Benson 2011; Beaverstock 2001; Fechter 2007), although, as O'Reilly correctly observes, 'we must not forget that these are often simply no more than post hoc justifications, constructed from the perspective of the new context within which they have found themselves' (2000: 28). In many of these narratives however, lifestyle reasons or career decisions are logically deconstructed to describe how the 'choice' for migration was made. Affluent migrants, it is therefore argued, are highly reflexive; effective students of the liquid modern condition, they do their research well in order to pursue, and hopefully achieve, their individualistic aspirations of 'happiness' (Giddens 1991; Beck and Beck-Gernsheim 2002; Bauman 2008; Benson and O'Reilly 2009a). But to what extent do these arguments, which extend across both lifestyle and labour migration, hold water in the South African context?

Lifestyle migration

That movement may be in search of contentment has been a particular recognition of the study of 'lifestyle migration', a category that encompasses various forms of purposeful migration from or within the developed world, but unites these in the understanding that they are all in search of a better and more fulfilling way of life (Benson and O'Reilly 2009a). Whether this is seen to exist in the touristic appeal of the coast, the 'rural idyll' of its hinterland, or in places that are seen to enable an 'alternative' lifestyle (Waldren 1996; Bousiou 2008; Benson and O'Reilly 2009b), lifestyle migrants tend to have a negative view of their own country and, often, an imagined and/or romanticised view of their chosen destination (Nudrali and O'Reilly 2009). For example, in O'Reilly's groundbreaking study of the British in Spain (2000), the United Kingdom's 'bad' features – weather, crime, pressure of urban life, routine dullness, poor education facilities and lack of community and care, as well as personal factors such as unemployment and redundancy, ill health and concerns for a pleasant old age – are all variously drawn upon as explanatory factors pushing the exit. Similarly, Spain is discursively constructed as 'good': having a more preferable climate and pace of life, offering the promise of better health and wellbeing, and crime-free, cheap, fun and anonymous – all are presented as strong 'pull factors' attracting a mixture of British middle and working classes to make the shift to move there. In Benson's (2011) anthropology of middle-class British residents in the Lot district of France, its appeal as a region of counter-urbanisation is revealed as a clear and dominant motivation. These are people looking for 'a better way of life' and, usually as a result of their holiday experiences as tourists, the rural charms of the French countryside, the beauty of the Lot landscape and a desire to be part of the local community are all imagined as offering a clear path to a more fulfilling and 'authentic' way of life. In contrast, but in common with O'Reilly's findings, Britain is positioned as being 'not what it was': high crime rates, the threatening behaviour of young people, failing health care, difficult and competitive working conditions, the absence of community, and a poor environment for children all add up to a conceptualisation of migration as a remedy for an unsatisfactory present and an unpromising future (Benson 2011).

For some, such as our respondent Ruth, the concept of 'lifestyle migration' did have some traction, interplaying with 'romantic migration'. While still in the pursuit of happiness (Bauman 2008), at least at first, romantic migration is often more accidental and spontaneous than many of the strategic plans outlined by downshifters, sun worshippers and rural idyll seekers. Further, as Trundle (2009) argues, this form of migration is almost by definition an unstable category, likely to be transformed either by marriage/long term partnership or by the end of the relationship. This indeed was the case for Ruth, whose relationship with the man who first drew her to South Africa did not last long. Rather than return to the UK, however, she decided to move to Johannesburg to find work, eventually becoming a successful businesswoman. In time, she also met another man, this time British like herself, and the two have now been married for over 30 years. Ruth's 'category jumps' (Dunn 2010: 4) from 'romantic migrant' to 'labour migrant' to 'marriage migrant' to 'retirement migrant' reveal how migration is itself an ongoing and constantly shifting process of identity-making over the life course.

Labour migration

Privileged migration also includes labour migration: 'mobile professionals' who are also understood to move abroad purposefully, in search of improved career prospects or personal professional development, or simply to satisfy the demands of employers (Leonard 2010; Fechter and

Walsh 2012). While once dominated by conceptualisations of a 'cosmocrat' ruling elite – a 'transnational capitalist class' (Sklair 2001) located at the top of the global hierarchy consisting of 'corporate executives, globalising bureaucrats, creative knowledge workers, politicians and professionals' (Leonard 2010: 7) – recent analyses recognise that most skilled labour migrants do not occupy such elevated socioeconomic positions (Amit 2011; Fechter and Walsh 2012). In fact, much global movement is not conducted by either the very affluent or indeed the very poor and, as such, to concentrate on those people who are seen to travel the world indulging in affluent lifestyles within a densely networked set is to belie the diverse yet broadly middle-class nature of most skilled migration (King 2012). As such there has been a growing interest in 'middling' labour migration and the 'banal' and everyday nature of their transnational engagements (Ley 2004; Conradson and Latham 2005). In common with the lifestyle literature, this research is also underpinned by assumptions of individualisation (Beck and Beck-Gernsheim 2002; Bauman 2005), with skilled migrants conceptualised as highly reflexive workers with multiple and global options in search of what is best 'for me' (Atkinson 2010: 414). However, this literature further reveals how, as technologies have changed, so have the forms of skilled migration. While at one time migration was for the whole of a career, especially for administrators, managers and other workers in the former colonies (Callan and Ardener 1984; Bickers 2010; Coles and Fechter 2008), increasingly, mobile professionals are younger people who move for shorter periods. Located on the lower rungs of the career ladder, a spell abroad is often viewed as a potentially important ingredient for personal development, knowledge accumulation and promotion prospects (Beaverstock 2002).

Privileged labour migration, like lifestyle migration, may also therefore be a key part of 'the project of the self' (Giddens 1991). For example, in his study of highly skilled inter-company transferees, Beaverstock (2005) found that while all viewed their transnational experience as highly beneficial to their career path trajectories, both with respect to promotion within the firm, and as regards intellectual and social capital accumulated through interaction within the business community, certain destinations such as New York were 'prized' and as such an intrinsic part of career planning. Nowicka (2006) describes the mobilities of the transnational professionals in her study of an international organisation as 'life projects': travel is perceived as a 'tool' for achieving better results and satisfaction from work, perhaps by taking on a new assignment or personal development opportunities, as well as often a means for getting a job done more effectively by being 'on the ground' in the country where the work is. More relevantly, longer term assignments 'are coupled with general life planning and discussed' (Nowicka 2008: 107), such that career decisions interplay with personal reasons such as enabling the family to experience another culture or enjoy better educational facilities. Fechter (2008) demonstrates how gender may be a further important component here. She describes an emerging group of 'expat girls': young career women working in fields such as international education and development, as well as accounting, marketing, management or IT, who have very actively sought employment overseas. 'The fact that she lives abroad is more important to her than the particular country where she is stationed for a while' (Fechter 2008: 193), as international experience is seen as an important career asset, as well as providing an enjoyable and meaningful lifestyle. Critical to this motivation is the desire to 'do good'; 'to make a positive impact on their host society' (Fechter 2008: 199). 'Expat' men, in contrast, were seen by the women as being chiefly motivated by making as much money in a short a time as possible. Yet our stories of British migrants to South Africa challenge the literature on privileged migration in two key ways: first, in terms of the place of 'strategy' in decision-making processes, and second, in terms of the dominant motivations and practices which are seen to frame migration.

A strategic decision?

The extracts at the start of this section illustrate that, for British migrants to South Africa, just as noticeable as the repertoires of exhaustive planning and careful deliberation that characterise privileged migration are those of serendipity and contingency. For many we talked to, South Africa is framed as where they 'ended up' rather than a symbol of initial desire; a feature which was also highlighted by the International Defence and Aid Fund's (IDAF) assessment of British migration in the 1970s which we discussed in Chapter 2. However, and as we also demonstrated in Chapter 2, this is certainly not to argue that migration to South Africa for the white British was, or is, a mere accident of history. Rather, it is to recognise, as Foucault argued, that while notions of 'chance, discontinuity and materiality' (1972: 231) characterise historical events, these are simultaneously framed by discourses, power relations and social structures within which individuals are both positioned and can position themselves. In the context of British migration, the (silenced) structuring discourses of white/national privilege and entitlement that have long governed global migration policies have enabled migration possible to a broad range of destinations by (white) British subjects. This group of migrants are, in Foucauldian terms 'instances of a type' (Hoy 1991: 47): in this case, white, British and highly mobile. Further, as Bourdieu argued, their narratives demonstrate that it is not always the case that what people *think* is the 'true explanation' of an action that tells the whole story, since individual intention is never a unique cause or motive (Callewaert 2006). Thus while themes of spontaneity, accidents, U-turns and leaps in the dark are drawn upon by our respondents' to construct their migration stories, this assumed serendipity is in fact, *'faux'* (Atkinson 2010): characteristic of the broader 'ignorance contract' that white people sign up to (Steyn 2012). In fact, this group of migrants possess particular forms of objectified and embodied capital that offer them 'fields of possibilities' (Atkinson 2010: 416), meaning that raced opportunity *masquerades* as accident or adventure. Skills, work colleagues, friends and relations, money in the bank, houses ready to be sold, even the South African Immigration Organisation 'Samorgan': all of these taken for granted and unacknowledged factors are forms of objectified capital that enabled Ruth, Paul, Barry, Susan, Rose and all our other respondents to migrate. Also important is the role of embodied capital, which includes the disposition towards migration as a possible opportunity, and the ability to 'fit in' to a white settler society with strong connections with Britain. In the 1960s, 1970s and 1980s in particular, it was of course the material possession of bodies with European ancestry and phenotype that gained white British people of all class backgrounds access to South Africa in the first place (Andruki 2010). As Andruki goes on to argue,

> 'transnational mobility is not incidental to, or an epiphenomenon of, whiteness in South Africa, but is immanent in it. In the contemporary period the formulation of whiteness as a "passport of privilege" (Kalra et al. 2005) cannot only stand abstractly for the transcendent power consistently bestowed on and associated with whiteness across the globe, but must also be stretched to indicate the emergence of whiteness as a congeries of bodies characterised by their capacity to move across borders, and how this is linked both to earlier histories of movement and the current globalising era'. (2010: 360)

For some, this was acknowledged in their accounts, while for many others it remains a tacit aspect of the migratory habitus. However, as Steyn (2012) argues, this 'ignorance' of the white entitlement to mobility, an opportunity that is often not available to racialised others, is in fact a social accomplishment. It is based on an epistemology that involves 'misrepresentation, evasion and self-deception on matters related to race' (Mills 1997: 19). As Charles W. Mills adroitly puts it, there is some irony in the outcome 'that whites will in general be unable to understand the world they themselves have made' (1997: 18).

However, while stories of 'faux' serendipity or impulsiveness dominate our respondents' 'arrival stories', we did encounter several people for whom coming to South Africa was very much a part of an individualistic and strategic project in pursuit of the 'good life', improved career prospects, or a mixture of both. We will explore their stories more fully in the following chapters, but important features of their narratives are the distinctive pleasures that South Africa are seen to offer. Like the British migrants in Benson's (2011) study of the Lot, France, these migrants in the stories of their migration draw on the touristic constructions of the country: its beautiful landscape, wonderful climate and outdoors lifestyle, its animals, food and wine. For example, Moira and Ted, now in their late 60s, own their own small game reserve outside Johannesburg. Their patch of 75 hectares abuts land put to similar use by their group of like-minded neighbours: 'We've managed to persuade other people to join in, take their fences down,' Ted says. The reserve is well-stocked with zebra, giraffe, wildebeest and buck: the fulfilment of a childhood dream for Moira. As Pauline bounces along in the back of their Land Rover, clinging on desperately as it lurches over tree roots and rutted, unmade tracks, Moira shouts over the noise of the engine: 'Can I tell you something? When I was nine or ten, there was a programme on the television – I mean television was very new then, I can't even remember what it was called now, but it was about a game farm.[4] I think it must have been in Kenya, and I saw that. And then I wanted to live on a game farm!'

Moira recognises how unlikely this dream was: 'I was southeast London, in a place called Sidcup,[5] you know a kid from Sidcup! It's impossible if you think about it, absolutely impossible! And okay, it kept surfacing throughout my life "Oh! Wouldn't it be nice!"...but you've got to earn your money, you've got to have a job!'

Moira recalls the moment when, in her 30s, she was offered a job in South Africa. Married then to her first husband she remembers, 'I had to look my husband straight in the eye and say, "I've got a job." And he said, I'll never forget it, "If it's in the north of England, I'm not coming with you!" And I said, "It's in South Africa!" and he said, "I'm coming with you!"'

While it was still many years before Moira finally realised her dream of owning her own game farm, migration was an exciting first step in that direction. At the same time, however, Moira denies that this was strategic:

> Absolute chance – there was nothing strategic about it whatsoever. I'm not a strategic person, I hate to tell you. To give you an example, well, to give you some idea I'm actually the sort of, and I was all through my school career, I was the sort of girl that sat at the back of the class with the arms folded, staring out of the window. I think that's as far as my strategy went. Terrible to have to admit, and it was chance.

In contrast, other respondents recognised that they had been highly strategic in the way they planned their migration. For example, Victoria, whom Pauline interviewed in a London pub in 2011, had migrated to Johannesburg in 2005. Single, upper-middle-class and in her early 40s, Victoria had first lived in South Africa as a child, migrating from Britain with her family when she was ten and living in Kwazulu-Natal until she left in her late teens to come to London, like many other young white people from the Commonwealth (Conradson and Latham 2005). She ended up staying longer in the UK than she had planned, but 'for 20 years, I literally always had this longing to go to South Africa, longing! I went back 17 times in 20 years!' Working in public relations, South Africa's developing international business scene post-1994 seemed to promise her exciting opportunities in spite of its changing local employment policies. However, while it was 'probably the only country in the world that I could work without having visa issues!', Victoria recognised that the move demanded careful planning and negotiation:

> I thought, 'I must go, because I really want to go because I love it, so let me go there,' but I hadn't really thought it through. So from that time I said, 'Right, I'm going to give myself a year' – so I sold my flat and bought a bigger one so I could rent it out for more money. I got all my ducks in a row in terms of business…then I said, 'That's it, I'm going. I'm going.' And I was filled with this enormous sense of excitement: from the word 'go', there was nothing that stood in my way.

She started by going on a visit to reconnoitre the opportunities and 'filled it full of meetings with people in the industry that I wanted to see'. Her strong translocal connections in Johannesburg were clearly to be put to good use:

> 'On my "reccy trip" I met this one chap who was the general manager of a big insurance company. He signed this business card and said,

"Year end party!" So then when I got to South Africa, I literally had emailed him a week before I was flying saying, "I'm arriving, and I need to come and see you." And he said, "Absolutely brilliant!"'

For many of our life-style shifters, coming to South Africa in an attempt to better the quality of life was a step made upon retirement, once the fetters of work in the UK were shed (Oliver 2008). Clearly this is part of the larger trend of residential mobility for Westerners in older age, instigated by radical improvements in older people's incomes and assets as well as through major transformations in older people's preferences and opportunities (King et al. 2000). While there is an increasing 'taste' for retiring overseas, southern Europe is the most popular destination for British people, often as a result of their holidays there (King et al. 2000; O'Reilly 2000; Oliver 2008). Two types of destination are popular: either 'sunny coastal locations or rural areas which are attractive havens of tranquillity or valued cultural landscapes' (King et al. 2000: 92). In an effort to feel 'less old' (O'Reilly 2000), older Britons tend to migrate to find 'warmth, good health, enjoyment, company and friendship' (Oliver 2008: 1). But it is not only the fact that there are communities of other older British expatriates ready and waiting in many of these destinations which draws new migrants by making the decision, on the face of it, less risky (O'Reilly 2000). In contrast, many retirees are looking for the opportunity to join a new, often idealised local community, which is emblematic of what they feel has disappeared in the United Kingdom (Oliver 2008; Benson 2011). This community is imagined as closely knit, caring, and safe – such that doors can remain unlocked, and neighbours will know if you are ill.

In addition to the geographical and social drivers, there are economic ones: the cost of living is lower in southern Europe and so, in spite of the anti-materialist rhetoric that is commonly drawn upon by migrants in their explanations of migration, this is often at root a consumption-led migration to improve material conditions (Oliver and O'Reilly 2007).

Yet while the economic motivation is one that appeals to both the working-class and middle-class British, clear social fissures are revealed to appear within British communities in European contexts. Oliver and O'Reilly noticed how 'distinction' was forged through class contempt, either downwards for the 'uncultured Brits' from the 'wrong background', who were often conflated with being 'chancers' and 'scroungers' (2007: 58), or upwards, for those who seen to be 'up themselves': 'The Rogers and the Daphnes!' as one migrant puts it (Oliver and O'Reilly 2007: 61). Some of 'the toffs' include ex-colonials, emigrants from Southern

Africa amongst them, who fail to fit in 'because they're only used to bossing servants around' (Oliver and O'Reilly 2010: 61). There is little socialising across these social divides. In France, Benson (2011) found that many British expatriates also strove to become indistinguishable from the local community, and that 'distinction' was gained by having little to do with the British community. While comfort was clearly to be gained from the familiarity of their compatriots, efforts were made to distance themselves ideologically in order to emphasise how close migrants were to 'a better way of life'.

In contrast to the findings of these studies, we found that, in South Africa, attitudes towards compatriots and distinction are formed very differently (Bourdieu 1984). Many of the British here actively seek one another out, preferring to spend time and build networks with each other. As Samantha, a long-term resident of Pietermaritzburg who migrated to South Africa in the early 1960s put it, 'You gravitate towards those, especially newly out, because you didn't have to explain things to them. Like you still do to a certain extent.' It would appear in this regard that South Africa stands as a highly distinctive context in which to seek lifestyle improvement.

A distinctive context

Whereas the British in Europe are conceptualised as attempting to minimise ethnic/national differences, having ambitions either to become indistinguishable from the local, indigenous community or at least to live a similar lifestyle, this is often not the case for the British in South Africa. Rather, 'distinction' here (Bourdieu 1984), at least for many of our respondents, is seen to derive from British nationality and whiteness, and embracing the identities and communities these offer, and not through denial of these subject positions or a distancing from other compatriots. Migration to South Africa is therefore often motivated by its perceived similarity to Britain, in terms of the symbolic and material culture of the British community, the lifestyle that is possible and the consumption opportunities that are available. As such, we argue, the search for a better quality of life in South Africa is often less about an escape from the perceived negative aspects of Britain, and an attempt to find somewhere that is perceived as 'the antithesis of the lives they are leaving behind' (Benson and O'Reilly 2009b: 615) in order to make a downshift to an alternative, simpler, slower, less materialistic and more authentic way of life. In contrast, it is often underpinned by an imagined opportunity to enhance a British way of life, based on increased opportunities for consumption and distinction. Thus, while on the one hand, our research supports the arguments made in the existing literature that, through consumption, migrants are enabled to construct and sustain a particular lifestyle and narrative of self-identity, on the other hand, we argue that the South African context challenges the assumption that this is achieved through a 'fundamental change in lifestyle...a break, a contrast, a turning point', often through attempts at a less materialistic way of life (Benson and O'Reilly 2009b: 616). As we demonstrate in the later chapters of this book, consumption is often a key means by which 'being British' is performed in South Africa and as such is a mechanism by which to continue an old lifestyle rather than building a new one.

Second, while South Africa clearly offers migrants pleasures similar to those cited within the European context – the beautiful landscape, good weather, an outdoors lifestyle, relatively cheap property and (sometimes) advantageous interest rates are all mentioned as important pull factors by our respondents – these have to be negotiated alongside the complexities of the political and historical context. These include features that are often discursively positioned by 'white talk' within South Africa (Steyn and Foster 2007) as antithetical to the migration 'goods' understood to be offered by Europe, such as 'community, security, tranquillity' (Benson and O'Reilly 2009b: 616). A negative discourse of 'hopelessness, crime and decline' (Steyn and Foster 2008), emphasising aspects such as a high crime rate, the perceived needs for high-level security and awareness of personal safety, and supposed political instability, is so well-rehearsed by South African whites that no new migrant would fail to hear its ululation. Furthermore, even the declared 'pull' of an economically privileged lifestyle is brought into question when the reality of unstable exchange rates, private health fees, a frozen British state pension, the financial costs of return, even for short visits, and other material factors are considered. As some did admit, long-term British residents may become 'priced out' of the option of return because of the low value of their South African assets when exchanged into sterling. The neat dichotomy of 'Britain equals bad' and 'migratory destination equals good' is thus fundamentally challenged by South Africa. Migration here is a much more complicated affair, and the ways in which race and nationality are drawn upon to negotiate this complexity are made more or less visible within our respondents' stories, as the following examples illustrate.

Saul, an energetic and urbane 75-year-old, arrived to meet Daniel in a sports car with Arsenal football stickers in the window. Saul enjoys volunteering for a child literacy programme in an underprivileged school in the informal township settlement of Kyayelitsha in Cape Town twice a week. Although he retired to Cape Town from London in 2004, his connection with the country began in the Second World War, when his father encouraged his family to leave the UK to avoid the threat of Nazi invasion and the consequences that this would bring for them as Jews. Saul, his mother and brother stayed with relatives living in Johannesburg. Upon returning to London at the end of the war, when he was 10 years old, Saul had no thoughts of returning. Indeed, as he grew older and started to understand apartheid, he told Daniel that he had decided, 'I would never come back to South Africa.' However, when the uncle he had lived with in Johannesburg died in 1992, he went to the funeral and 'stayed with my cousins behind the walls' there. This visit did little to foster a desire to return because as he was driving along, a bullet smashed through the window of his car and narrowly missed him. 'A week later, I came home, never thinking I'd come back again!' Saul declared.

His life changed considerably when his marriage began to fail in the early 2000s. He decided to take a break and visit his cousins, then living in Cape Town. This time, he thought 'it was really nice', and returned six months later to rent a cottage for three months. It was then Saul realised, 'I really did like living out here and loved the relaxed atmosphere. It was easy-going. I didn't find anything to be frightened about... By that stage, my divorce was almost complete... and I decided to come here permanently.' Saul had by then sold his furniture business and arrived in Cape Town with his 'car, bike, clothes, the lot!'

Alex portrays himself as a man of wealth and influence: he built up a successful business in the UK and was a parliamentary candidate for a British political party as well as a senior party activist. In South Africa, Alex was on a national accountancy committee and met Nelson Mandela. Today, he chairs his neighbourhood's management committee and negotiates security and amenity contracts with the city council. Since 1991, Alex has lived in Cape Town's 'millionaires' row' in Constantia and then Wynberg, alongside other wealthy British residents, such as Sir Mark Thatcher and Earl Spencer. Alex tells Daniel he could live anywhere in the world, but chooses Cape Town because it is 'England by the sea' and has the 'perfect climate'. Alex had retired to the south of France, but the trouble with that, he quips, was that 'It was full of French people!' When Daniel asked Alex about Cape Town's 'Englishness', he talked about the familiarity of South Africa's shops: 'You've got Woolworths – which is Marks and Spencer's; Clicks – that's

Boots; CNA – WH Smith; Pick and Pay – that's your Tesco's. It's all the same.'

As a former politician himself, Alex is well aware that Cape Town is politically and demographically different from the rest of South Africa, and he will move again should political circumstances in the city and Western Cape change to his inconvenience. For the time being though, Alex enjoys eating out at Cape Town's many European cuisine restaurants for a much lower price than he would 'ever pay in London, Paris or New York', indulging his wife's expensive love of horses, and sitting by the pool in the sunshine. Whether this wealth and influence could be sustained to the same degree in a different context, or in the United Kingdom, is debatable, but South Africa affords Alex considerable material fulfilment.

In this section, we have argued that British migration to South Africa complicates the existing literature on privileged migration in three key ways. First, in contrast to the literature that stresses migration as the result of processes of strategic decision-making in order to achieve either a better quality of life, career enhancement, or a mixture of both, we have shown how British migrants to South Africa often frame their arrivals as being the result of a complex combination of chance, accident, indecision or reluctance. However, we argue that this is in fact a sort of 'faux' serendipity, as behind the individual biographical circumstances lurk the powerful discourses and practices of white Western entitlement by which migration policies are framed. Second, while examples of more careful planning and deliberation do exist, we have emphasised how the ambition is usually not to distance oneself from other British people or to assimilate with the local population. Rather, the British often celebrate ethnic and national difference as a form of distinction, and South Africa is for many seen to be attractive because of its perceived similarities to Britain rather than its difference from it. Third, therefore, is the fact that British migration to South Africa is not necessarily the result of a dichotomous 'Bad Britain'/'Good South Africa' discourse, and as such migrants are not inevitably looking to make a break with national culture and relations. This may be further complicated by the realities of contemporary South Africa, which have to be negotiated after arrival. Here, as we explore in the following chapters, connections with Britain, whether material, symbolic or imagined, continue to frame British migrants' everyday lives and are often important resources in the making of identities, social relations and social performances. As such, the theoretical insights of transnationalism and translocalism, which focus on the ways in which migrant lives and experiences are forged through the interconnected spaces of their biographies, are also central to the theoretical approach taken to the research (Basch et al. 1994; Levitt and Schiller 2004). Crucial here, too, are the intersections that exist with whiteness studies.

Transnationalism, space and race

Transnational research focuses on the ways migrant lives and experiences are constructed through an ongoing connectedness between the spaces, people, culture and institutions of origin and settlement (Vertovec 2001). Drawing frequently on poststructural and postnational epistemologies, the aim is to investigate in detail the processes by which migrants develop and maintain 'multi-stranded relationships – familial, economic, social, religious and political – that span borders and link their societies of origin and settlement' (Basch et al. 1994: 7). Transnationalism thus takes a pluralistic approach to researching the multifaceted, fluid and ongoing negotiations between, and identifications with, the spaces and places of both 'home' and 'away', understanding migrant experience and activity as transcending national borders to occupy a hybrid 'thirdspace' (Soja 1996). However, a tendency in the early literature to use migration as a metaphor for movement and dislocation and the crossing of borders and boundaries, and the migrant as a trope for placelessness, disembeddedness and the inherently transgressive, has been challenged by more recent research that argues for a 'respatialising' and 'regrounding' of transnational migration processes (Mitchell 1997; Ahmed 1999; Dunn 2010). Focusing on 'the importance of grounded attachments, geographies of belonging and practices of citizenship, both within particular places and over transnational space' (Blunt 2007: 687), this important development acknowledges that it may not be nations and nationalities that are the primary focus of transnational connection-making, but local spaces, places and communities. Steve's spatial identification with Tyneside rather than 'the United Kingdom' and Lottie's claim that she 'did not want to live in London all [her] life' remind us of the different scales and locales that need to be taken into account in considering how migrants bring their original homes into play with their place of contemporary dwelling. Further, different locales of South Africa were viewed very differently as potential places of settlement; we were interested for example how some Capetonians reacted in horror at the idea that they might live in Johannesburg, perceiving it as too 'African', while some of those in Johannesburg had a corresponding abhorrence of what they saw as the parochialism and colonialism of Cape Town. A 'translocal' approach thus considers the range of spaces and places that become significant during the processes of migration, which include the interstitial spaces that are part of the itinerary of movement as well as the corporeal body that moves across these (Brickell and Datta 2011; Dunn 2010; Farrer 2012).

Drawing on Burawoy's 'global ethnography' (2000), grounded transnationalism or translocalism is therefore both a micro- and a macro-level approach, connecting the material, corporeal and subjective detail of migrants' everyday lives with the diverse global histories, forces, connections and imaginations that shape them. This is achieved by paying close attention to the ways in which identities are negotiated and transformed in the local spaces and places of everyday lives: examples of 'banal, ordinary and middling transnationalism' (Dunn 2010: 3), while also acknowledging the 'multiple and hybrid histories' of these local spaces, their politics and social constructions, their material geographies, and their connections to other scales, places and times (Brickell and Datta 2011). Included here are the different encounters with 'others' that migrants have, which are mediated further through their own individual transnational histories, cosmopolitan attitudes, diasporic belonging, national identity, and particular positionalities of gender, race, ethnicity and citizenship (Silvey and Lawson 1999; Brickell and Datta 2011: 6). Coles and Walsh's (2012) exploration of the ways in which Britons in Dubai construct a collective sense of what it means to be British in relation to 'locals' through such everyday practices as clubs, dress, food and excursions; Findlay et al's (2004) analysis of English migrants in Scotland and the ways in which they position themselves within different subject positions of English/Scottish nationality; Wise's (2010) discussion of the emotionally complex ways in which Anglo-Celtic residents in Australia are responding to the changing landscape of their Australian suburb due to large-scale Chinese migration; and Korpela's (2009) study of ageing Western migrants in Varanasi, whose youthful search for 'alternative', 'bohemian' lifestyles gradually transforms into unemployability in the labour markets of home, all give a taste of the rich diversity of recent research within this approach. Further, they reveal how, when moving to a new place, race, ethnicity and nationality may take on new meanings, and notions of 'home' and 'away' become reconfigured.

These realities of settlement and the 'localising strategies' (Clifford 1994: 303) within them also raise the question of the extent to which migrant communities such as the British can be considered as 'diasporic'.

While this is a term that has traditionally been used in relation to marginalised and socially excluded racial and ethnic minority communities in the global West and North (Alexander 2010), at the heart of the term is an ideology of separation from, and a longing of return to, the homeland (Knott and McLoughlin 2010). As a consequence, the concept has been extended to other groups with a variety of experiences of displacement, voluntary as well as forced, such as immigrants, ethnic minorities, exiles, expatriates, refugees, guest workers and so on (Tölölyan 1991). Recognising that not all mobility and resettlement leads to a homeland consciousness and/or a sense of community based on this (van Hear 2010), diaspora can thus be usefully conceptualised as a 'stance' (Brubaker 2005) or process that includes the multiple and fractured practices of 'homing' undertaken in the place of settlement (Alexander 2010). The extent and manner of such practices, the existence of diasporic subjectivities within British communities in South Africa, and the shifting notions of nationality and whiteness on which these draw, are all questions which are central to this book.

Whiteness

In keeping with the multi-stranded perspective of translocalism, recent understandings of whiteness have highlighted the ways in which this is both a discursive and a grounded, embodied, material accomplishment (Saldanha 2007). Thus, not only is whiteness a socially constructed, discursively mediated set of identities, which offer ways of knowing, evaluating and interacting with the world (Steyn 2001), it is also a material and embodied actuality (Knowles 2003; Saldanha 2007; Andruki 2010). This is thus a theoretical approach to whiteness in which space is intrinsic; it is through the spatiality of whiteness that the materiality of bodies, 'their appearance, genetic material, artefacts, landscapes, music, language, money and states of mind' create and practice their effects, enabling the 'heterogenous process of differentiation' that is race to be enacted (Saldanha 2007: 9). While recent research on whiteness focuses primarily on these effects in order to examine and expose the often invisible or masked power relations within existing racial hierarchies (Twine and Gallagher 2008), the extent to which whiteness varies considerably between and within contexts is now also well recognised. Whiteness is a multiplicity of identities that are 'historically grounded, class specific, politically manipulated and gendered social locations' (Twine and Gallagher 2008: 6), and it is these often nuanced and locally specific performances that have formed the central focus of much of the most recent research. The ways in which 'whiteness as a form of power is defined, deployed, performed, policed and reinvented' (Twine and Gallagher 2008: 5) have been categorised as a 'third wave' of whiteness studies (Twine and Gallagher 2008). While the first wave concentrated on naming whiteness as an issue and making its supremacy visible (DuBois 1977; Dyer 1997), in the second wave, scholars turned to examine the discursive practices that render whiteness undetectable, enabling the structurally privileged positions of white people to be normalised and taken for granted (Fine et al. 1997; Frankenburg 1997; Roediger 2005; Steyn 2012). Within the third wave, a range of innovative research methodologies is producing some exciting empirical accounts of highly contrasting white identities. These reveal how whiteness importantly intersects *inter alia* with nationality in its heterogeneous constructions, and an important shift is emerging within the literature to explore white identity formations in contexts beyond the dominant US myopia (e.g. Jackson 1998; Knowles 2008; Essed and Trienekens 2008; Basler 2008; Leonard 2010; Walter 2011: 1296).

In South Africa, the successive 'waves' of whiteness studies have led to some inspiring scholarship exploring white/indigenous and gendered relations, both historically and more contemporaneously (e.g. Gaitskell 1983; Walker 1991; McClintock 1991; Hetherington 1993; Dagut 2000). This literature recognises that 'whiteness in South Africa differs from Western contexts in that it is more obvious in its potency: self-conscious rather than deliberately obscured, and accepted rather than veiled as a site of privilege' (Salusbury and Foster 2004: 93). At the same time, it recognises that there is no such entity as the 'whites', but that white people are divided geographically, politically, religiously and economically as well as by language (Steyn 2001; Salusbury and Foster 2004; Lambert 2009). Of particular interest have been the different cultural identities that the English- and Afrikaans-speaking communities have cleft for themselves and the extent to which these continue to be constructed as meaningful. The dominant narrative here has long been that each considers the other group 'an unworthy custodian of entitlement' (Steyn 2001: 26), and the British, with their history of empire and their sense of superiority, have regarded the Afrikaners as more rural and often illiterate and, as such, racially distinct and 'not quite white'. In turn, Afrikaners have regarded the British as imperialists who subjugated them alongside the indigenous black people, such that the 'texture of the Afrikaners whiteness, then, was coarsened by discourses of indignation and rebellion toward the more confident whiteness of overlordship assumed by the English' (Steyn 2001: 26).

Since the collapse of apartheid, and with it, the singular, dominant 'master narrative' of whiteness, Steyn (2001) suggests that the diversities between whites have become more multiple and nuanced. There are now 'many shades of whitenesses' available, subject to context and situation. While there are those who still assume and live by the old patterns of power and privilege ('still colonial after all these years'), others see themselves as victims in a reversed order, while still others accept the change and are trying to find new ways of being white. There are also those who never internalised the racial hegemony embedded in the old order, and even others who are moving away from their whiteness in different ways. The key point emphasised here is that white identities in the contemporary South African context need to be understood as multiple, through which the meanings of race are dynamic and subject to renegotiation. More recently, Steyn and Foster (2008) have explored the discursive strategies by which this is achieved. Through the 'white talk' that white people use to maintain their privileges, two key repertoires are identified: 'new South Africa speak' (NSAS) and 'white ululation' (WU). In the face of the global attention that the 'path to freedom' attracted, any lingering racism or affinity with the past social order needs to be denied, while an overt engagement with the new regime needs to be emphasised. To this end, NSAS stresses democracy, social development, non-racialism and non-sexism, equality and freedom; however, in the process of, for example, decrying black poverty and eulogising 'good blacks' such as Nelson Mandela, this repertoire implicitly criticises those in power and 'bad blacks'. The second repertoire works through stacking up negative tropes such as 'crime' and general 'decline', thus demoralising the struggle for change and encouraging alienation from the new regime. A further strategy is to claim 'ignorance' of the realities of apartheid in order to gain distance from the role of (other) white people active within this regime (Steyn 2012).

As was discussed in Chapter 2, research with a more specific focus on the white British has been more limited. In consequence, the British have been described as 'an unknown people' (Bond 1956: 1), 'seemingly without either role or identity' (Lambert 2009: 600; Salusbury and Foster 2004), and as 'the foil, never the star' (Sparks 1997: 51). Much of the research which does exist takes a historical approach to explore the construction of (gendered) British settler identities (e.g. van Helten and Williams 1983; Erklank 1995; Dagut 1997, 2000; Lester 2002; McKenzie 1997; Saunders 2006; Lambert 2009). For example, Lambert (2009) attempts to identify a hegemonic British identity, which he claims rests on social and cultural values such as a common Protestantism, use of the English language, and a web of habits, laws, ideas, collective memories and institutions holding people together. 'Home' for much of the nineteenth and twentieth centuries was a nostalgic concept, indicating a lost world, a rural idyll rather than the grimmer realities of industrialised Britain. Lambert (2009) argues further that such was the pervasiveness of, and enthusiasm for, 'Britishness' among British South Africans, it was difficult for a vibrant new British South African culture to take root. This was further complicated by strong North American influences on lifestyle and in business practices, television and film in South Africa in the second half of the twentieth century (Saunders 2006). Combined with their political marginalisation, these factors combined to mean that that many British failed to either identify with South Africa or to see that they had a long-term future within it. However, while the British might have failed to identify socially or culturally, some did identify with its landscape (McAleer 2010). Through the writings by British South African authors and poets such as Olive Schreiner, Alan Paton and Guy Butler of their love of the beauty of South Africa, a broader white South African ideology started to emerge; its proponents self-identified as '(White) English-speaking South African' (WESSA) rather than 'British'. This group widened to incorporate other English-speaking ethnicities apart from the British.

Due to the specific social circumstances of the contemporary context, Salusbury and Foster (2004) argue that WESSAs have 'clung' to each other, consolidating a 'group' that might otherwise have dissipated. Indeed, now that whites have very little overt political power, the characteristic of speaking English may be the only socially acceptable means to claim the privileges of whiteness. Salusbury and Foster (2004) point out that through the primacy of the English language in the global context, WESSAs' transnational connections with Europe and the West are emphasised, confirming their unique position as appropriate leaders to assist with the international 'development', which is seen to be so important to the future of South Africa. At the same time however, WESSAs are techniques 'to obscure ongoing racial privilege'. First is the strategy of downplaying any potential hegemonic cultural 'identity': by drawing upon a discourse of 'culturelessness' or 'cultural normativeness', WESSAs are prevented from being seen as a distinctive minority identity. Rather, it is claimed, by being culturally void or neutral, they are perfectly positioned to take an objective position within the current politically complex context. A further tactic to retain power is to identify by class rather than race. By constructing 'white' culture as middle-class, WESSAs are able to redefine what it means to be 'white' in the new social climate. Black people may be allowed limited entry into this group as long as they take on a set of 'white' ideologies and practices. WESSAs also tend to identify as a business-oriented and commercially successful collectivity with international links. In the face of their limited political influence, economic power is claimed as being more important for South Africa's success than internal political affairs.

While some interesting work is emerging that explores the discursive strategies of English-speaking, if not necessarily British, people in the contemporary context, there is little that combines this with a focus on their material, embodied and emplaced experiences and practices in and with South African spaces. This book is an attempt to fill this theoretical and empirical absence: to combine explorations of the extent to which 'the British' still self- identify in nationalistic terms and how they locate themselves both discursively and materially. Our focus is on ways in which race and nationality operate as practices, in both speech and talk, and in the ways in which bodies move through and use space and draw on its material artefacts. Through the exploration that follows, Britishness and whiteness reveal themselves as heterogeneous processes, but ones that operate as resources by which to achieve differentiation. As we now turn to show, in the shifting amalgamations between embodied selves and other bodies, both human and nonhuman, as well as the landscape, different spaces and places in the city, homes and domestic life, food and consumption, the diverse ways in which 'Britishness' is styled and achieved in contemporary South Africa are revealed.

4
Space and Place in South Africa

The final approach to the Mimbangu[1] Eco-estate in Kwazulu-Natal is a good half-mile of rutted and dusty unmade road through the bush, and the small car Pauline is driving bounces along it, up to the thatched security booth and firmly locked, high-level wooden gates. A smiling guard appears, gun in holster, and laughs at the reason for the visit – 'Why you want to research us right out here?' – before letting her through with a friendly wave. The other side of the gate is more established: in the distance a rolling golf course stretches out over the cliffs to the dazzling blue sea in the distance, horses graze in fields with the sun on their backs, and vast colonial-style mansions, surrounded by acres of beautiful gardens, dot the landscape. Pauline drives several miles along the road flanked by a 20-foot high metal perimeter fence, topped with the ubiquitous barbed wire and security cameras, before eventually pulling in in front of her destination: a luxurious modern villa with verandas, surrounded by rolling lawns.

Bert is already waiting outside: Pauline's visit is the result of many months of emails and arrangements, and to have finally made it out to this remote and beautiful location feels like something of an achievement. Inside, the house is spacious and open plan: we walk across white marble tiles out to the garden for our interview while Bert's Afrikaner wife serves us coffee. We can see for miles: as we sip our drinks in the morning sunshine, the sea sparkling in the distance, beautiful sub-tropical birds flying through the trees, the soft muted colours of the bush contrasting with the green of the manicured gardens, we can easily understand the estate's publicity descriptions of a 'paradise'. But with the prices of houses averaging at well over 5 million South African rand, this slice of 'paradise' is only available to the very wealthy few. 'All my neighbours are white,' Bert explains, an observation confirmed by a later visit to the estate's exclusive country club for lunch.

It's very difficult to actually see the houses in the northern suburbs of Johannesburg, and even more challenging to photograph them. While the roads are attractively broad with grass verges and beautiful jacaranda trees, the walls and fences are high, topped by spiralling barbed wire. Fixed notices offer dire warnings: 'Top Security', 'Armed Response', 'Tactical Support', 'Guard Dogs'. Sometimes tantalising glimpses of the opulent residences of the neighbourhood can be seen behind their fortifications, through the gaps of heavy metal security gates, or over the high-level walls. Many residential roads are defended by blockades, with gated communities especially well defended by their security booths and barriers. Black security guards walk towards you as you approach to ask what your business is; at road junctions, signs scream: 'Criminals Beware! Professional Armed Reaction! This area is being monitored 24 hours by CCTV cameras!' Pictures of roaring lions, guns and security cameras reinforce the clear message: 'Keep Out!'

Oliver had been a policeman in Northern Rhodesia (now Zambia), and returned to the United Kingdom a few years after independence. When he retired, he came back to southern Africa with his Dutch wife, settling in Somerset West in the Western Cape in 2009. Sitting by their pool, the couple talk about the better standard of living they can enjoy in South Africa, and although they deny crime affects them personally, Oliver explains that he is part of a neighbourhood safety group:

> I find it quite interesting. It's almost like being back on police duty doing night shifts. So, twice a month I go out, once in the evening and then a second time during the night for three or four hours, normally from 1 'til 4 or 2 'til 5, with two guys in our own cars, and we go round in radio contact with the local police and security companies. And we keep an eye on the residents and react to any incidents that the police ask us for assistance with. So in that way it's quite nice to be involved in the community. We've not really had any problems since we've been here.

While this voluntary activity is framed through involvement in the community and a return to a job Oliver had previously enjoyed, Daniel is struck by the extent to which the threat of crime influences the couple's everyday life. As Oliver's wife drives Daniel to the local shopping mall after the interview, she explains that she's always careful to check in the car's mirror to see if she's being followed back from a shopping or cinema trip after dark. Once or twice she has thought that she may have been and has either driven an extra time around the block, rather than stop at her home, or has even called the armed response unit the couple pay towards before arriving home.

The couple are far from unusual: Saul, a retiree in Cape Town, explains how when his partner goes walking through the nature reserve on Table Mountain 'I make sure she takes with her a stun gun... You feel you need to take a stun gun with you just in case. There are too many little incidents, or big incidents that happen. And while they happen in all parts of the world, one feels it more here.'

In this chapter, we argue that while difference is produced through multiple social mechanisms of South African life, it is the materiality of space that makes its daily operations starkly visible. Exploring who owns what, who goes where, how this or that person travels and why, helps to expose the texture of racialised privilege and its performances. In South Africa, the management of the spatial has long been the key means by which racialised identities and positions have been constructed and entitlements secured. From the early days of the mid-seventeenth century, the colonial settler elites of both the British and Dutch immigrants attempted to inscribe the spatial landscape in their own terms, seeing it as a key means by which to achieve national, ethnic and racial distinction.

It was, however, after 1910 that systems of racially segregated space became more firmly entrenched. With the need for more labour in the British-owned mines and on British and Afrikaner farms, African access to, and mobility within, land was squeezed, meaning that many had little choice but to come to the cities to seek work. Yet the 1923 Urban Areas Act established spatial segregation practices by designating 'white' spaces and preventing the entry of black Africans into these, while also regulating their movements elsewhere. The NP's accession to power in 1948 further consolidated racially exclusive places of work, residence and leisure as policy (Murray 2011). Indeed, the racial demarcation and management of space was a fundamental tenet of apartheid, and cities such as Johannesburg and Cape Town were quintessential examples of how the urban environment in particular was used as a resource to segregate people by race and establish white privilege. Black squatter camps within the cities were destroyed and replaced by segregated satellite 'townships' adjacent to the main urban conurbations, and many black people were forcibly removed from 'incorrect locations' to newly created Bantustans or 'homelands'.

Ultimately, however, the system of spatial segregation was unsustainable. While the black population fell in white urban areas, it grew rapidly in the Bantustans, resulting in substantial overcrowding and impoverishment (Butler 2009). The political incidents of the 1980s led to a progressive breach and disintegration of support for the system and a few liberal whites, as well as blacks, started to challenge the racialised exclusivity of the metropolitan areas. This constituted a profound crisis for apartheid governance (Conway 2009), resulting in a relaxing of some segregation laws. Black Africans were able to use a few of the lower classes of public facilities and transport, and the government turned 'a blind eye' (Thompson 2001: 221) to black occupation of some of the white residential areas such as Hillbrow in Johannesburg.

Since 1994, land reform has been slow and early promises of changing the positions and identities of people/space have only been very partially delivered. In many ways the landscape has changed little: the blacks still live predominantly in the townships and squatter camps on the urban fringes, and most white people have resisted the full democratisation of space in a number of ways, remaining nestled in luxurious accommodation behind their high walls and barbed wire fences and in their gated communities (e.g. Ballard 2005; Lemanski 2007). However, the rise of the black middle class has started a slow process of change to the residential and commercial spaces of cities such as Johannesburg, Cape Town and Durban. In addition, considerable energy has been put into the redesign of such symbols of modernity as vast shopping malls and high-speed transport systems in an attempt to reflect the 'new South Africa' and its ambitions for industrial development and a mixed and multicultural society. Multiracial environments are increasing, offering new spatial resources to their residents. The extent and manner to which change is occurring in the ways people of all races embody, construct and imagine space and place is therefore a key barometer of changing social and political positionings and identifications (Leonard 2013).

For the British, the most popular places of settlement remain just as they have been since the nineteenth century: Johannesburg, Cape Town and the Western Cape, and Durban and Pietermaritzburg in Kwazulu-Natal. These three regions continue to offer distinctive opportunities for the construction of identities and social relations. While Johannesburg lacks the dramatic beauty of Cape Town or the colonial British heritage so evident in parts of Kwazulu-Natal, it is certainly not constructed by its British residents as in any way a 'poor relation'. On the contrary, it is seen by some to offer very specific and attractive resources for the making of (transnational) identities, everyday lives and, in the process, race. The British come here to work: as the metropolitan and economic 'power house' of southern Africa, it offers good employment and cosmopolitan business opportunities. Yet it has, of course, long been a deeply segregated city, and indeed, in the apartheid era was perhaps the quintessential example of a city where everyday lives were organised into racially distinct spaces and places. As such, it is still a city of deep contrasts. Its echo is found in cities in the United States such as Detroit and Los Angeles: downtown, central Johannesburg was deserted in the 1980s by a 'white flight' of industry, business and finance, entertainment and leisure (Sugrue 2005). Now physically deteriorating, its reputation tarnished by some whites as a tense, dangerous and litter-ridden place of crime, drugs, violence, homelessness and fear (Murray 2011), it is, simultaneously, a vibrant and cosmopolitan African space (Simone 2004; Tomlinson et al. 2003). Furthermore, recent attempts to attract business and commercial enterprises back into the centre, in ways similar to the development plans of major US conurbations, have been successful, and shoots of regeneration are emerging. To the south, southeast and southwest lie the townships and informal settlements that stretch out to Soweto, mirrored in the northwest by the township and informal settlement of Alexandra, which closely abuts what is now the main business and commercial district, Sandton. It was in such townships that the bulk of black residents were forced to live under apartheid and still remain to this day. Many of these areas lack social amenities, and in certain cases, even the most rudimentary services, although other parts are becoming distinctly more middle class (Murray 2011). In stark contrast, to the north, white South Africans, English-speaking, British and Afrikaners intermingle in the white-dominated, leafy and luxurious suburbs, although their proximity to townships such as 'Alex' fuels discomfiture for many.

Cape Town presents a contrasting spatial, racial and socioeconomic context. It is South Africa's oldest city, established in 1652 as a trading post for the East India Company and is often lovingly referred to as 'the Mother City' (Lemanski 2007). It is dwarfed by the iconic Table Mountain, and surrounded by beautiful beaches and the green hinterland of gently rolling wine farms. Considerably less populous and geographically smaller than Johannesburg, it has a higher proportion of whites resident in the city and surrounding areas (Lemanski 2004). Since 1994, the Cape has attracted further intrawhite migration from Johannesburg and Zimbabwe as well as becoming a popular tourist destination, voted 'best foreign city in the World' by the 2004 British

Telegraph Travel Awards (Lemanski 2007). These developments have driven major transformations in its central business and commercial districts as well as a growing demand for high-end residential accommodation. At the same time, however, 'Africa is coming to the Cape' (Lemanski 2004: 103; Western 2001). Black in-migration is also radically altering the city, with the contrasts between the 'sprawling informal settlements and desperate poverty' (Lemanski 2007: 451) and the affluent, but heavily fortified gated communities in the suburbs (Turok 2001; Robins 2002) meaning that it is becoming increasingly polarised. Further, the push for Cape Town also to become a 'global city' alongside Johannesburg means that spatial divisions have been ruthlessly entrenched as poorer (black) people have become 'hidden' in settlements away from 'the tourist gaze' (Urry and Larsen 2011).

The province of Kwazulu-Natal, and the city of Pietermaritzburg in particular, provide yet another contrasting landscape. Long coined by the British as the 'the last outpost of the British Empire' (Lambert 2010: 150), this area, for most of its British residents, is seen as different from anywhere else in South Africa – as a distinctly 'British' place where, for much of its more recent history, white English speakers have formed the majority and have been dominant politically, socially, culturally and economically. Architecturally, Pietermaritzburg retains many of the features that were used in the recreation of a quintessentially British market town: an impressive Victorian town hall, tree-lined streets named after British people and places with English-style homes and gardens, a range of Anglican churches of various denominations and small businesses, libraries, leisure clubs and voluntary organisations that resemble those of 'home', both physically and imaginatively. The surrounding countryside where many of the British live is green, lush, and beautiful, and many British settler authors and artists have professed a love of the place and identification with its surroundings (Lambert 2010).

Yet while connections between landscape and identity are almost a defining feature of South African nationhood (Foster 2008), this has never been a uniform relationship. The ways in which space is multiply constituted and represented at a range of spatial scales, from urban to bush and from neighbourhood to home, means that South African space is many 'types' of landscape, differently framed and eliciting a diversity of responses. McAleer (2010), for example, identifies that for the British, Southern Africa was historically viewed variously as a place of 'convenience', a stop-off point on maritime routes and journeys for recuperation and restoration; a place for development and settlement, due to its considerable natural resources; and a place of penal potential, a solution to rising 'problems' of crime and punishment at home.

Similarly, our respondents drew on space in highly diverse ways to conduct their everyday lives and construct their identities and their place in the world. In this chapter, we show how five key tropes dominated their narratives and influenced the ways in which they engaged and identified with space in embodied and imaginative terms. For the British, South Africa is at once a space of desire and anxiety: a place of spectacular consumption, to be encountered and gazed at for the uniqueness of its landscape, animals and peoples; a space of distinction, by which 'race', class and nationality are constructed and status sought; a place of fear, in which mobilities are restricted both imaginatively and physically; a space of connection, by which local and transnational links are established; and a space of change, by which, in the present moment, their hopes or fears of the 'new South Africa' are imagined and managed.

We conceptualise space here as active, therefore, a medium rather than a container for identity construction and social action. Space is simultaneously socially producing and socially produced: as different groups and individuals act out their lives in different spaces, different social and spatial outcomes are produced due to the transformative capacities of human agency and the environment (Tilley 1997). As Massey (2005) has argued, it is the ongoing and dynamic articulation of these processes and practices in particular locales that produces place: a distinctive and meaningful space, which involves specific but unstable sets of linkages between the human and non-humanly created world, at a range of scales from the very local to the global. While this interactive world is thus very much a socially constructed one, in which responses and experiences are mediated and structured by race, nationality, gender and class, it also phenomenological, involving bodily senses, emotions and kinetic movements (Merleau-Ponty 1962; Smith et al. 2009). Through the ways in which we saw that daily routines, activities, journeys and communications were both described and embodied, individual and collective identifications of Britishness, whiteness, class and gender were imagined, performed and maintained (Knowles 2003).

'It gets into your blood'

Not one of our respondents was emotionally unaffected by the splendour of the South African landscape. Even those who claimed to have 'had enough', desiring to return to the United Kingdom, still positioned

South Africa as one of the most beautiful countries in the world (Foster 2008), delivering specific pleasures to the emotions and the senses. Indeed, Foster notes that, 'over the centuries, few European visitors to southern Africa have been prepared for the affective power of its landscapes' (2008: 3; also McAleer 2010) and as such South Africa as a place of powerful and aesthetic beauty has long been a key synedoche by which the country has been represented to the West, and the United Kingdom in particular. As described in Chapter 2, from 1820, when Lord Charles Somerset described it as a 'land flowing with milk and honey' (Edwards 1934: 31–32) in order to lure the first British settlers to the country, to a 1970s Barclays Bank guide to emigration, which describes it as a 'country with much space, sun and fresh air' (Barclays Bank 1971: 12), to today's billboard, newspaper and online images of wondrous landscape scenes and promises of 'paradise' (SAT 2012), the space of South Africa is iconic.

This representation of South Africa as a set of breathtaking and 'picturesque' landscapes is thus firmly implicated in the West's relationship with, and consumption of, the region. The deployment of a discourse of pleasure has long been used to attract European settlers, rendering the landscape as a touristic attraction that, through the tropes of wildness and primitiveness, offers new emotional and sensory experiences (McAleer 2010: 74; Urry and Larsen 2011). Historically, white settler presence was further justified by the selective racial 'special optic', which saw Africa as a vast and empty space, an 'aesthetic sensibility [that] threw blacks out of focus while zooming in on landscape, plants, and animals' (Hughes 2010: 24). Through this representation, Europeans were able to overcome the limitations of their minority status by obscuring and delegitimising the indigenous African population (Hughes 2010: 24; also, Armbruster 2012; McAleer 2010). As such, this was also a common theme of the apartheid state's presentation of the country to the world: one in which South Africa was a beautiful backdrop for white lives and in which the indigenous black population was largely absent (see Bureau of Information 1989, iv–xxiii).

Framing the landscape as vast, unfilled and beautiful thus requires cultural work that is deeply implicated in the historical and continued racial construction of the South African state and society. 'Depictions of landscape as empty', writes Foster, 'allowed narratives to be inscribed onto them that would have otherwise been impossible' (2008: 230). Images of 'unowned' landscapes, providing distinctive phenomenological engagement, enable them to become vehicles for the collective white imagination (Foster 2008), and it was clear that this process was still working in the narratives of our respondents, many of whom conceptualised South Africa as offering uniquely physical and almost mystical or spiritual pleasures: 'Sun, space, everything...South Africa gets in your blood...you know, it gets in your blood. Africa's in your blood. It's just magical!' Louise, a 40-year-old Johannesburg resident explained. Some went even further, positioning their response to South Africa as akin to an almost religious experience, sacralising its landscape as 'blessed' and 'God-given'. As Victoria eulogised: 'I feel South African in my soul...I love the country, I love the people. I love its beauty, its majesty; it's just amazing. I'm a Christian, so what's been created is just spectacular.'

On one level, the topophilia (Tuan 1977) revealed by our respondents' experiences of embodied and sacralised senses of wonder at the beauty of the South African landscape reflects their attachment to place. On another level, however, this emotional engagement is also actively producing that place, reaffirming it as a touristic space that offers an opportunity to gaze at its 'out of the ordinary' geography (Urry and Larsen 2011; MacCanell 1999). While only a few of our respondents had come to South Africa specifically for such touristic engagements, the pleasures of unusual, even 'liminoid' scenes and encounters were highly memorable even for people who had lived there for many years. Maureen, a Johannesburg resident who had come to South Africa more than 30 years ago as a single woman, and had subsequently married (and divorced) a South African man, recalls some of the most special moments of her time there as being in the Kruger with her children and acquiring a love for the landscape and its extraordinary qualities, where the cares of everyday life could be forgotten (Shields 1990):

> So we stopped the landrover and sat....This young leopard was watching some impala, and every so often, her head would come up, and she would go towards it. Now to see a leopard, it's just very, very special...To me, this is the fun of Africa. Okay, well, let's have a drink. Let's have a sundowner! To a newcomer, it's dry, and it's dull, but I think the longer you are in the country, the longer you become accustomed to Africa, you begin to see the beauty of the wildness.

As Urry and Larsen note, 'People gaze upon the world through a particular filter of ideas, skills, desires and expectations, framed by social class, gender, nationality, age and education' (2011: 2), and the privileges embedded in Maureen's visual and embodied experiences were often reinforced in the narratives of our other respondents.

In Cape Town, the landscape features as a particular draw of the city, and its apparently self-evident pleasures were often used to express a sense of belonging and distinction. The dominance of Table Mountain in the urban area, and the fact the peninsula is surrounded by beaches and the sea, inevitably led to frequent references to the landscape as an enabler of 'the good life' that lifestyle migrants, in particular, search for (Armbruster 2010; Benson and O'Reilly 2009a). However, as Field and Swanson note, this 'postcard view of Cape Town' relies on a whitewashing of the landscape, typically 'framed by Table Bay in the foreground, with a central scene that includes Table Mountain... This image of Cape Town dominates how visitors and locals imagine the city. But so much is excluded' (2008: 7). In fact, this touristic rendering of the city's landscape is taken from Blaauwberg beach, which for decades was whites-only. This is, therefore, a particular standpoint to the landscape that for many years was not accessible to the country's black and coloured population. Avoiding this reality, and the everyday socioeconomic problems of the area, many of our respondents described the Western Cape as 'a paradise' because of this illusionary landscape. Further, they drew on its distinctive and extraordinary qualities to justify their reasons for living in South Africa and why their remaining stay there would be indefinite: 'Well, just look at it!' they would say, with a nod or pointing to Table Mountain or the sea, bathed in sunshine.

In recent years, the attractions of the landscape have fuelled a new fashion in residential living: 'eco-estates'. Alternatively labelled 'game estates' or 'nature estates', these gated communities attempt to market and manage the indigenous landscape for the consumption of the wealthy elite seeking to flee from the changing racial spaces of the city (Ballard and Jones 2011). Making a special feature of native or indigenous plants, grasslands and forests, these estates deploy the natural environment in the production of place to encourage residents to purchase 'a reconnection with the land' (Swart 2008: 204; Ballard and Jones 2011). Some even feature a mini game reserve, so that at the weekends, over-stressed workers can spend their leisure time spotting 'wild' animals on their own doorstep. Some of our respondents had retreated to such enclaves in order to escape from the unsettling post-apartheid changes. For example, Bert, now retired and living in an eco-estate on the stunning Kwazulu-Natalian coast, explains that he is only able to cope with changing South Africa because he lives in 'an oasis... It's a way to go if you are worried about the future... This is the way forward.' A further appeal of the estate is its exclusivity: 'It's very expensive, that's the first thing! A plot of land here is going to be about a million, which is a lot of money for South Africans.' Even more attractive for Bert is that such estates are havens for the British:

> So a house like this to build is going to be like five or six million, on top of the cost of the land. And there aren't many people who have got that kind of money. There are a few black people who have bought into these estates; a lot of Indian people, but the bulk of them are white people. A lot are from Britain. We'll have about 500 houses here, of which probably 50 or 60 are owned by people from Britain, who come here for six months in winter there, and go back to Britain.

As we discuss more fully in the next chapter, the African landscape and, more particularly, its management, is a key means by which the British construct a sense of 'belonging' in Africa. In its ability to attract communities of British people to live in close proximity to each other, it becomes a key means by which 'being British' is not only negotiated and performed, but also made distinctive in both its imagination and its embodied practices.

'A space that is clearly the space that I fit into'

Bourdieu (1984) demonstrates how taste, lifestyle, a place within social structures, and a sense of self are all actively constituted through space, consumption and the material environment as part of the practice of distinction. Part of learning to be white in South Africa is understanding the specific places of whites – where they are and what these look like – as well as how to perform within these in ways that produce and maintain power, distance and authority over other people in other places (Frankenberg 1993; Kothari 2006). As Said (1979) has argued, people define their identities in part through the identification of 'the other': by defining what they are not and by creating physical and imaginary borders around what they see they are (Easthope 2009). However, while the spatially divided nature of South African urban space was accepted as an almost inevitable state of affairs by most of our respondents, there were differences and inconsistencies in terms of how this was used as a resource to construct identification. Some unabashedly delighted in the polarised nature of space, seeing it as a means for achieving status and the sort of upwards social mobility unavailable in Britain: this is what they came to South Africa for! Others expressed more unease with how divisions played out in both public and private spaces. While discomfort did not always lead to action, some did draw on space in an attempt to forge identities and lives by which to challenge the social geographies constructed through apartheid and after.

Stephen, a wealthy professional in his 50s, drew on difference – race, class and nationality – as a desirable resource to produce and maintain his extremely privileged lifestyle. Having lived in Johannesburg for 30 years, coming out in the early 1980s on the assisted passage scheme, he describes himself as 'not a great Johannesburg fan'. However, Stephen was very keen to pick Pauline up from her hotel and spend several hours driving her in his large and luxurious car around the greater Johannesburg area in order to give his special guided tour. It was clear that the landscapes of privilege animated him. Leaving Sandton behind, they drove over 'The Ridge' towards 'the old town, which is where we're going; when the mine bosses, you call them Randlords, chose to build a house they picked the best location … so there's some marvellous houses that I can point out as we travel along here.' Passing the mine dumps that punctuate Johannesburg's landscape as a living reminder of its gold mining past, the ultimate destination was The Rand Club in the old central district. The fact that this is now for many whites a completely 'no-go' area means that the club is on its last legs, struggling for membership. However, Stephen still comes here often, loving its colonial past, what it represented and can still deliver:

> The Rand Club is very interesting. It was started in about 1890 by Cecil Rhodes. And he began the club, to my knowledge, really as a bit of one-upmanship. The club was intended to appeal to people like me: white, male, Anglo Saxons. The people that we don't want would effectively be blacks, Jews, women. Anybody non-white. You'll be pleased to know that the club voted to admit women members only just before I arrived! And I can now use my reciprocal membership to get into a club that wouldn't have me as a member in the UK. That's the joy of colonialism, a bit of class hopping!

Stephen has indeed class hopped – he has made a great deal of money by setting up his own business and sees that Johannesburg is distinctive in terms of the resources it offers to whiteness: 'This to me is one of the things that you can do in a place like this that you cannot do in a place like London. So occasionally I ask why am I still here. I know the answer: it's because my kids go to fantastic schools, and it's because I'm now 50-something, and it'd be very difficult to adjust back to working in London'.

However, in spite of this, and the fact that he has a white South African wife and his children have been born and brought up here, nationality remains very important to him as a marker of his difference. He remains resolutely British, and the space of clubs such as the Rand are drawn upon to perform this identity:

> I am British, and I will always be British.... So I sort of styled myself and quite enjoyed the concept of the Rand Club. I'm a member of the Rolls Royce and Bentley club. I have ten cars – I have three Bentleys – so I can choose which one I want to use. You can't do that in England. So what's happened here is that for me I've enjoyed moving into a space that is clearly the space that I fit into.

It is clear that this is very much a 'white space', and Stephen is unabashed about the continued segregated nature of his life. He tells Pauline of the need to live in 'the right suburb', by which he means the 'very expensive ones'. Here, within the cocooned environment of his luxurious home, space continues to be segregated at the micro-level: 'I can't relate to these people. So, the gardener is from Zimbabwe; the maid is from Lesotho. Lovely people, but they're in completely different space to where I'm at. So I'm in the privileged white, you know, monied, my kids go to the best schools.'

Stephen's wealth clearly enables him to spend most, if not all, of his time in the spaces of privilege, and from this he defines his identity, his tastes and his lifestyle. His is a life of separation: as he sweeps around the city in his expensive car, he enjoys observing the landscape and lives of his fellow citizens but remains spatially distanced from them, both materially and imaginatively.

In some contrast is Louise, a Johannesburg resident who longs to return to Britain. There is much she does not take to about South Africa, and transnational connections are constantly made in the ways that the country is negatively compared to the UK. Thus while she lives in a 'normal suburb', by which she means a middle-income, white neighbourhood in the northwestern part of the city, she dislikes the way 'they put palisade fencing around all the entrances and exits to the suburb, with security guards... It's a nice suburb, but it's not pleasurable because all you've got to do is walk past people's houses, and dogs bark all the time... There's no concept of walking your dog like in England!' Louise explains that if she and her family want to

> 'do something nice and get our taste of nature, we go – we ride all the way round to the other side of the M25 equivalent [a major British ring road], round the highway. We go up Fourteenth Avenue. There's a wonderful botanical garden there called Walter Sisulu Botanical Gardens.

It's got a wonderful waterfall there. It's the source of the Crocodile River. It has an admission fee. It's very controlled, very privileged, very safe. Beautiful place. Absolutely wonderful! Perhaps, you could argue, way in excess of what you could find in Britain. That's where we go all the time – that's our coping mechanism. You have to pay to get in, so it turns out to be quite pricey at the end of the day. So you pay, but you're sitting there in this beautiful environment. But, you know, you're sitting there being privileged. You're privileged... the have and have-nots.'

Although Louise's use of space is clearly less elitist than Stephen's, it is still a key means by which she attempts to forge the sort of life she wants to live while she must be in South Africa. Apart from her visits to the park however, Louise claims that she 'never leaves our house... you don't go anywhere in Africa.' She longs for 'a British club or a British pub' that she could go to, but in the meantime her home does offer some respite in terms of its luxury: 'We just live in this peaceful environment- you know, there's palm trees, swimming pool and such charm, and it's just all so peaceful,' while also affording her some social mobility in the eyes of her friends and family at home: 'You have to be nobility to have a pool in England!' However, at the same time, she has never quite got used to the lifestyle, finding the presence of a maid 'very difficult because somebody's in your private space'. Distinction, for Louise is an ambivalent and contradictory affair: on the one hand, she recognises with some discomfort that she is enjoying a privileged lifestyle but, on the other, she longs to give it all up by returning home.

For some of our respondents, space is used as an important resource to confirm the uniqueness of their British identity. In Pietermaritzburg particularly, certain neighbourhoods are imbued as being particularly 'British', both materially, in terms of the configuration of the landscape, and socially, in terms of the number of British expatriates that live there. For example, Dick and Susan have lived in a small village outside Pietermaritzburg since the early 1980s. The approach to their house is beautiful: wooded and hilly, it is reminiscent of the west of England at springtime. Dick explains that they chose this area carefully, as it is 'more English up here... we weren't happy with, lower down towards Durban. So we decided to get out of there, and we just came up here. But we much prefer a bit higher up, too... ' At this point, Susan interjects. It appears from her interview that Englishness is particularly important to her, and she elucidates:

The ambience here – oddly enough, it is more English up here. Now you see that's another thing, down where we were, which is about a 20-minute drive, it's a very Afrikaans area. It's strange, but there's a completely different atmosphere and background to the people. But we just didn't like the area: end of story! We had pleasant neighbours, but it wasn't us. And I don't care whether that sounds snobbish or not, it wasn't us.

Occasionally, space was used by our British respondents to fashion an alternative, more resistant identity and lifestyle. Andrew, now in his early 50s, came to Johannesburg in the early 1980s, specifically to find out more about apartheid first hand. He was immediately struck by the stark differences between black and white space: 'There'd be lots of nice white houses with their swimming pools, then half a mile away, the other side of the electricity pylons was the township: in those days it was all dusty roads, no cars, not really very much to speak of and little boxes that they used to live in'. Andrew was also struck by the fact that none of the white people he met had any real knowledge of what life was like within the townships because 'they'd never been there'. This is what Andrew had come to see, however: 'I didn't think anything of it in those days. Didn't have any fear of getting into trouble or being caught doing something that I could be told off for! Didn't really cross my mind because it was like, Well, that's what I wanted to find out about, and I did'.

Working in the construction industry, on a project building a school in Soweto, gave him an entry permit; just as black Africans needed a pass to come into the white areas, it was also illegal for whites to enter the townships. 'You would get into trouble if you did,' Andrew says. 'It allowed me to see what I was really coming to see.' Andrew was always the only white man there, 'So I was very lucky in that respect. And I met a lot of great people and really got a good feeling about the place.' He made many friendships, although maintaining these was not always easy at that time: 'I used to travel with them in the same vehicle, which might sound like it's nothing, but there were laws.'

Andrew also met a black woman from Soweto with whom he fell in love. At first, finding it 'impractical' to live together in Johannesburg, they moved to Lesotho where mixed relationships were not illegal. However, in 1987 they returned, as Johannesburg was where they really wanted to be:

So we had a look around Jo'burg to see whether it was feasible, knowing that obviously it would be difficult even in '87. Basically, it wasn't really practical. The only place that we could have lived in those days was in Hillbrow, which I guess you've probably heard is... It was very bohemian in those days, that was like the nightclub area, the party place, and lots of nice but not mega-expensive hotels. It was a nice place. ... It was the first to sort of mix. So by '87, instead of being white-only, which it was in '81/'82, it had started mixing. And obviously the first thing that crossed my mind was, 'There's a lot of black people around here, and they're quite free to move around,' whereas previously there very much hadn't been.

For Andrew, therefore, space was used to position himself very differently from his white compatriots. He is proud of the fact that he resisted the spatial restrictions imposed on him to create a very different lifestyle and set of social relationships. As it was more to his taste to drink in the bars of Soweto on a nightly basis, this is what he did. He remembers, 'It was great, because you really felt what African South Africa was like. And even to this day, if I speak to South Africans, maybe the ones who are in England now, and even the ones here who stayed, but still don't really mix, they have no concept of what was going on then or now for that matter in the townships. They just had no idea.'

'I can't live in fear!'

As Andrew explains, the contrast between the townships and the suburbs is vast, and this helps to fuel the dominant discourse by which many of the British, along with other white South Africans, frame their lives: fear. As formal spatial segregation has declined, crime has increased, and both of these features have been accompanied by an 'explosion' in the depth and extent of fears expressed (Lemanski 2006: 787). In response, urban landscapes have changed considerably: the once open-fronted gardens of the 1960s and 1970s have become gradually secreted away behind heavy duty fortification: high concrete walls topped by curling razor wire, electric gates, security cameras and patrolling guard dogs. There has been a dramatic increase in gated communities: private residences that range from

> total security estates (residential or commercial) with impenetrable boundaries and 24-hour security guards monitoring access and patrolling the interior, sectional title developments and blocks of apartments with perimeter fencing and a gate accessible by remote control, the 'booming off' of existing streets (enclosed neighbourhoods) and everything in between. (Lemanski et al. 2008: 134)

While heavily criticised for creating a new form of 'urban apartheid' that promotes inequality and separation by 'entrenching existing patterns of socio-spatial urban fragmentation and protecting the wealthy at the expense of the poor' (Lemanski et al. 2008: 134), such developments are fast defining the shape of the urban landscape of Johannesburg, Cape Town and Pietermaritzburg/Durban (Lemanski 2004, 2008). Ballard (2004) notes that 'semigration' to these cantonments reflects a desire to remove oneself from civic engagement: behind the perimeter fencing, a separate 'European' lifestyle can be maintained and the increasing 'Africanisation' of public space avoided, without actually having to leave the country.

In this way, (segre)gated communities form a response to two key fears: the fear of mixing and the fear of crime. By constructing highly controlled environments, whites are enabled to both circumvent areas where they feel they lack control, as well as make a show of 'mixing' with members of the new black middle class in a contained environment where assimilation rather than difference is a key requirement (Ballard 2004). Further, they enable residents to feel they are relatively 'safe', less likely to be victims of property or violent crime, in spite of the fact that, in reality, crime remains concentrated in the poorer black spaces (Shaw and Gastrow 2001).

However, this is not to deny the incidence of crime in South Africa, which is significant and most, if not all, of our respondents had been victims of crime. Yet while fear is a key discourse into which British migrants are quickly socialised, there were significant differences in the ways they chose to be positioned by this. Undoubtedly, the dominant position was to become subject to it, and we met many whose whole lives were subsumed by the threat to themselves, their families and properties. One such person was Neil, a computer programmer in his late 20s, who has lived in Johannesburg for six years. Married to an Afrikaner woman, they are expecting their first child, a fact that has only served to escalate Neil's fears. They live in a smallish flat in a middle-income white neighbourhood; on the corners groups of black men cluster, waiting for offers of work or chances to sell things through car windows. Driving past them on a daily basis makes Neil nervous; his conceptualisation of space is full of danger and crime, and as such he positions himself as ever on the brink of victimhood. This defines his spatial practice: he, like many of the British residents in Johannesburg that we talked to, has never been to Soweto, for example, and his pathways around the city are confined to car journeys between his house, his workplace, the mall and a British-style pub where we meet for lunch.

At home, Neil enjoys the 'luxuries you have behind the barbed wire fence – swimming pool, greenery, somewhere to park my truck', and he is willing to defend these privileges: 'No one's going to get in my house. I mean I have weapons, and I'll use them if anyone does get in the house, not a gun and stuff, but I've got an axe, and I've got a knife, and they're strategically placed. Because all the horror stories that I hear – it's unbelievable.'

Yet, while his daily life is largely produced in some comfort behind these defences, Neil resents what this does to his engagement with space:

> There's no freedom: where do the children play? She can go round the corner there, but it's all within security fences, it's all electrified, you know. Then you'll worry about them. We've got a sliding door to the back garden, and there's a gate that anyone can get through, and I just keep saying, 'Keep the door shut!' and my wife's like, 'Yeah, but it's not dangerous,' and I say, 'It just takes once. It just takes once, that's all. Then it's very, very unpleasant.'

As Neil does not want to spend his life feeling threatened, he and his family are returning to live in England. Other respondents also refused to live their lives subsumed by fear, but managed this by rejecting the discourse of crime and violence. For example, Geoff and Yvette, now in their early 50s, have lived on 'a lifestyle estate' on the rural fringes of Johannesburg for 25 years. This is of course a highly secure environment, but one of its key attractions is that 'we don't surround ourselves with barbed wire and high walls, which is what a lot of the sort of image is about South Africa.' Geoff remembers that in the early days of their migration, however, they became caught up 'with the crime thing': 'We were Police Reservers when we first came out as well: the mounted police! So we loved that and doing our bit and ridding the streets of crime, until we found that just nothing was happening! It was boring actually, going out on horseback and nobody was doing anything naughty!'

Since then, they rebut the discussions that dominate their dinner parties: 'We refuse to get into that debate, if... there's people been hijacked today, there's people being shot and burgled or whatever...' While they recognise that their teenage sons are relatively immobile compared to their peers in Britain, they cite the lack of public transport rather than a fear of crime as the cause of this. As Geoff reasons,

> It's everywhere, and there's so much of it goes on that we don't even hear about in other countries. I mean, I've had friends that have

moved from here and have gone back to England and had crime and want to come back! You know? It's everywhere. And in Australia – I have friends that have moved out and they've only been out there a few weeks and had their house burgled.

Phil, a more recent migrant who has been in South Africa since 1998, also refuses to join in the dominant mindset. He doesn't live in a gated community of any sort, finding them 'a bit too much in your face'. Instead he lives in 'just a normal South African house' where, as he explains,

> I stick my head in the sand sometimes and pretend that we don't [live in a dangerous environment], but at least it's some measure of normality. I'm more concerned of my children, the little one anyway, drowning in a swimming pool – than being attacked by someone. So I don't live in fear of someone jumping into the house and holding us all at gunpoint, although I don't deny these things happen. But, I can't live in fear – if I felt like that, I'd have to leave.

Our green and pleasant land

> Home is a mythic place of desire in the diasporic imagination. In this sense, it is a place of no return, even if it is possible to visit the geographical territory that is seen as the place of "origin". On the other hand, home is also the lived experience of locality, its sounds and smells. (Brah 1996: 192)

While migration demands that new identities, homes and lifestyles are reconstructed, these are not necessarily transgressive but often a continuation of the homes and lives that existed before (Ahmed 1999). The unfamiliar is made more comfortable by making transnational and translocal connections with the landscapes of home at a range of scales from the imagination of the scenery and the embodied negotiation of the neighbourhood to the management of the garden and the decoration and furnishing of the home (Walsh 2006). By making ongoing material and imagined transnational connections between the spaces and places of Africa and home, Britain becomes an important political and social symbol to many British expatriates, working to inscribe not only their nationality but also to define and maintain their distinctiveness within the broader white communities of South Africa: theirs is a very particular form of whiteness.

In many of our interviews in people's homes, we were struck by how almost inevitably they would be decorated in 'the English style'. Dick and Susan's 1930s 'mock Tudor' bungalow on the outskirts of Pietermaritzburg was a quintessential example. The house was approached by a carefully designed, well-stocked garden of European as well as indigenous plants, the visual similarities with the homes of middle England further emphasised by the sight of an exuberant Labrador dog bounding across the lawn. In the living room of chintzy sofas and Victorian antiques, walls laden with paintings of English landscapes and hunting scenes, the symbols of nostalgic attachment to 'home' were palpable. On the footstool was a pile of *This England* magazines, its byline, 'for all who love our green and pleasant land', tapping into the emotions of loss and longing with which many of Dick and Susan's British neighbours also strongly self-identified, as the interviews confirmed. But 'home' in this context was not the reality of contemporary industrialised, multicultural Britain: it is a sentimentalised, fantasised place and time of belonging, of which collective acts of remembering serve to bond the British here (Ahmed 1999). As cups of tea are made, dogs scolded, long-awaited weekly newspapers read, and *Coronation Street*[2] watched, the routines and habits of daily life work to solidify the white and British connections of Pietermaritzburg, South Africa with Britain still further. As Tuan describes, 'what begins as an undifferentiated space becomes place as we get to know it better and endow it with value' (1977: 6), and the inscription of meaning in places is achieved through the intertwining of both the embodied performances and the discursive practices which take place there, by which people make relational connections with other spaces and times, both local and global (Smith 2001).

Many of the embodied practices of home are echoed in the new contexts of migration, such that transnational connections are continuously imagined and reproduced through the iterative spaces, places and embodied practices of everyday life. In the ways that people can simultaneously experience social relations corporeally in the place of inhabitancy and imaginatively in places elsewhere, the 'translocality' of place is articulated (Appadurai 1995; Gielis 2009). As we discuss more fully in the next chapter, shopping malls in particular were places by which powerful translocal connections were made with home, as shops closely equivalent to those in Britain were sought out and frequented. Often, however, these were framed as pale versions of 'the real thing', as Lizzy attests: 'Here we've got Woolworths, which is basically Marks and Spencer's, but it's the small version of it…It's like shopping in a

Sainsbury's Local at home. You can guarantee, if you've got a shopping list, you can't get everything on it!'

The spaces of leisure are also places by which connections with home are maintained and performed. In Pietermaritzburg, Susan, Gill, Aggie and Patricia, all British, regularly meet to walk their dogs around the lanes of their local neighbourhood and chat about 'home', or the latest episode of the imported British soaps they all watch avidly. Aggie and her husband Martin are both sporty and, through their memberships of the local sports and social club, dominated by British compatriots, their transnational connections are grounded and maintained through such embodied activities as fruit pie making, darts playing and football. In the lifestyle estates north of Johannesburg, British-style 'pony clubs' organise gymkhanas and show-jumping competitions, in which full British riding apparel is a must, despite temperatures reaching the 30s. As the judge announces, 'And it's four faults for Lucy on Badger' in a clipped British accent, the ways in which 'the local is as much a process and a project' (Appadurai 2002: 33) are clarified.

While South African space was often reproduced to enable embodied practices of Britishness, it also acted as a constraint. The perceived lack of ability to walk freely within many of the everyday spaces of urban life was a protest made by many of our respondents. Nostalgic memories of the relative freedom in the local places of home are often drawn upon in some frustration: 'Walk! In this country? Normally the most you would walk is from your car to the shop, or car to work, or car to the garage. That's all you do. Nothing else, don't do walking!' Neil complains, as he contrasts the restrictions of his Johannesburg life with that of his parents who live in a small town in northeast England: 'My mum and dad live in a little town outside of Scunthorpe... It's just the walking they do! The little town that my mum and dad actually live in is great. I mean, they're walking round that. It's just here, I can't even think of a place you would walk without worrying about it!'

However, while Britain is often paid homage to, it is also positioned negatively in comparison to South Africa. As we discuss in the following chapters, people's relationships with Britain were often ambivalent: a complex coexistence of belonging and unbelonging. Negative comparisons were often mobilised through space, and particularly through the trope of the 'great outdoors'. The British obsession with the weather is a recurring motif in this talk: while Britain is conceptualised as cold, wet and windy, a place where 'you didn't go outside very much', South Africa in contrast is 'outdoorsy', where 'braais' (barbeques) and sport are the norm. Martin, a close neighbour of Dick and Susan's, 'lives in shorts all the year round!' his wife Aggie tells me, a far cry from their native Scotland where 'we lived on the west coast of an island, and it was wet! We would manage to get the sausages and burgers cooked and then have to shoot indoors because it always rained!' Dick and Susan laugh along with such memories but, while it is clear that a return to Britain is treated with some ambivalence, the ways in which the spaces and places of Britain continue to have such clear co-presence in both talk and embodied practice reveal how the translocal states of 'inbetweenness' (Ang in Zournazi 1998: 161) prevent a full allegiance to South Africa by many of its British migrants.

A space of change

'The landscape is never inert, people engage with it, re-work it, appropriate and contest it. It is part of the way in which identities are created and disputed, whether as individual, group, or nation-state' (Bender 1993: 3).

The discussion so far has referenced some of the dramatic changes that South Africa's urban space has experienced over the past 20 years (Nuttall 2004). Desegregation means that cities are now home to a multiracial population (Popke and Ballard 2003), and the rise of the black middle class means that some, if not all, formerly white enclaves are slowly becoming 'deracialised' as new black neighbours move in. How, and whether, this actually changes daily life for the whites is a moot point; however. as Steve, a resident of Johannesburg's northern suburbs summarises:

> The whites still go to their pub, the blacks still go to their pubs. You go to the up-market restaurants, there's a mixture. But if I go round the corner and go to my local watering hole, I would say about 90%, 95% were whites. You know? They tend to stick to where their friends are and what they want. So in that way, there's nothing changed much.

In spite of this, for some of the white British, along with others in the white population, the perception of change is a source of some anxiety and fear. This was particularly striking in 'the last outpost' of Kwazulu-Natal. Durban, the large city close to Pietermaritzburg, has experienced some dramatic spatial transformations, which have become a particular source of anxiety and concern for many whites (Popke and Ballard 2003), as Bert's narrative exemplifies: 'I had to take my car in for service in Durban; it was a Volvo – only place to go – and [my sister] came with me because she wanted to do some shopping, and she was shocked. Because the area used to be white, and it's just 100% black now. And she didn't actually want to walk amongst them.'

Retreat has been a key white response. As blacks move in, they move out (Durrheim 2005). From his secluded life on the eco-estate, Bert is uncompromising in his clarification:

> What has happened is there's been a migration north. What was a white city in Durban has gradually become blacker and blacker and blacker and Indian; white people moved to Umhlanga, La Lucia, Durban North, and now they're moving to places like this. Or they've moved abroad. I would guess offhand, and I don't have any figures to corroborate it, that probably half the white population of KZN has left.

It is not only at the larger scale of residential living that white/British retreat is in process. It is also in the daily choices that are made about where to go and where to avoid, as Bert goes on to explain: 'Umhlanga Gateway is the biggest shopping centre in the Southern Hemisphere ... you walk bloody miles, and is it worth it? There are actually more Indians than white people there and fewer black people. If you go to La Lucia Mall, which is the other side of that, it's a very smart mall; there's like 85% white people there.'

Martin and Aggie agree: 'We're careful ... we don't go into Durban very often. We certainly don't go there at night ... we tend to sort of do things here.'

In the American sociological literature, the exodus of whites from spaces that were historically viewed as their preserve is termed 'white flight' (Frey 1979; Sugrue 2005). As we discussed above, in South Africa, Hillbrow, a suburb in Johannesburg, was one of the first examples of this process. Although never one of the most exclusive areas, prior to the mid-1970s, almost all of Hillbrow's flat-dwellers were white, and many were newly arrived white immigrants. Then, from 1977 onwards, 'Coloured', Indian and black people started to migrate into the area, pushed by a shortage of accommodation in the townships (Conway 2009; Morris 1994). The subsequent renting of flats irrespective of race represented an early crack in the apartheid regime, and the response of most whites to the 'influx' was to flee, taking their wealth with them. Processes of white flight have since been repeated in all of South Africa's major metropolitan areas. The result can be that a once-thriving space may slowly become derelict and run down. Many of Johannesburg's beautiful parks have been afflicted, as Louise describes:

> When we first came here, and everything was still sort of very – what's the word? – colonial, we had a beautiful municipal park with a wonderful restaurant in it... a very high-class restaurant. And I remember when we came here, the park was lovely. They had craft fairs once a month in the park. The restaurant was beautiful. You could have the things that, like, switch you on. You know, you think, oh, isn't this wonderful? And now, the place is derelict, totally derelict. Not safe at all. The restaurant has gone. So there's no place to walk. There's no public area. It's because I don't believe they're allocating the priority to the budget to maintain the park properly.

However 'white flight' is not the response of *all* whites, and now, for some, the new spatial identities emerging offer exciting new opportunities. In contrast to the Kwazulu-Natalians discussed above, we found that in Johannesburg some British residents are welcoming the changes occurring in their suburbs. Ruth, in her early 70s, has lived in her 'lovely' housing estate in Western Johannesburg since the 1970s. She outlines how it has changed at a range of spatial scales:

> It's a very established suburb, almost 50 years old.... used to be a lot of ex-pats but not so many now, we've got multicultural... multi-ethnic, we've got neighbours from all backgrounds. Brandenburg itself has become quite Africanised, but not to the extent that I wouldn't want to go there. I certainly do, and we've got some big shopping centres... The church we attended for years, you know there wasn't a single black person in the church because no black person lived around us, and it was a local church. There was quite an old-fashioned reformed attitude about in Johannesburg, whether black people were second-class citizens or not... and we found that a bit difficult. But it has gradually changed. What we find in our church, we are members of what's called the Church of England in South Africa... We made a big drive when black people started to move into our suburb. We made a big drive to encourage them; in fact, they even came voluntarily to our church. I mean, we also visited them in their homes around us and so on

For Lauren and Matt, a young couple in their 30s who have lived in the city for six years, Johannesburg's special attraction was its multiracial dynamic, and the ways in which they felt they would be able to engage with this. Lauren explains,

> At one level, everything in me wanted to go to Cape Town, because it's like, 'I don't really want to emigrate. I don't really want to go to South Africa!' I had very mixed feelings because I'm quite English really! Cape Town just feels like, 'I could do that.' But at the same time, I also felt it was almost *too* English. If you're actually going to make a difference, really engage in South Africa, Jo'burg feels more... This is where South Africa is really changing!

They live in the southwest of the city which, as Lauren explains is 'a nice area but it's not normal suburbs'. By this she means that it is a more racially mixed community than some others: 'Down the road is Sophiatown, which was the classic place where in the 50s, where all the black people were thrown out of the township. Sophiatown is definitely multicultural, whereas Auckland Park would still be more white than that. But it still feels very mixed.'

Seeing Johannesburg as a contemporary and multicultural space is important to the couple, and this is reflected in the ways in which they embody their local space. Lauren pushes their young baby in her stroller to the shops or to see friends, and Matt cycles to work. They are full of excitement about the possibilities on offer:

> In Jo'burg, the walls are high, but the thresholds are low, whereas in Cape Town, the walls are lower, but the thresholds are higher. Jo'burg's this place where everybody's looking for a network, everybody's looking to know people, and there's less of an old boy's network and that sort of thing going on. There's just this high energy to everybody that's willing to engage and connect.

Lauren is 'grateful that a lot of our friends are different to us, and I feel really enriched by that'. Having actively chosen the neighbourhoods and social circles that many white people in South Africa seek to avoid, Lauren and Matt are keen to put a moral distance between themselves and the white majority. However, at the same time, their narratives reveal that they are still enmeshed in a colonial sense of entitlement to the best of what Johannesburg has to offer, whatever that might be.

In Cape Town, changes in spatial organisation of the city are also related to political and social changes in the country. Today, the city markets itself as a 'world city' and has invested heavily in high-end tourist developments, shopping malls, high-tech business parks and an enlarged international airport (Lemanski 2007: 451–453; Marks and Bezzoli 2001: 29–32). The centre of the city has conspicuously gentrified with Manhattan-style residential developments and shops. Along the coast and surrounding suburbs Mediterranean style villas, apartments and large shopping malls have rapidly developed. As we will discuss in subsequent chapters, some of the people Daniel interviewed believe they have played a role in this spatial project, as property developers, municipal managers or as beneficiaries of being able to use Western, 'British' spaces in the city.

Yet this was not a universal response. James, who retired to Cape Town in 1991, warned Daniel against walking in the city because of crime. James believed that 'things were changing quite dramatically' in Cape Town after he arrived. 'The main shopping street', he continued,

> Adderley Street, in the old days was very European: it had big department stores, and nobody was allowed to trade on the pavement, and I remember women used to come in from their homes round in Newlands and Claremont in normally Mercedes cars with chauffeurs, and they used to meet their friends and have coffee and have lunch in, for instance, a big department store. Well, that was already all folding, and if you go there now, the big department stores have gone, a lot of the shops have gone, and there's a lot of street trading…it became more African.

Walking along Adderley Street, Daniel notices that there are street traders, but the large department stores also remain, albeit considerably quieter than the branches at high-end and tourist-focused malls at the V&A Waterfront and other suburban and out-of-town locations. The uses and perceptions of space by British residents draws from broader discourses and practices of whiteness that frame the South African landscape, inform practices of everyday life and create perceptions (and misperceptions) of broader sociopolitical change in South Africa.

In this chapter, we have discussed the importance of space and place as resources in the construction and performance of white, British identities in South Africa. The complex spatial frameworks by which the country is inscribed reveal how the legacies of former periods of colonialism and apartheid intersect with newer discourses of globalism, postcolonialism, industrialisation and multiculturalism in multiple and complex ways. Within the ever-changing pleats that are emerging, white British residents must fashion their everyday lives and practices and make reflexive and unreflexive choices about where to go and how to comport themselves when they get there. While former distances and segregations are in many ways impossible to maintain, the presence of the African 'Other' can be minimised through a constrained and highly constructed relationship with space and place or accepted and even enjoyed through a reimagining of established habitats. Through the ways in which spaces are made into meaningful places and through the everyday, mundane activities such as working, shopping, dog walking, horse riding, gardening and home decoration that are conducted within these, Britishness becomes operationalised in all its diversity. As we turn to explore more fully in the following two chapters, it is in these performances that notions of belonging and unbelonging to Britain and South Africa are articulated.

5
Landscapes of Belonging: Negotiating Britishness in South Africa

> I am still, technically, a British citizen, but inside me, I'm South African.
>
> —Susan, emigrated to Johannesburg in 1963, now living in Somerset West, Western Cape

Susan had returned to Britain with her husband and young daughter in the early 1970s, but faced with an economic recession, they returned to South Africa within a few years. Now living in retirement on her own, she explained, 'I say I am South African...I haven't got my citizenship, and I intend doing something about it, even now at this stage in my life, because I still say, no, I'm South African.' Asked what she meant by this statement, Susan replied that if she was watching a rugby match on the television, she would always support South Africa if they were playing against England. Susan has no desire to return to Britain, a country that she feels has changed beyond her recognition, but Daniel noticed in her home a large picture of an English country church and village and beside it a watercolour painting of that same image: 'That's the village I grew up in,' said Susan. A nostalgic and personal connection remains at least, even if there is a conscious and stated disavowal of Britain.

Shane, a chef in his early 40s, first met his South African-born wife when she was living in London. As he explained, 'We basically had a decision to make: Were we going to stay in London or move to South Africa?' Shane had visited the country on a number of occasions in the 1990s and 'felt a connection with South Africa. I don't know what it was. I had lots of South African friends; they always used to rave about the place.' However, his South African friends in London would also say to him, 'It's the most beautiful place in the world, but you're white, you're foreign, just leave it. You know you can't live there and everyone wants to leave.' Nevertheless, he decided to emigrate to South Africa in 2001, and as he reasons, 'I got here, and most people don't want to leave was the reality. All the things that they warned me about, I just have not seen, even in the 11 years I've been here. I still don't see the issues that they warned me about: the crime, the education, all those issues. I just don't see it.'

Shane elucidates that 'I don't feel that England is home anymore. I only go back for funerals and weddings.' Shane has two young children, and his sense of belonging to South Africa is also expressed in the life he feels the country can give them:

> I want my children to grow up in a country where they feel that they are citizens of that country... I'm just another person in the UK. Here I have better standing; my family have a better standing. My children will know that they're Afrikaners (Shane's wife is Afrikaans-speaking), and South African children, very proud to be that.

However, this sense of belonging for Shane and his family is complicated by worries about the 'unknown' future of South Africa, and he has made sure his children have British passports.

Daniel visits Mark at his newly built home in Somerset West, outside of Cape Town. Mark is in his 30s and runs a small wine production business and bespoke tourism company. As he talks, his heavily pregnant wife sits at the computer working for her online wedding business. Mark learned his winemaking skills while living in France, but as he explains, 'in France at the end of a seven-year tenure, or seven years of French living, four or five of which were with my girlfriend, French girlfriend... my French was totally fluent – I was still a foreigner. Whereas in South Africa, it's very strange, I don't feel a foreigner.' Mark knew little about South Africa's history before moving there in 2001, but he has become fascinated with it and talks at great length about the histories of the different population groups in South Africa, particularly the role of the Dutch and British settlers. When Daniel asks him if he has noticed the country changing since he arrived he replies, 'Yes, magnificently... It's very moving.' He then adds, 'You watch sport on the TV, well, I'm not supporting England. I'm most definitely supporting South Africa. And you just feel – you feel a part of it, proud to be part of it... and a need to be part of it.' Mark looks forward to his child being raised as a South African, but he admits his British-born wife 'misses a lot of her friends and her Mum and Dad. She specifically misses British, or English mentality...I'm not so bothered about that because I enjoy mentalities from all over the world.'

'Belonging' is at the centre of contemporary debates on whiteness and white identity in South Africa. How to belong in a country now governed by black people? It was white British people's sense of belonging that had initially drawn us to the project. Shortly after moving to South Africa to study, Daniel vividly remembers talking one evening in Grahamstown in 2001 to a university friend's parents who were originally from the Home Counties in the UK. They emigrated to Johannesburg in the 1960s and had later been joined by their parents. Following the rise in violent crime in Johannesburg from the late 1980s onwards, all three generations had moved to the rural Eastern Cape area of the country. Being schoolteachers, they had felt keenly the changes in policy following the fall of apartheid and the efforts the new government has made to incorporate black students and staff into the former whites-only schools.

'We feel the country we moved to has been taken away from us,' said Daniel's friend's mother intently. 'We feel we are not welcome here anymore. I'm reminded of that so often. Everything has declined: education, the arts, the country. Everything!' Some months later, her elderly parents' home was broken into, and they were tied up and beaten by the intruders. Today, like many white families, the generations are scattered between the UK and South Africa. Daniel's friend's parents have now returned to Britain and are living with one of their South African-born children. Speaking with white British residents in South Africa over ten years later, this narrative of alienation and decay was not often articulated in such stark terms. Indeed, many of the people we spoke to expressed a deep sense of belonging and embraced South Africa as home. Alienation from a contemporary 'Bad Britain' (O'Reilly 2000) was a common theme, but as the opening case studies indicate, belonging and home are not absolute, indefinite achievements. Everyday life, considerations about the future, both in national and personal terms, differences in familial attitudes and the constructed notions of what kind of space, place and nation British people think they belong to introduce ambivalence and varying levels of anxiety. Belonging, as such, is a shifting and contingent state, constructed and specific to place and time. It is also not fully expressed, and many of the narratives we collected were contradictory in their stated senses of belonging, home or alienation.

The 1970s Barclays Bank guide to South Africa highlighted the experience of a British couple who had emigrated to Cape Town. It explained that 'the first piece of advice Richard and Hazel Baigent have to offer English people considering emigrating to Cape Town, is that they should not expect to find it little England. It is a totally different country, and that is what they will soon realise' (Barclays Bank 1971: 34). However, for some of Daniel's interviewees, Cape Town was 'England by the sea' and thus feeling 'at home' was apparently effortless. Others acknowledged that 'belonging' in South Africa was achieved through a process of work and adaptation, and feeling at home in South Africa was at risk of 'failing' if they did not make this effort, and were unsuccessful. Migration as a challenge to be overcome underpins many immigrant narratives, and the ultimate failure is to return home.

As discussed in Chapter 2, many thousands of British citizens experience South Africa as tourists, where belonging can be a fleeting experience, or not experienced at all. However, for some British tourists, South Africa evokes such strong emotions that they return as longer-term immigrants. Such 'lifestyle migrants', who usually chose Cape Town as the place in which to attempt to achieve their dreams, can and did present their life as 'one long holiday', except with the added advantage that they would not be returning 'home'. Others considered the transition of holidaymaker to permanent resident to be a challenging one. Karl was one such immigrant, coming to the country for the first time in the 1990s, when he was in his 20s. Karl's decision to move from London to South Africa emerged as a result of visiting the country, but he soon realised that his main challenge after having finally moved to Cape Town was

> trying to adjust to the fact that, you know, the experience of being here as a tourist on holiday for a couple of weeks, I think I realised after a while of living here, that it's not all like that, because as a tourist, you get a particular perspective clearly ... and I think the biggest adjustment for me was adjusting to living here, and the additional aspects of living in Cape Town, which aren't things you notice or experience maybe when you're on holiday. You know, on holiday it was like beach and kind of fun stuff, and I suppose the realisation that it's kind of, it sinks in after a while that actually, okay, now I've actually got to actually make this work because I don't come from a wealthy background or parents that are going to be able to support me. I've got to kind of make this happen myself and make it work for myself. And I suppose it was that gradual realisation that, okay, I'm no longer on holiday. I've actually got to really make things happen for myself and live here and survive.

Karl eventually achieved the need to 'survive' the transition from tourist to long-term resident, even to make South Africa home. However, he explained how his mother missed him, and during their weekly Skype chats, she would become upset if she couldn't see him properly. Karl had not returned to the UK for three years and had no immediate plans to do so.

Jeremy, who emigrated to South Africa in the early 1970s, also discussed the effort required to make South Africa a 'home'. Jeremy's IT qualifications were highly sought after in the republic's growing economy, and a significant number of his colleagues at the time were British immigrants. Jeremy recalls that a majority returned back to Britain after two or three years. When asked why, he replied, 'I just don't think they tried. I don't think they tried hard enough.' Jeremy explained that this 'not trying' amounted to still wanting 'to be British in South Africa', something he claimed he had never wanted to do, as South Africa was 'a foreign land'. Today, Jeremy strongly identifies South Africa as home and has looked forward to coming back to the country on every occasion he has visited Britain. While working at belonging was consciously expressed by those who considered South Africa to be foreign, different, or an adjustment, for others, belonging in South Africa was not a challenge and 'fitting in' was more effortless. But how did this scale of belonging to South Africa affect feelings of 'Britishness'?

South African belonging and Britishness

As discussed in Chapters 2 and 3, Britishness and Englishness in South Africa is a politicised white social identity: British residents have historically been considered to assimilate with English-speaking whites, and been marked out as different from Afrikaans-speaking whites. Despite the historic currency of British and English-speaking whiteness, Britishness or Englishness could cause disruption to belonging, mediating and framing migrants' sense of place and identity. Many of the people we spoke to expressed some degree of ambivalence, or certain moments when their Britishness became salient, even if they considered Britain itself to be remote.

Karl, who has established a successful career in Cape Town and enjoys living and working in the city, explained that Britain seemed almost 'alien' to him: 'When I read and hear what goes on there, it is like "little Britain". It's like this strange quirky island, overcrowded island as well.' Exchanging South African rands into pounds sterling for occasional trips back added to his sense of going on 'holiday' rather than returning 'home', and he has lost his sense of the cost of living in the United Kingdom.

However, he said, 'I feel, as time's gone by, I feel *more* English, because I can identify my Englishness or whatever you want to call it, I think, so I actually feel more English, but I feel less connected to that country and to the culture there and what goes on there.' Karl's 'Englishness' was further reinforced by other people's perceptions of him:

> I suppose the first thing that crops up is when I speak to anyone, or most people here, whether they're friends or clients that meet me, very regularly I have clients come down from Jo'burg. and people who meet me for the first time, and they say, 'Oh, you're from England. You're British, aren't you?' just on my accent. And yet when I speak to family and friends, they tell me I've got a South African accent... because over there they say I've got an accent, a South African accent, and everyone here tells me I've got a British accent... I do feel more English than when I lived in England. I think I can – I can understand my identity as an Englishman, and I am an Englishman. The other thing – I correct people on things like when they talk about British stuff... I'm born and bred in England, so therefore I'm an Englishman, and I have a greater sense of that as an identity than I did before I moved here.

Karl explained that when Cape Town hosted the football World Cup, he had gone to see England play Algeria with a group of friends from London:

> And it was this huge army – I mean, the stadium was like 95% English fans. You know, the flag of St George, red and white everywhere you looked, there was a little kind of section of Algerians in the corner, absolutely phenomenal... I kind of felt connected to that whole group of fans, and afterwards I went to Long Street, and Long Street was one huge party of English fans being English and downing six pints and falling over. They're my people, that's kind of where I come from, a little bit embarrassing some of it, but kind of, nonetheless, I'm also proud of my fellow countrymen and supporting England.

This enduring sense of Englishness and belonging to the UK, or England in particular, while disconnected from it as a physical space, was also expressed by Roy, who was retired from a senior managerial position in Cape Town Municipality. He explained:

> I haven't lived in the UK for 36 years, really, apart from sort of bits and pieces. In the end, you become a sort of stateless person. I mean,

clearly, I've got, you know, British roots. With virtually no family left there anymore, I haven't really got ties. I feel I'm as South African as you can be, short of not being fluent in eight languages, at least, the ones that are here. But without having a passport, I still feel that my loyalties are very much South African. I'm not disloyal to the UK, and I'll stand if the Queen comes in the room. I did find myself bursting into tears a few years ago when they had a Proms night at the City Hall [in Cape Town], and they played 'Land of Hope and Glory', and we were all invited to sing it. I just found that I collapsed in tears. It was really quite amazing. You know, it was an emotion that just came out quite involuntarily. So there's obviously something still there.

Despite ostensibly making a home in South Africa and experiencing an increasing disassociation from the United Kingdom, these two case studies reveal how, as time progresses, Englishness or Britishness may remain an identity, emotionally held at least, and a means by which some British migrants differentiate themselves from other South Africans and mediate their sense of belonging.

Differentiation from Afrikaners

All the British immigrants we spoke to talked about their perceptions of and relationship with Afrikaans-speaking whites and/or Afrikaner culture. For long-term residents these narratives were often related to the history of apartheid in the country and a sense of differentiation and alienation from Afrikaners. For newer and also younger immigrants, these accounts could be less fraught (although this was not always the case), but belonging was always expressed in relation to intra-white differences as well as the differentiation between other ethnicities in the country.

'Did your Dad face problems with Afrikaners when he first got here in the '60s?' asked Barry.

Daniel explained that his father had once been stopped by the police while driving towards the South Africa border and was questioned why he had what was then a 'banned' book in the car (*Catch-22*). By answering the policeman in Afrikaans, the policeman's demeanour completely changed, and Daniel's father thought what could have been a serious problem had been avoided.

Barry explained that when he and his wife first moved to a predominantly Afrikaans-speaking area in one of Johannesburg's southern suburbs, they faced a certain level of hostility:

> We were the only British people, and the only English-speakers, on the street. I had a problem with the guttering, and I saw that a neighbour's [black] gardener had done some work on his roof, and he was out there that day. We hadn't been there for that long. I went across to ask him if he could just fix the gutter, and I'd give him some money. He said yes and came across. Within a couple of hours, the police were there. Of course, we didn't have the right work papers for him – he worked for our neighbour, and it was apartheid. It was someone else on the street had informed on us. They were like that.

Barry's wife, Jane adds, 'We used to get called *rooineks* [rednecks – a common insult for English-speaking whites] and the kids at school...when the kids used to go up the street to go to school, I would say to them, you know, "Just ignore the kids on the street corner. Don't get involved."'

Barry and Jane moved to a predominantly Afrikaans-speaking suburb on Cape Town's Atlantic seaboard in the 1990s. 'Obviously, you try to fit in to society as best you can,' Jane says. 'And obviously, your children go to school, and the friends they bring home are South African, but we've never run a typical, traditional South African lifestyle. We've still kept to our own sort of British way of life...That is what we have stuck to and, you know, been happy that way.' Barry expands on what this means:

> If you look at a typical South African household, you know, you've got helpers, whether it's the old housecleaning girl or whatever you want to call it, the garden boy. That was typical South African lifestyle when we arrived. Now, what we decided to do then was not get too carried away and become used to having that lovely facility. So Jane has always done her own housework, and I've always done the garden. We've never fallen into the trap of relying on or falling in to what I call 'a typical South African lifestyle'.

Daniel speaks to them as they cook a South African *braai* [barbecue]; the braai has not been used in awhile, and they explain how they find meat to now be expensive. It's clear their social life revolves around their family and the other remaining British immigrants they knew from the 1960s and 1970s. Their daughter married an Afrikaans-speaker and they go to great lengths to say how friendly and family-minded Afrikaner people are after sharing these anecdotes.

The next day, Daniel speaks to Alex, who lives in one of the wealthiest suburbs of Cape Town. When Daniel says where he interviewed the day before, Alex replies, 'You don't want to go there! Very Afrikaans-speaking – above the *boerevors* [farmer's sausage] line, I call it!'

Many of the people we interviewed who went to South Africa during the apartheid-era reflect on their negotiation of white Afrikaans-speaking culture and their realisation of difference and feeling out of place in light of it. Julie moved to Johannesburg in the 1960s, having spent part of her childhood and adolescence in Kenya:

> I remember very, very clearly having the feeling that I was actually in a totally foreign country, because you used to hear far more Afrikaans spoken around you than you do today... All the shop assistants were white in those days, and they were virtually all Afrikaans-speaking people, in the bigger stores anyway... I was utterly miserable here, having no friends, being quite shy, having spent three years in an all-girls boarding school. Unless you played sport, you had no social life at all, and I was not a tennis player, and I was not a interested in watching cricket or Rugby or swimming in large swimming parties and stuff like that. It was very restricted for a single girl because it was socially not acceptable for you to go out on your own and also you were expected to sit at home... The Dutch Reformed Church held sway, and they were very Calvinistic in their attitudes about women. For instance, in those days, women weren't allowed in bars – might see the bottles – so you used to have to sit in the dingy lounge, and there was a hatch, and the bar man would pass the drinks through.

Julie secured a job as a secretary in central Johannesburg and began to settle in South Africa. Today, she lives in retirement in Hout Bay, an upmarket, sea-facing suburb of Cape Town, and although she misses Johannesburg, she would never leave South Africa.

Catherine, who first moved to Durban in the late 1960s as a teenager recalls,

> The Afrikaners were very much another race. There were no Afrikaans people at parties or anything else like that. The schools were divided into Afrikaans-speaking schools and English-speaking schools. So the children – because after all the people I knew were only a few years out of school – they didn't have Afrikaans friends. They didn't meet them, at all. So an Afrikaner was similar in a way to somebody who was black or was not white: you didn't meet them in the social situation. They were there for other reasons. And you'd get this sort of thing, like, 'So and so, he's Afrikaans. You know, but he's quite

nice.' Even though, despite the fact that he's Afrikaans, he's still a nice guy! So very much a very separate group of people, and we just didn't come across them.

Many anecdotes about Afrikaner attitudes towards British people are situated in the apartheid past, but some were much more recent. Vernon and Veronica moved to South Africa in the early 1990s, when their daughter started studying at Rhodes University in Grahamstown. They now live in Riebeck Kasteel, a small village in the Western Cape. The couple faced a challenge 'fitting in' to the Afrikaans-speaking community there. 'One of our neighbours even set her dogs on Vernon!' quips Veronica. Vernon was asked to help resolve a dispute in the village. He did so, and the couple noticed an immediate change: 'One day, my neighbour turned up at the door with a beautiful cake she had made for us and that was that: we were accepted.' Veronica explains with some relief.

Bob, who retired to South Africa from the Merchant Navy in the 1990s, lives with his South African wife in a small community outside of Hermanus in the Western Cape. He explains that in his social and family life, 'If you didn't speak Afrikaans, I'd have to sit there, one out of ten, and everybody would have to use English because I didn't speak Afrikaans, so in that context, anybody who wants to get into the society has to learn Afrikaans. It's not easy to learn a language when you're older, but you have to do it.'

When Daniel speaks with investment bankers Nigel, Paul and Vanessa about race relations, Nigel, who has been in South Africa since 1986 and first worked as a mining engineer, replies that it is better to think in terms of class. He gives the example of speaking with a white Afrikaner who is living in a poor working class area because there's just nothing in common. 'And that was probably the biggest battle I had working on the mines,' he says. 'was with some of the white Afrikaners who had a very sort of entrenched view of history and virtually, you know, almost hated the English.'

Vanessa, who has lived in South Africa since 2003 adds, 'Hmm, we've experienced that, too.' Nigel continues, 'and when I first came out here, you know, memories of the Boer War were still very, very strong, and....' Vanessa chips in: 'That gets mentioned here. I mean, that was mentioned in my book club. I had a really scathing "You guys invented the concentration camps" comment, which I found deeply offensive, and I didn't feel I could even reply. And you get it, like, with the odd taxi driver will make a snarly comment about hating the British.'

Other British residents also talk about their shock at being told (or confronted) about British concentration camps in the Boer War[1], an historical fact that variously affronts them, engenders resentment, or helps them understand South African (and British) history. Shane, whose wife is Afrikaans-speaking says,

> I've never come across any direct racial prejudice because I'm English from Afrikaners, but then I never really understood the history. I've been taught what I was taught, and then you come here, and you actually read about it, and you actually realise what did happen during that scorched earth policy, etc., and I'm surprised that they even allow English people in after a certain period because it was horrific, what happened, and of course, they're taught that, or were taught that, in the old Afrikaans education system, so yes, I can understand why there would be that, but I haven't come across it.

British residents thus continue to negotiate intrawhite linguistic, class and ethnic cleavages. For some, it adds to their fascination with the society they live in and informs them of its history. For others, it creates dissonance, resentment and a sense of being 'foreign'.

Belonging where?

If belonging is a process of work, adaptation and becoming accustomed, where do British migrants consider themselves to belong? In other words, in a fragmented society such as South Africa, there may be multiple spaces and realities through which British residents create 'home'. As we showed in Chapter 4, living in the centre of Cape Town, leafy Pietermaritzburg, or in one of Johannesburg's wealthy but car-dependent northern suburbs, within a gated community, behind barbed wire and electric fences, or in a small village along the Western Cape coast, or on an eco estate on the Eastern coast, dramatically affects the place where people consider they belong. Some residents we spoke to were convinced that the South Africa they lived in was quite different from the South Africa elsewhere in the country. Bob, who lives outside of Hermanus, was particularly clear that his home was completely unlike the rest of South Africa. Indeed, he denied that he had noticed any change since the end of apartheid. As he explained,

> My friends are white. If I went to eat in a café: all white. If I went into a shop to buy: all white. My clientele? 99% white. The people I buy from? A 100% white. If we go out to a restaurant, we'll see 98% white.

If I had to say, 'I have a black acquaintance,' it would be nonsense. I'd have to really go out and work hard to find a black acquaintance because we're just not in the same area...I mean, our social life is a 100% white. It's not that we specifically want it that way.

Bob wondered, 'Maybe I'm living in a fool's paradise, but long may it continue!' Indeed, many of the British people Daniel spoke to in the Western Cape considered the province to be very different from the rest of South Africa and from Africa. The racial demographics and political dynamics marked it out as distinct. Some could never countenance ever living elsewhere in South Africa.

In contrast, many of the people Pauline spoke to in Johannesburg considered it to be the 'real' South Africa – more multicultural, more edgy, more 'African' – and that was the space they belonged to. Thus, integration into society is also distinguished by region in many British residents' minds. Catherine, who lived in Durban and then Pietermaritzburg until 1985, says that she has found living in the Western Cape to be

> completely different from Natal. They're not friendly people [here]. And I've been absolutely gobsmacked by how – they're very – they're nice – the photographic society I've belonged to for three years now, and not one person – I'm not that bad, not one person has said, 'Why don't you come round for coffee? Shall we meet for lunch? Oh, we're having people round for drinks on Friday, would you and your husband like...?' – not one. Not one! And I was talking to another girl in the photographic society, and I said, 'You know, I've been here this long – how long have you been here?' She said 12 years. I said, 'Oh, so you're part of the scene?' She said 'No!' They've very unfriendly. They don't bring you in...No, Cape people are terrible. They are not friendly people, but Natal people are. And most of our friends here we're not very gregarious but most of our friends here are fellow Brits.

James, who lives in Cape Town, concurs that the region is considered 'A bit snobby...I don't know why it's got that reputation, but in Johannesburg you can quite rapidly meet people and be invited to their house; here, it would take a long time for them to invite you to their house, and it's not the fact that they don't have servants or something like that. It's just they like to keep their life private.'

Vanessa and Sean, also in Cape Town, do feel integrated into Cape Town society, however. They draw a distinction between themselves and other British residents: 'We don't choose to be with ex-pat people,' says Sean. 'Whereas in Jo'burg, it was pretty much all of our social life, wasn't it, was with ex-pats?' 'With ex-pats, but not British ones, though' Vanessa adds.

As we discussed in Chapter 3, South Africa has been considered a 'landscape of convenience' for the British since the first colonial occupation. For Alex, Cape Town is a place where he can maximise his income and lifestyle. 'I work and concentrate on things that interest me and get maximum return,' he explains. 'There's a big demand if you're English and you're educated. I'm a very happy bunny!' He admits his emotional connection is with 'Africa' (or at least Cape Town):

> Africa is – you should ask my wife: she says it gets into your soul. Africa gets into you. I mean, you lived here. There's something about Africa; there's something different about South Africa. I mean, Cape Town, this is heaven on earth. It really is. You've got everything in Cape Town: superb restaurants, [the] winelands, beautiful scenery, relaxed way of life. It's great.

For much of the interview, Alex stresses his wealth and international mobility. As he explains, in South Africa, 'there is a freedom here which I certainly don't feel anywhere else.' This freedom is conceived in personal economic terms: 'Nobody interferes...One of the advantages of living here in my situation is you don't pay any tax here on your social security pension; you don't pay any tax here on your private pensions, which are earned solely outside of South Africa, nor do you in the UK, so basically you live tax free.' Alex explains that

> My mother-in-law has just been out on her twenty-second visit. And she was in tears: she didn't want to go back. She just sits by my pool with her red wine and her gin and tonic, and she just says, 'This is wonderful.' We go down to the Waterfront [a shopping, hotel and restaurant complex] and we have a superb meal. The food is magnificent, and you can eat top quality food, nice wine for three of you, and it's expensive in South African terms – it costs you £70. It would cost you £70 each in Britain!

Cape Town is the space in which Alex can maximise his lifestyle and his income, and he sees little difference between the United Kingdom and Cape Town, apart from the weather. He has no sense of being 'foreign'. He explains: 'If I was to leave here, because I felt I wanted to leave – I can't imagine what would trigger that – I would go to either Cyprus or Malta for a very simple reason: They speak English and have old English influences, and they're exactly the same latitude north as we are south, and there's nothing like a Mediterranean climate!'

Alex is more than a tourist, however, and he is involved in his local community, although the South Africa he lives in is very specific to his lifestyle and tastes. As such he can be considered a 'knit-your-own world global citizen' whose 'actions are a form of global individualism' (Knowles 2003: 153). Such a citizen 'wants, expects things to basically operate for his personal convenience and betterment. His life and his requirements are the vantage point from which the world is judged... belongs, not in a country, but in a set of circumstances that promote, or at least do not impede, the things he wants to have and do: the things he regards as entitlements' (Knowles 2003: 153).

Alex's whiteness, in a context where whiteness equates to socio-economic power, his Englishness in a city where it is linguistically and socially dominant, and his enjoyment of good weather make Cape Town the perfect 'landscape of convenience' to which he feels he belongs.

However, even if migrants consider themselves to belong to South Africa, there are still things they may miss about the UK. Vanessa admits she gets

> nostalgic from time to time, but I just need a trip there and then it kind of gets it out of my system, and I think, 'Oh, I want to go home.' I call this [Cape Town] home now. I miss – we were just saying, Nigel and I like the humour. Nigel was sat next to me on a flight to Jo'burg and, suddenly, to be able to chat about the British-type of humour, we don't get – I don't get that with any girlfriends here. It's not the same. The humour's not the same.

Vanessa also misses the clothes sales that British shops have, particularly when shopping for clothes to wear for work, although she has noticed how European designer shops have been opening in Cape Town in recent years. Vanessa's husband Paul mentions he misses

> the cosmopolitan-ness of London, and the rich diversity of stuff, urban stuff, from, you know, galleries to museums and theatres, or whatever you like. Going to see bands and stuff is happening, where we're a bit out of the loop here. So I miss that, but that's nothing compared to what you do get here and, you know, especially with

Cape Town with its mountain, beaches, woods. So for more sort of rural/urban stuff, there's a greater diversity here.

Pensively, he adds, 'I miss the countryside a little bit. It's gentle, you know, to drive around the country lanes and stop at a country pub: that sort of overly characterised idyllic sort of thing that John Major was going on about.'

In similarly nostalgic vein, Nigel remarks that

> in some ways, I miss certain periods in England, like Christmas – the feel of Christmas around England – summer in Yorkshire where everything's just beautiful and green. There is always a certain familiarity for me in Yorkshire, in the people and just going into shops and that and talking to people. And, you know, it's a different mindset and a different sort of culture that I enjoy, you know. So it's nice to go back and experience that.

Missing English humour, landscape, culture and specific aspects of everyday life was common, and it was often this romanticised construction of the United Kingdom that was juxtaposed with a strong identification with South Africa. Vanessa remarks, 'I think it's interesting that all three of us [her husband Sean and business associate Nigel], our history is that we all travelled a lot, and then we've chosen to settle in this country... We've all lived all over the place.'

Nigel adds, 'You have a very different global outlook,' and 'It's not that much to sort of up and go off and live in another country', because they had all lived in different places throughout their lives. This ease of transnational relocation and belonging belies the displacement and difficulties such moves entail. In particular, homecoming to the UK (as a number of informants had attempted at one time or another), could end with failure, or at least a return to South Africa. For example, Catherine went back to the UK with her husband and family because of her fears of South Africa's future in the midst of the chaos of the State of Emergency. However, it was an unhappy experience:

> I never made any friends in England. I had acquaintances from work. And one or two guys, you know, came round for dinner, and that was fine. But it was, as you say, extremely formal. And no, I didn't make any friends in England, none at all, and we were there six years living, working, being part of the community, taking the children to school and all that sort of stuff.

Catherine gives an example:

> We went to a [British political party] barbeque once. And I said, 'Well, you've got to meet people, so I'll go to all the barbeques. I don't care which party they are!' And so we went to one, and it was absolutely horrific. It was like, 'Hello, we're new. Yes, we've just arrived in the village, or a few weeks ago or whatever. Oh, how do you do, how do you do. This is Jill, and this is John, hello.' And then just carried on. If that had been in Natal, it would have been, 'Come, sit over here. Make room chaps, these guys have just arrived.' And maybe you wouldn't have got on with them ultimately, but everybody would have made an effort. And you had the opportunity to meet people and to see if you had some shared ground somewhere along the line. Not a bit of it, not a bit. The only people we met were our neighbours and they usually complained. Unbelievable!

Catherine believes there may have been political motives for this, and what she was perceived to have been 'involved in' or 'supporting' by living in apartheid South Africa. As will be discussed in greater depth in Chapter 7, she also noticed that her family 'didn't ask anything. Which is absolutely extraordinary. They just, "Oh, you're back home, nice to have you back home."' Daniel asked why they didn't seem to care. 'I don't know', she replied. 'Either they don't care about South Africa – you know, there are countries all over the world doing strange things with their population. I really don't know. I think I changed too much for them, because I'd left as a child and come back clearly with two children as an adult and everything else like that. And they never asked anything.'

South Africa: Landscapes of opportunity and mobility

Roy meets Daniel at the large golf club where he is a committee member. Roy explains, 'I was brought up in a two-up two-down terraced house in a town in the north of England, an industrial town in the north of England. You know, no bathroom and an outside toilet.' Roy obtained a financial qualification and started as a junior finance assistant in the local town council. By 1975, he had migrated and was working on public sector projects in West Africa. In 1984, he moved to Cape Town and became a senior city official: 'I know I've contributed to the change in Cape Town. And because I was at management level, senior management level, I was able to affect a lot of those changes', he explains. Roy tells Daniel how he helped enable the highly successful

V&A Waterfront development to happen and how he protected the city's tax base against a potential 'white flight' that has affected other cities. The main point Roy wants to make in the interview is how much agency he has had in South Africa, and with his British qualifications and multi-national experience, 'it wasn't difficult to shine, you know, and, more importantly, provide solutions.'

Roy ends the interview with an anecdote about returning to the town where he grew up. A school friend who lived in a neighbouring street and started at the same level as him in the local council is still living in the same type of terraced housing in the town and working in a middle manager's job in the council. For Roy, this symbolises the success his decision to migrate has been and his belief that he has made a difference to a major city, a difference he could not have made to this extent in the United Kingdom.

Roy was not alone in emphasising the heightened agency and increased opportunities for social mobility South Africa afforded, compared to the United Kingdom. Karl, who moved to Cape Town in the 2000s after visiting as a tourist in the 1990s, contrasts the very 'structured' life he had as an NHS manager in London and the successful career he has built in Cape Town:

> I'm a known name and [his company] is. [Karl] is [his company] I suppose, and there's nothing wrong with that – it's good for business! But, yeah, I'm very involved in the city centre. I spend 7 days a week walking and talking the city centre, showing clients around, giving them bits of history and stuff, kind of as we walk between buildings. I'm very fortunate because we walk 90% of our appointments... So it's like living and breathing the city centre. I love it, and there is a lot of change – there's a continual change, all for the good pretty much, I would say. It's exciting, and it's fun to be part of that, and to be, to see the changes and things going on around you, and it's my passion: I'm obsessed with the city centre and what's going on here, so yes, I'm very much part of that I suppose, and I'm not being pretentious about that. I know that I'm just part of it, and things like the property magazine and stuff is... I'm well known for what we do in the city centre and so on.

Over 40 new apartment blocks have been built or converted in the centre with over 3000 apartments, and Karl was involved in the first major conversion. It is a life he could hardly have envisaged when he lived in London. Both Karl and Roy thus believe South Africa gave them freedom to do things and make an impact, beyond what they could have achieved in Britain. This agency has, in their view, changed the nature of Cape Town. These accounts are, of course, discourses of whiteness, and both men are material beneficiaries of whiteness: Roy because of apartheid and Karl because of the funds built up from the sale of his London apartment, which went further in South Africa, allowing him to experiment with careers when he first arrived. His vision of gentrification of the city also suits the broader political and social management of the city, a white spatial project that has prioritised neo-liberal forms of economic and social gentrification in the city centre; albeit that this has been been criticised by some for privileging the needs of international tourists and wealthier members of the middle class (Marks and Bezzoli 2001).

Not only did South Africa give British immigrants the opportunity to make an impact and be socially mobile, but as some of those spoken to argued, it *necessitated* this. With a much reduced welfare system compared to the UK's, British immigrants had to 'sink or swim'. Jeremy, who moved to South Africa in 1971 and now runs an IT business, made a direct comparison between South Africa and the UK. Jeremy's sons now live in the UK: one works in a junior administrative role in a university, and the other is on unemployment benefits. Jeremy thinks that even his son with a job 'would have done so much more for himself had he been in South Africa. I tell him, so this is no secret.' He continues that for his other son, who has been unemployed for 18 months,

> I know he would have done more for himself; he wouldn't have relied on the system to support him. Because you have to if you're going to get anywhere in this country – you've got to do it because of your ability. Nobody's going to look after you. There isn't a supporting infrastructure. I can't stop work. There's no dole! There's no unemployment benefits. I mean, my youngest brother, who is 54, has worked for less than 10 years of his life. Lived on the state... you can't survive like that in South Africa. So by definition, the people who were here were people who were self-starters by nature; otherwise they ended up going back to the UK, and most of those people that weren't self-starters, I watched go back to the UK for exactly that reason, you know?

Such accounts sharpen claims of the effort that belonging requires and the perceived failure of return. While this may be a return to a more cosseted and less respectable existence, an easier life, it would, in these terms, be considered a less successful one. Again, such accounts partially obscure the automatic benefits of whiteness in South Africa that open to English-speaking whites in particular: access to a superior education, social and economic capital, and access to influential networks. British residents can often point to the 'difference' they see they have made to the society around them and the 'success' they have made of their lives in socio-economic terms. However, the extent to which this agency and mobility was dependent and enabled by whiteness in a racist context is rarely acknowledged.

Children and the future

Children, whether young, adult or expected, brought many of the questions about belonging and the future into sharp focus. Apartheid-era South Africa based part of its appeal to British migrants on a better future for them and their offspring. However, we spoke to residents who began to doubt their decision to migrate to South Africa in the 1980s because of the danger they believed the disintegrating apartheid state had put their families in and the uncertain future they now faced.

Today, longer-standing British residents in South Africa often have children and grandchildren who have moved away: to Britain, Australia or elsewhere. Those with young children or who plan a family, are posed with a number of questions about the society their families live in. What education will they receive? What impact does living in a complex and divided society have on their children? Will their children's whiteness have consequences for their future ability to find employment and build a life in South Africa? These questions revealed doubts about their personal futures, but also statements of commitment and belief in the future of South Africa. For some, talking about children underscored an ambivalent and a complex relationship with the country.

Susan explains: 'My son and his wife and their young boys have gone to live in Australia because of the life here.' Her home is full of pictures of them:

> They feel that they're the wrong sex and the wrong colour, and they fear for the future for them. David took over the agency business of my husband and had a very good business, and my daughter-in-law is a doctor, a GP. They didn't like having to be, you know, surrounded by high walls, electric fencing, keeping the children in... and I could understand that. And I mean, even right at the beginning, we – Harold [her husband] – when Harold was alive, we said to both of

our children, 'If you do feel you want to go, leave the country, you go with our blessing, you must do what you want to do.'

Susan is adamant that she's happy in South Africa and would never leave, but Daniel wonders if there is an unspoken sadness that her son and her grandchildren feel they do not belong in South Africa.

Contemplating the future of South Africa is an abstract question, but it is made more real and revealing when British migrants consider what the future holds for their children in the country. Vanessa and Sean, who have young children, want them to be highly mobile and not tied to South Africa:

> I would like them to go to university in the UK. I'd like to buy an apartment because I think the economy's at its worst at the moment, so I feel it's a good time to buy a sort of flat in London, and then I'd like them to go there to university. I'd like to have enough money saved that we can afford to send them there. I think that would be amazing. I don't want them to go UCT [the University of Cape Town]. Not that I don't think it's brilliant. I don't want them on our doorstep; I want them to spread their wings and have a more cosmopolitan life.

Sean adds:

> I don't totally share that viewpoint, but the end goal is the same. I want the kids to kind of go anywhere in the world and have very much an international outlook and the ability to go and work anywhere. I'm not sure that that is predicated therefore on getting a degree in the UK. I think they can get a degree here and still go and work in London or wherever. And I think they should make their own minds up, but I'd certainly encourage them to go to the UK to do their degree. And I certainly wouldn't encourage them to think they're going to spend their whole lives here now. I don't want them to think as either particularly English or South African but, you know, are able to go wherever they want.

Sean and Vanessa have both lived in different countries across the world, and their professions in the financial sector give them considerable mobility. Both express a deep sense of belonging in South Africa (albeit specifically Cape Town and not Johannesburg, where they have been victims of crime), but they also believe it is important for their children to be internationally mobile. This could be an expression of their class and own background, but it could also be due to unarticulated concerns for South Africa's possible future directions and the need for children to be able to leave.

Daphne, who has lived in South Africa since 1984 and now lives on a vineyard in the interior of the Western Cape with her husband and two teenaged sons, expresses less anxiety about their future:

> When they [her children] were born, I really sat down and gave it long thought how and where I was going to bring them up, when my first one was born, and I look at what they have here and the life they've had, and my seventeen-year-old is turning eighteen this year: it's definitely 100% the right way. It's a healthy country to bring up children in respect of the climate, the diet. I think they had more challenges with the political change in schools, but that's not a bad thing because the change in going in the right direction, but for them yes, they had a very healthy upbringing. I find now when I go back to the UK, last August I was back there, I find the children in the UK unhealthy, I find them rude, and I find them disrespectful to their peers and to their adults. I think the standards are higher here with respect, within the family unit.

Daphne's sons now attend a private school in the province, a fact that changes considerably the broader questions about education in a different society. Daphne expects her sons will attend a South African university, such as the University of Cape Town. Similarly, Shane also believes he is able to give his children a 'brilliant future' because he has sent them to a private school,

> which I would never have been able to do in England...I have lots more opportunities here for my children than they would have had in the UK. They would have end up stuck in some state school because of our postal address, not being able to afford to live in the right area. Here we can send our kids to private school. They follow an English curriculum, so from an education point of view, I think their future's fantastic! I think they will get the best education available to them.

However, when he thinks about their future in relation to the country's future he is not so sure:

> It's very difficult to say what it will be when they're 18. You know, we live in a country where – it's like that powder keg, it's almost, at

any time – I don't know, if Mandela dies, who's going to be the next president. You know, you think about stuff. I don't care who's the next prime minister in the UK; we know that all the same things will happen. The political differences are so minor that we wouldn't really notice that much difference, I don't think, if you live an everyday life; whereas here, political changes do affect you.

Shane has made sure his children have British passports: the reality for all white South Africans is that an increasing number of their children have left the country. For many British residents, this is a prospect that some expect and even encourage. South Africa may give their children a 'better future' via its presumed better education system (or at least via a more affordable private education), but many do not expect their children to 'belong' in South Africa in the ways they claim to. This reveals tensions and contradictions in their own narratives of belonging, and deeper anxieties about the future of the country and the extent to which they and their families will be able to make a home there.

British-born immigrants negotiate everyday life in a context where their race, nationality and class carry considerable historical, economic and social significance. Belonging in this context is complex and shifting, and sometimes it is expressed in a contradictory narrative. Contemporary residents of South Africa, particularly in the tourist landscapes of the Western Cape, continue to draw from colonial conceptions of the African landscape and consider the area to be a lifestyle 'paradise'. However, the ability to realise and sustain this paradise is complicated by the socio-economic dynamics of South Africa that restrict and interfere with the everyday use of the landscape.

As Armbruster discerned in her interviews with German immigrants in Namibia: 'The enthusiastic appropriation of "Africa" as nature, co-existed with the "expulsion" of, and dissociation from, "Africa" as people and culture; often in the same conversation' (2010: 1235). This contradictory logic is difficult to maintain in contemporary South Africa, and the accounts we heard belie the lived material reality of how these landscapes are used and experienced. Focus on the material, everyday experiences of the landscape thus reveals tensions, anxieties, fear and alienation as well as some contrasting engagements and enjoyment of it.

The post-republic South African state encouraged the British to think of South Africa as a home away from home, albeit one where the sun always shone and where they would have the space and socio-economic ability to fulfil their lifestyle ambitions. The fractures in whiteness in South Africa meant that the lived reality was, however, quite different, and any British claims to 'home' in South Africa were treated with suspicion by Afrikaans-speaking whites. Today, intrawhite tensions can still be present and make British people feel 'strange' and foreign. For others, the ongoing 'whiteness' of certain spaces – in shopping malls, restaurants and in tourist landscapes – creates an apparently seamless sense of comfort in place and belonging.

This raises the question of where such people think they belong in twenty-first century South Africa. We have seen that belonging is a process of work and adaptation, and a process where failure results in unbelonging and ultimately return. The agency and mobility of British residents is often framed around their resourcefulness and resilience in a country where you 'sink or swim' but, as with all else, whiteness underpins and enables these narratives of upward mobility and significance.

Attitudes towards the UK raise further questions about place and home. For some, alienation towards an unrecognisable Britain underpinned their sense of place in South Africa and justified their move. Yet the complexity of South African society and the whiteness of British residents rendered the extent to which South Africa really was home unstable. Discussions about the future of family and children further revealed ambiguity and anxiety about the future and their family's place within it.

6
The Landscapes of Un/belonging in South Africa

Louise came to Johannesburg in 1996, after marrying Alan, a South African man she had met through work. Although Alan was happy in England – he had left South Africa in the 1980s because of 'all the troubles and difficulties' – Louise, then in her mid-30s, was ready for adventure. Alan still had family in the poor white suburb to the east of Johannesburg in which he had grown up, and had even been offered his old job back by an ex-boss who missed him. So Louise persuaded him to return: 'I said, "Come on, Alan! Let's go and do it. Let's go and see if we can make a go of it!" ... because I wanted to find out all about South Africa and what South Africa was all about.'

Keeping Louise's modest Victorian terrace on in the UK, they could still afford a 'huge four bedroom, two bathroom, South African house – you know the picture – with a massive swimming pool, which is the shape of Africa, in our garden. Palm trees everywhere!' Although at first Louise 'absolutely loved it', because 'South Africa gets in your blood', she admits that at the same time 'it's very much a complicated mesh of positive and negative influences', and has been 'all the way through'. For Alan, 'it was just like putting the fish back into water again ... you could just see him come alive!' but Louise experienced real problems finding work over the years, which she puts down to two key reasons: 'I'm white, so I'm not an affirmative action employee, and also I was British ... I wasn't a South African citizen.' Her lack of citizenship is a particular issue, she feels, for the Afrikaners who in many cases were on the selection panels of the jobs she was applying for in the civil service and academic settings: 'My experiences with [the civil service] have been really desperate, really desperate. And there's a lot of Afrikaans people who work in [the civil service]; same as there's a lot of Afrikaans people who work in education. Okay?'

In addition, their son, now 12, has learning difficulties that she feels have been poorly dealt with by the education system, despite her constant battles with various schools and teachers over the years. She now feels that here it is *she* who is the 'fish out of water', due to the fact she just doesn't belong: she feels she is saying and doing 'things that don't match up with their belief system and their way of doing things'. Missing Britain 'intensely' and having had her adventure, she now desperately wants to return.

Stephen has been in Johannesburg for over 30 years, is married to an English-speaking South African and has two teenage children. Extremely successful in business, he lives in the most prestigious and expensive area of Johannesburg, has a suite of cars in the garage, children at the top private school, and properties all over the city. However, in spite of his considerable economic achievements and domestic relationships, Stephen does not feel he belongs in South Africa, nor does he want to. By way of explanation, Stephen compares himself to his brother, another expatriate, who lives in America, and who, 'the minute he arrived in America and put his foot on the tarmac decided – and I think he was generally accepted – to be an American...so he has naturalised to the point where he is an American.' Stephen could imagine doing this himself in Australia, a country where he spent two years, because 'Australia is very inclined towards British. The Queen is still the monarch, the figurehead. You arrive in Australia, you want to be Australian, the minute you hit the tarmac you can be Australian.' In contrast, he feels that in South Africa, people cannot move on from their nationality, race or class: 'Here you arrive, and I am British, and I will always be British...You 're pigeonholed without even being asked. And I'm pigeonholed into "British South African", and there's an element of me in there, obviously – I don't want to let it go. I quite like being seen as the English fellow.' For Stephen, not only are different identities mapped onto people, but the gaps between different cultural groups are vast. He thinks he will never feel that he belongs in South Africa, because he will never understand or relate to its people or problems:

> How can somebody who's been here this long feel like he's British? It's quite easy. So with all respect to Mr Jacob Zuma, the President, he has 3 or 4 wives and 20 children. And really I can't quite relate to that. HIV, you know, I can explain why it's so prevalent here, is that my problem? Well, no. I don't think that's my problem. Julius Malema[1]! You know this gentleman?...So it's quite easy to distance

yourself from these things, and think, well, you know, it's going on, but it's not my problem. Now in Australia, you would find it very much easier to take on Australia's problems and consider them to be your own. Because you're there and you're fitting in...

As soon as Samantha picked up the article on Daniel and Pauline's research on 'The British in South Africa' in the *Daily Telegraph* online, she made contact. Loving Britain and feeling British to her very core, she just had to be involved. Many emails followed and complex arrangements were made so that Pauline could spend the day interviewing not only Samantha and her husband Dick, but a good selection of their British neighbours who lived nearby in their green and wooded suburb of Pietermaritzburg. Although not grand, their houses were located in an impressive location: dotted amongst trees on an undulating hill, they looked out onto views of the African landscape. At the same time, there is something quite 'English' about the ways in which the houses and their gardens are designed and, as the neighbours nip easily through their gardens to see each other for coffee, chats and news from 'home', their dogs trotting at their heels, a corner of England is recreated in both performance and imagination. 'We know all the neighbours in the street,' Samantha tells Pauline. 'Excuse the "Hallo", but I make a point when people walk in of asking them if they need help, do they know where doctors, dentists, wherever....'

Now well into their 70s, Samantha and Dick have been in Africa for nearly 50 years, coming out separately to 'Rhodesia' (Zimbabwe) and marrying once Samantha's first marriage 'went pear-shaped'. They have had a colourful life that has been dominated by their involvement with animals: they have owned their own safari company, kept horses and run stables, and worked for a travelling circus where Dick was the elephant keeper. When this sort of work was short, there were always the more humdrum occupations of painting and decorating or office work.

However, in spite of their exciting and unusual experiences, Samantha in particular has never stopped feeling thoroughly 'British': 'We fly the flag; during the World Cup, I had the flag on the car. We keep in touch: we blow our top about Brown, Blair, not too sure about Cameron, poor man, got an awful job. We're very English in that respect!'

Pauline asks if they are proud of being British. 'Ooh, yes!' Samantha gushes, while Dick is more temperate: 'We wouldn't change it, let's put it that way. We'd never fiddle with a passport.' Samantha concurs: 'When the opportunity came here, we categorically didn't even take dual.' Dick turns to Pauline to explain: 'A lot of Brits here take dual South African citizenship. We wouldn't!' 'Born English!' Samantha summarises.

Neil meets Pauline in a British-style pub in a small, unglamorous business park situated next to a busy six-lane highway on which the thunder of traffic is continuous. For many expatriates, working life is spent some way away from the glamour of Sandton, in one of the more industrially-oriented suburbs of Johannesburg where the offices of IT, construction and manufacturing companies intersect with run-of-the-mill shopping centres and middle-range housing. British or Irish pubs regularly dot these landscapes; artificially forged in the African sun, they provide local expatriate office workers with pints of beer, pie and chips, the television inevitably on in the background, showing the latest British football, rugby or cricket match. Though ostensibly meeting for 'lunch', this turns out to be nothing more than several pints of warm British beer in Neil's case.

Neil tells Pauline he has 'had it' with South Africa: always perturbed by the levels of crime during the seven years he has lived here, the imminent arrival of a baby has firmed his resolve to take his Afrikaner wife and new family back to the UK: 'I don't see it growing up in this country,' he explains. 'There's no freedom...I don't want it to not be able to trust people; I don't think that it's a good way of growing up.' Although his wife calls him 'paranoid', he feels it is his job to be always watching out for the possibility of attack: 'I can tell, three roads down, the same car is still following me. Some things you've got to be careful of.' While Neil says he knows 'all the tricks', and indeed fills Pauline in on many of them, he's got to the point where the crime and the corruption 'annoys me, because I see too much of the bad in this country to then find the good anymore'. But it is not only the level of crime that Neil feels will prevent him from ever relaxing, or belonging. It is also the behaviour of other white people that alienates him:

> Service also is another reason I want to go to the UK! We're so spoilt in this country, you know, just snap your fingers and you've got a beer on the table, and I see the worse side of it as well. I've seen a bloke come in, he'll sit down, and he won't say his 'please' or 'thank you', and he'll complain that his glass is slightly warm, and then 'Can you take my beer back, and you'll not bother us,' you know? I mean that's not me; that's not my lifestyle.

In the last chapter, we showed that nationhood and national belonging, while usually constructed from above, cannot be understood unless also analysed from below: that is, in terms of the assumptions, hopes, needs, (be)longings and interests of ordinary people (Hobsbawm 1990). National and ethnic belonging 'happens' in a variety of everyday settings, embodied and expressed in 'everyday encounters, practical categories, commonsense knowledge, cultural idioms, cognitive schemas, interactional cues, discursive frames, organisational routines, social networks, and institutional forms' (Brubaker 2004: 2). The journeys of migration to a new variety of such everyday settings involve a splitting of the practices and spaces of national belonging, from those conducted at home to those continued or sometimes newly forged away. In South Africa, as we saw in the last chapter, home, and any ongoing sense of belonging, are worked for: achieved and maintained through the imagination, the senses, the embodied performances and material objects of everyday life, which draw on the familiar routines of home. However, the ways in which home and senses of nationhood continuously 'leak' into people's narratives and performances revealed how these may work to prevent or mediate full integration into South Africa (Ahmed 1999). For many of our respondents, the United Kingdom is the lens through which South Africa is framed and judged, and while certain aspects are rendered as sources of potential belonging, others come into focus as emphasising difference and, consequently, unbelonging.

In their research on 'global Brits', Finch et al argue that British migrants are less likely to integrate successfully if they are retired or work for British or multinational companies, have limited family or friends locally, live in enclaves and have poor language skills (2010: 8). Based on research primarily undertaken in Bulgaria, India, Spain, Dubai and the United States – all countries with significant inflows of British migrants – they found, conversely, that those who had integrated successfully tended to work for local companies, have family or friends locally, engage in community activities and speak the local language. Perhaps even more important, they conjecture, is an emigrant's 'outlook': 'Those who are positive, entrepreneurial and looking to broaden their horizons do well'. Those who take a safety first approach, and are living overseas primarily because they can enjoy as better standard of living have a more limited experience' (2010: 8).

While our research to some extent corroborates these findings, South Africa's history and contemporary society once again present a challenge to general 'mainstream' findings such as these. However, rather than adopting a position of South African 'exceptionalism' (Nuttall 2001), we would reinforce the fact that the acknowledgement of context, in all its specificity, is always of key importance, nuancing issues or even understandings of integration, rendering it inappropriate to discuss these in deterritorialised or individualised terms. For example, as we have shown, the historically ambiguous and contested place of the British within white South African society, as well as their position now as part of a racial minority, means that (dis)integration, or senses of un/belonging, cannot be seen neatly as something to be necessarily achieved or not achieved according to a set of predetermined criteria, but are often more slippery, fractured and partial, negotiated according to time, space and place. For many of our respondents, feelings of unbelonging were not consistent or continuous but had a complex coexistent relationship with feelings of belonging. In contingent and highly selective ways, British migrants simultaneously expressed allegiance to, and disaffection from, the social, political and physical landscapes of both the United Kingdom and South Africa.

For some of the longer-term residents – those who had emigrated during the apartheid period to witness and live through the dramatic social and political changes – feelings of unbelonging may be replacing previous senses of engagement. As we saw in the previous chapter, many are unsettled by their uncertainty about the future, no longer sure what their place might be, and relieved by their possession of a British passport that allows them to leave with relative ease if necessary. Shifting senses of unbelonging were also demonstrated by some of our younger participants, such as Neil, whose new identity as husband and father was both positioning him more solidly within the white discourses of fear, while simultaneously alienating him from what he saw as the entrenched racism of white South African society. While Neil's fears about crime and security reflect a pervasive and general white concern about the future and position of white people in South African society, his decision to flee rather than push for change confirms the ambivalence of many of the British to long-term settlement and belonging.

The biographical stories used to open this chapter reflect the key themes that frame British senses of unbelonging in the new South Africa. As well as issues of crime, also important for many are their experiences of public services that may have been coloured by corruption or inefficiency; politics and the new black South African government; work, particularly in relation to affirmative action and other work-place policies; education for children; as well as relationships with other South Africans: black, Coloured, Indian, English- and Afrikaans-speaking. As stated above, many conceptualised these aspects through a transnational lens, such that Britain and the imagined landscapes of 'home' provided the ontology by which their South African experiences were constructed as alienating and they positioned themselves as 'different'. Further, for those who possessed a strong and continuing loyalty to, and longing for, Britain, everyday life in South Africa was often conducted against a sense of loss and belonging elsewhere.

Crime, security and corruption

> And so, around white dinner tables and at the corner cafe, a very different story about South Africa's transition began to circulate, and, while the finer details varied, the heart of the tale did not: it was about somebody who had been held up at gunpoint, another who had been shot, another who had been kidnapped in her own car. The anecdotes of guns and blood spread like an airborne disease, becoming something of a contagion. By the end of the millennium, much of white South Africa had died a thousand deaths in their own homes, around their own dinner tables. (Steinberg 2008: 26)

For many of the longer-term British, 'the rot started with law and order' (Johnson 2009: 445). The post-apartheid opening up of urban space meant that 'a criminal culture, whose appetite for commodities and for violence was legendary in the townships, arrived in the suburbs' (Steinberg 2008: 26), with the result that, as we saw in Chapter 4, the urban landscape became shored up and fortified, and the routine activities of everyday life were reconstructed as fraught with danger. Despite the fact that crime is rarely aimed at whites (Ballard 2004; Lemanski 2004; Steinberg 2008), the bulk of the older generation of British residents, in common with other white communities, have ratcheted up their approach to personal security since 1994. In addition, newer migrants, both young workers and older retirees, are given strong advice: always lock doors and windows on houses and cars, never walk anywhere, be careful where you go and certainly never venture into the townships and poorer suburbs unaccompanied. For some who had once felt at ease or at home in South Africa, now reconceptualising it and, in many cases, experiencing it firsthand as a landscape of criminal activity, was part of a broader shift in their relationship with the country.

As Ballard (2004) argues, this is fundamentally fuelled by the decline in their status in the post-apartheid state. For newer migrants, who are less likely to arrive with the same sort of ambitions for social positioning as their predecessors, the powerful discourse of violent crime may mean that they may never feel fully at home or that they 'belong'.

And indeed, it must be acknowledged, while their experiences of crime rarely, if at all, realised their imagination, all of the British we spoke to had personal experiences of crime. Most had, at one time or other, had their houses robbed, been accosted through their car windows, been held up at gunpoint or with another weapon, or been hijacked or forced to drive to a cash point to extract money (Steinberg 2008). As Stephen explains: 'If it goes badly, you get shot. If it goes well, they just make off with your phone, watch, wallet and car.' In spite of government evidence to the contrary, Stephen is among those who feel that experiences such as this are becoming more ubiquitous and as a result his response is sharpening:

> So it's getting worse, the numbers get bigger, the walls get higher. Instead of – you know somebody who's been affected by it – it's now us. It could happen to us! I had a hijack issue, and my employer was very keen that I went for counselling afterwards. So eventually I went to counselling, and I chatted to the fellow, but by then my view had come to the point that, the counselling is not because I was in shock, as to this happened to me; the counselling is that I would have killed him. If I had a weapon, I would have shot him; if I had a knife I would have stabbed him; if I had a brick I would have hit him. The counselling, in my case, was a bit of letting off steam as to what energy and desire there was on my side to take him out.

Stephen's stark response highlights his lack of connection or empathy with his South African compatriots, but this was not uncommon. Jane, who lives in Cape Town with her husband Barry, has witnessed her daughter being shot in a 'car jacking' when they lived in Johannesburg. Jane's daughter recovered, but Jane remarks, 'A black person can smile and help you put your shopping in the boot when you're at the mall, but you can never be sure they won't hit you over the head and rob you the next minute.' As we saw in Chapter 4, Neil also has a range of weaponry that he is prepared to use if necessary. However, while Stephen does not seem uncomfortable with the acknowledgement that he would kill if necessary, for Neil, this is a stark change in his identity that he is not happy with. Stephen, a long-term resident who has never felt he belonged but is unworried by this, regards crime as just another facet of his alienation to the country in which he resides. Neil finds it more difficult to accommodate; not only the crime, but also the corruption that is attendant in some quarters of public life, including the police. Although he realises that the reason for this is partially due to inadequate pay and conditions, he feels that he will never get used to incidents such as the following, by which embodied performances are abruptly shifted out of their normal habitus:

> And so there's a lot of corruption because there isn't the money or resources to give to people. I mean, one time I was driving back from work, Friday afternoon about 2 o'clock, and I was pulled over by... there's different types of police in this country, but it was a metro cop for the cars... and then there's different ones for like, the gun smuggling and the drugs. I was pulled over by a metro cop, and he was asking me the questions: 'Where you come from?' I said, 'Just come from work,' and he says, 'It's Friday, isn't it?' and I'm like, 'Yeah.' He says, 'I think I'm gonna have some beers tonight!' And I was like, 'Maybe I will as well.' You know, and he was like, 'Do you have any money?' and it was like begging, begging... Metro police begging. It makes me annoyed, and when I go to the UK, and I see the police pull someone over, I feel like that is how it should be done, you know, not like what you see in this country.

Public service

Neil accuses the police not only of corruption, but also of general incompetence and even ignorance of the appropriate performances of public service. For Neil, it is the British police who set the standard, and deviations from this merely confirm his sense of unbelonging: :'I've seen cop cars stop within a 4-way stop. I know you don't get them in the UK, but it's like a junction. They stop in a junction to buy ice cream! I mean, "Come on! You're supposed to be teaching people how to do things!" and things like that annoy me.'

Others, too, drew on the activities of the police as representative of their sense of unbelonging in the country. However, for most, unlike Neil or Stephen, unbelonging was a fractured rather than consistent identity, at times exacerbated, but at others rationalised, as the unfamiliar becomes more accepted. Laura explains this well:

> You're initially interested, then it plateaus, and there's the hostile phase, and then you get your humour phase when you get, 'I accept it's like this,' and I can laugh at it rather than get annoyed by it. I remember going through a very cross stage about things (pause) –

things like police stops. I got stopped by the police and pranged for a massive fine for something I really didn't deserve, and that whole thing – that sense of how you relate to the police is very different here. At the end he said, 'I hope you remember I didn't ask you for a bribe!' I said, 'I hope not!' So then, people have said it's possible to get the fine squashed if you go directly, and you offer to pay it off there, and then they'll squash it. And I went, and they just would not budge, and I thought, 'I'm sure 100 rand note would do this, but I'm not going to do it,' so there was definitely that feeling. Whereas in the UK, I just never felt any attempt of 'Oh no, it's the police. I need to be careful.' I remember having that moment then, and then once going out, seeing a police stop, and I didn't have my driving licence and thought, 'I've got to go home and get this because if I get stopped, this is just a nightmare.' Whereas I never – that sort of feeling just didn't happen in the UK.

The police are not the only public servants whose activities produce senses of unbelonging for British migrants. Although certainly used to the bureaucratic red tape of the UK's public administration, at home, British-born residents are positioned differently and, as such, they are much more confident of their rights and expectations. Since 1994, as the entitlements of whites are felt to be more uncertain and up for question, white interactions with the state are becoming less sure-footed than they once were (Steyn 2001). This is not least in terms of the right of abode and settlement, where the shift from Temporary to Permanent Resident for newer migrants may take some time to be confirmed. In order to live, work, benefit from public services, and travel freely in and out of the country, full 'Permanent Resident' status is needed. However, this is not always easy to come by, and the variety of conditions that are now applied to its award has led to a perception by some that there is deliberate discrimination at work against 'ordinary' whites who are not, for example, in possession of shortage skills or aiming to set up a new business. Many had become further frustrated from their interactions with Home Affairs over their residency, due to a perceived slowness and intransigence in African bureaucracy, which was sometimes tainted with suspicions of corruption. This is unsettling, and the extended uncertainty that some experience perhaps prolongs senses of displacement and feelings of unbelonging. Jill and John, for example, a retired couple who have been in South Africa for 15 years, had started to apply for their permanent residency three years previously. For various reasons, this has been dragging on, and they are now becoming increasingly exasperated by their interactions with Home Affairs. John takes up the story:

> Now the only problem we have is getting the Department of ... What do they call it? ... Home Affairs! To pull their finger out and give us our permanent residence. We think they've lost it. Because it's three years this November since we applied. And we were told 18 months ago via phone by the department that it had been approved. And then it went quiet and nothing happened. And then we started ringing, and it was evident they'd lost our files. We were right on the cusp of them going from a manual system to a computer system, and we have probably fallen through the cracks. One of the last on the manual system, and we just got lost somewhere! Because [it's important] otherwise every three years or whatever we've got to go down and get a new temporary residence ... and of course they can say no at any time. You can't go out of South Africa – we daren't go out, because you have to have that little stamp apparently in the back of your passport to say you were living here and you can come back in.

As a result of the perceived vulnerability of their position, Jill and John have not left South Africa since they first arrived in 1996. John's son lives here, too, and his daughter has visited, but for Jill this means she has not seen much of her family. While on one level they have got used to this – 'We chat all the time on Skype!' – and their touristic relationship to the country means 'We've got all of South Africa to explore', it was clear that this enforced immobility distanced rather than settled them: 'I would like to go and see my dad because he's late 80s, and, you know, he's on borrowed time, if you like, so just once I would like to go and see him' Jill tells Pauline, somewhat sadly.

Politics and 'The New South Africa'

The advent of democracy in 1994 ushered in new understandings and expectations of civic participation and engagement. For the New South Africa, there were high hopes that 'citizenship' would mean more than a mere expectation of legal rights, and would include a range of ideas and practices with more substantive content (Nuttall 2001; von Lieres and Robins 2008). This would involve changes in everyday performances and relations, by which the South African people could become more bound and connected to each other, irrespective of race. Participation was seen to be key to this: as von Lieres and Robins argue, 'Citizenship is not bestowed by the state or by a set of legal norms, but is enacted in a set of diverse practices and spaces, and involves multiple identities and struggles around complex issues' (2008: 50). While it is through full civic engagement with the multifaceted issues that face South Africa that an active sense of compatriotism may be produced, for many of the British, with their longstanding reputation of political disengagement and enduring identification with the homeland, this would require a substantial change in their positionings. So it is pertinent to ask: to what extent has the changed political culture increased their participation in civic and political affairs and, consequently, their sense of belonging?

One of the most striking features to emerge from our analysis of the interview transcripts was the high proportion of people who described themselves as 'not political', particularly in Johannesburg. A claim to be disengaged from any sort of political participation or identification was an almost ubiquitous and unsolicited ululation amongst our respondents, of both long- and short-term residence. For the long termers, a denial of political commitment, or recognition of any need for this, is often offered as an 'excuse' for their earlier tolerance of, or complicity with, apartheid, and their current lack of interest in political affairs. On giving their stories of arrival during the 1960s, 1970s and 1980s, a common position to take was that South Africa's political regime 'had nothing to do with me'. As will be discussed more fully in the next chapter, although perhaps forewarned and even shunned by friends and family in the UK for their decision to migrate during a period of global excommunication, adopting a position of complete lack of political interest or knowledge was often used to justify this. At the same time, the discourse of political disinterest reaffirms a sense of national unbelonging, and any consequent obligation to either take personal responsibility for, or engage in resistance against, the political system.

As we saw in Chapter 4, Moira and her partner Ted live on their own private game park, some way to the north of Johannesburg. For Moira, living in the bush surrounded by wild animals was the fulfilment of a childhood dream. Desperate to come to Africa, politics had meant nothing to her: it was the animals, not the people that mattered. When she saw a job vacancy in Pretoria advertised in the British press, she didn't so much write a CV as 'a begging letter'. Yet, on being offered the job, her British colleagues were horrified. This was 1975, when the UK was learning the realities of apartheid, and for left-wing activists such as her head of department, migration was inconceivable:

> He was hell of a nice guy. He took me aside and said 'Ten years.' I mean, he was really, really up with current affairs and what was going on, and he said to me, 'Ten years. Don't stay there more than ten years; there's going to be a blood bath.' Yes, that's what he said, 'There will be a blood bath in ten years,' and it would be very violent and very nasty.

However, as Moira explains, 'I wasn't really interested in politics.... Blow the politics, I wasn't interested. All my life, I think, perhaps a terrible thing to admit, but I haven't really been interested in people, what people do, how they act, what they do: let them get on with it. I'm interested in having animals around. So blow apartheid, I wanted an animal!'

Arriving in Pretoria, she found little reason to change her lack of political engagement. From what she could see, things had been exaggerated, anyway: 'I think that I would've been disturbed by the politics if it was as bad as it had been made out to be, but I didn't find it that way. I didn't find that. As I say, I saw well-dressed blacks walking around Pretoria, and it was fine.'

Denying the realities of the apartheid system, Moira buried herself in setting up her game reserve. Acquiring and caring for animals has occupied Moira's and her partner Ted's time fully since then. The only blot on the landscape has been the lingering question of whether there is a long-term future for whites in the new South Africa. Consequently, it was for instrumental reasons, rather than wanting to engage politically, that they took out citizenship in 1994. This would, they felt, help to minimise their chances of being 'thrown out' once the democratic government came to power. Nevertheless, like many British, she and Ted constructed an escape plan, 'just in case':

> Because we didn't know what was going to happen, and how the government would react to non-South Africans, we purposely took out citizenship so that we could vote in the elections. We didn't really know whether the new political powers would turn around and say, 'But you're not really citizens!' So we bought two vehicles – we bought a Rolls Royce and we bought a Land Rover – and the idea was: we weren't married, there's nothing to connect us. We would simply drive out of South Africa, and we'd go to Zimbabwe. This was the

plan. We would pack what we could into the cars, and Tony would – he's brilliant with all things mechanical – so he would just freelance doing repairs, either cars or industrial machinery, or anything else you'd like to mention, and I would use the Rolls to do weddings and occasions and things like that, and this is what we'd decided. We had made our plans, and we knew exactly what we would do. Picked the wrong country, but we didn't have to. We didn't have to, nothing happened. Our ordinary lives just went on; they just carried on.

For Moira and Ted, 'ordinary life' means going about their daily business in a way that is detached from broader political events. Living right out in the bush, everyday life consists of walking the dogs, daily drives to check on their livestock, and the occasional excitement of a new delivery of zebra, buck or giraffe. Their personal investment in, and sense of entitlement to, the physical and nonhuman landscape of South Africa is clear, but this does not extend to any sense of political or civic obligation. If they feel it necessary, they will just drive north. However, converse to their espoused lack of political engagement, this 'escape plan' can be considered a very political act. Their need to have radical plans 'just in case' illustrates that their first priority is to maintain a certain standard of living for themselves, rather than more equality for all, and they will decamp quickly if this is threatened.

Moira and Ted's professed lifelong detachment from South African politics was a common response for longer-term British residents in the Johannesburg area, in spite of the fact they had clearly benefitted from its consequences. It certainly did not follow that a change of government meant a positive shift in the extent or manner of their political participation or identification with the country in which many had lived for much of their lives. The picture in Cape Town was somewhat different, however. A number of respondents here talked at great length to Daniel about Helen Zille, the premier of the Westen Cape, the predominantly white Democratic Alliance, and how unprofessional the ANC were.

Conversely, in Piermaritzburg, Pauline met a group of 'liberal' whites, many of whom had been anti-apartheid activists and now, today, were largely supportive of the aims of the ANC and keen to see it succeed. The diversity in the amount and kind of political engagement underscores the differences between the cities and the types of 'white spaces' therein, as well as the 'white talk' that goes on within these.

For newer migrants, fresh from multicultural Britain, a sense of political distance was also often found, but for very different reasons. Like Neil, whom we discussed above, many were shocked by the blatant racism of much of the white community, and the divisions that exist between the different sections of South African society. As Lottie explains,

> Politically, obviously it's very different. There's some conversations you have with people, I think they're very racist, very racist. And it's like, Ooh, okay! Especially how some people treat their staff. I just think it's...yeah. I mean, I'm not putting all people in the same, but a lot of the Afrikaans are very...Some of them treat their staff so badly, so rude. It's just manners, you know, at the end of the day. Be polite to people. That was quite shocking.

For various reasons, therefore, very few of our interviewees described themselves as 'South African', although some admitted to supporting South African sporting teams over the British. On the other hand, 'being British', in one form or another, was both a subject position and a set of performances that all our respondents signed up to: some with pride, some with ambivalence, and some attempting to have it both ways: juggling a British identity alongside a South African one because of partners and children. For some, their sense of Britishness meant that they felt they could never fully belong to South Africa: they would always be 'different' and look at the country through a transnational lens.

While in recent years, within Britain itself, the very existence of a 'British', and especially, an English identity, has come under some debate (Alibhai-Brown 2000; Kumar 2003), amongst our respondents there was a very clear sense not only that it existed, but that it could never be lost or discarded. However, as we suggested in the previous chapter, what was also clear was that, for many of the longer-term residents in particular, their imagination of what this identity is was at odds with many of the debates on its constitution, which are being conducted within contemporary Britain itself (Parekh 2000). Theirs is an identity frozen in the past: historical, white and exclusive. Further, while other research on privileged migrants suggests that Britishness is an identity that, through migration, they attempt to minimise (O'Reilly 2000; Benson 2009), this is very much not the case for the British in South Africa. It is not necessarily that they want to return to live in Britain and certainly not the case that they all agreed with the politics there – indeed, many had nothing for derision for British politics and its recent decisions on, for example, immigration. However, the strength of their continued interest in British politics and all things British was a political position that sustained a lingering sense of unbelonging to South Africa.

Work and education

It is perhaps the landscapes of work and education that have been most fundamentally changed for whites in South Africa in the post-apartheid period. The exclusive access to jobs and career opportunities that had previously been assured and taken for granted have been intersected by the legislation on affirmative action and Black Economic Empowerment (BEE) that aims to empower those negatively affected by apartheid (Southall 2004). While at first whites were able to resist much of the full impact of this legislation in the workplace, Mbeki's 'Two Nations' speech in 1998 ushered in a 'broader based' version of the legislation which, amongst other criteria, strengthened equity in employment and skills development (Ponte et al. 2007). Many corporations are now taking the legislation seriously, and together with the improved access of black children to educational opportunities, workplaces at all levels of the labour market are becoming more multicultural with a consequent and substantial growth in the black middle class. While, on one level, the internationalisation of many of South Africa's businesses and the opening up of the economy to multinational corporations means that opportunities for white migrants still remain, as well as the continued presence of white South Africans in the labour market, long constructed as the economically inclined group with international links (Salusbury and Foster 2004; Jeffery 2010), some of our respondents, particularly the women, had negative experiences in regards to finding work and establishing businesses and, for them, this was a primary reason for feelings of unbelonging.

Louise considered herself amongst the hardest hit and was somewhat bitter as a result. Continuing her story from the beginning of this chapter, after having her son, Louise has tried long and hard to secure work and develop some sort of professional career that befits her experience and qualifications. As a trained management consultant and researcher, she felt she had a good skill set to offer, but the combination of what she sees as bureaucratic intransigence combined with discrimination has made her attempts to secure permanent work opportunities 'an absolute disaster'.

Her first hurdle was to gain a work permit, given that she had migrated as a spouse rather than for reasons of work:

> The only way that you can get a work permit to come into South Africa, and I believe it's still the case, is to enter into South Africa for the purpose of work. So it's not entering into South Africa as my

husband's wife, or being my husband's wife, or just being here and having permission to work and do odd bits of consultancy when I want to. That doesn't exist. We only found this out afterwards, after we'd been through the whole sorry process...Because I thought a work permit gave you permission to work and to go and seek work, and it doesn't do that at all. So I fell foul of that, and then there was a big hoo-hah about trying to get the next work permit because I'd already had a difficulty with the first one. And it was just amazing what we were doing. It was just the hoops that we had to go through.

Her lack of a work permit meant that her first attempts at securing work became very 'messy'. From the start she felt she was at a disadvantage

for two reasons: I'm white. I was white, so I'm not an affirmative action employee, which is what they were looking for, and also I was British, and I wasn't a South African citizen. And in the end, the whole thing almost came to fisticuffs because they then said that they understood that I was a South African citizen. So I'd made it clear all the way along that I was British. I said, 'I've made this jolly clear all the way along. The whole point is that you're employing international skills that you don't have available in South Africa,' you see. But it was very, very messy – because I needed to get a work permit in order to work for them, and then that went into the huge Home Affairs black hole, which is indescribable in terms of bureaucracy and the difficulty navigating around when they don't give you any instructions. And I had already tried to get a work permit before in order to have permission to work.

With a difficult pregnancy, she decided to give up the idea of working for a few years:

It's been a struggle right from the word 'Go', from the beginning. So I basically just said, 'Stuff you, job. I'm not going in for this because I've got a much bigger problem going on here'...I'd tried so hard, because as you can see, I'm very motivated, and I just want to make a contribution. That was one instance of a lot of times of trying and giving up through one thing and another, and I strongly believe that it's to do with my Britishness.

On trying to enter the labour market again several years later, things were no less frustrating. However, rather than blaming the policy of

BEE, Louise puts her lack of success down to the competitive aspects of British-Afrikaner relations, and the fact that the Afrikaners 'consider themselves to be superior', as well as because of the environment here: 'They don't value you. They don't value your skills and abilities.' Although she managed to secure some consultancy work, unfortunately this did not lead to anything more permanent, as she had hoped. Although the Afrikaner management 'paid the money for me, they did not understand it... or give me one moment of thanks or acknowledgement for it'. Other 'difficult' experiences followed, such as being asked to apply for jobs, only to see them being filled by internal Afrikaner applicants. 'And my issue is, I can't even bloody well pronounce Afrikaans names, for heaven's sake! So I'm not in the culture... I'm just not in the culture here. And if they want to – if they want to talk about anything at all, they can just switch into Afrikaans, and you're totally clueless!' Feeling that she has 'basically come up against a brick wall time and time and time and time again', Louise now feels that she must return to the UK.

Her feelings of unsettlement and her rationalising of this as being due to discrimination by Afrikaners are further bolstered by her experiences with the educational system. Her son, Andrew, has learning disabilities, and these have necessitated many meetings at his school in order to discuss his progress. Her first issue is with the timing of these meetings, a factor of embodied practice that underscores how she has never really adjusted to the South African habitus:

> Because your British clock is on things starting at nine o'clock or eight-thirty, that's what your British clock is, but things here mostly start at seven or seven-thirty! So if you're going to have a special meeting at school about your child, it's seven a.m. in the morning. And I've always resisted against that. I said, 'No, lunchtime. Half past one, thank you!' Because this is an important meeting about my child, and I want to be geared up for this, and I'm not going to stress like crazy to get there, dump Andrew half an hour earlier for school, completely overturn everything, probably get no sleep the night before just to get to a meeting at seven o'clock. But they regard this as completely normal! I don't though, because I'm always on a British clock, and that's never changed. It's never changed!

In spite of the very regular meetings she has with the school, she feels that they have failed to address or meet Andrew's needs to her satisfaction. She longs for him to be 'sorted for the future' and be at a school, which is 'giving him all the opportunities and maximising his strengths and addressing his weaknesses'. Unfortunately, from her perspective, 'this is patently not happening over here'. As a consequence, she feels she has had to 'fight, fight, fight'. The school claims that the problem is due to anxiety:

> Anxiety! Well, of course it's bloody anxiety. You would be anxious if you were trying to cope in grade four with this problem. You would be anxious. Anxiety comes from somewhere. And then of course, no, it's the mother that's anxious. I'm a neurotic mother! Because, 'Oh, it's Mrs Miller complaining again.' You know, 'Here she goes again.' That type of thing. But I actually found this is not uncommon to South Africa.

Louise feels that Andrew's needs would be much better met in the UK, where there is a nationally benchmarked approach to the teaching of reading. In contrast, in South Africa, Louise feels that 'they will quite happily run with huge margins in between chronological and actual reading age without perceiving it as a problem'. Another problematic issue for her is the fact that he has to learn Afrikaans:

> He has to spend all of his time, regularly, as a part of their curriculum, on Afrikaans, whereas what I want to do is get him literate in English, thank you very much! And then aged 16, if they fail Afrikaans, they fail their matric! There are 11 official languages in South Africa, so why isn't there a second language option on Zulu or Hausa, or any one of the other 11 official languages? Why is that?

Louise not only resents the fact that Afrikaans has a dominant place in the curriculum, but also in part blames his Afrikaner teachers for detecting her son's issues: 'For grade two and grade three, he had Afrikaans-speaking [teachers], and they waved him through and said "There's absolutely nothing to worry about." Grade four, he went back to a white, English-speaking teacher, and she said his word attack skills are very poor, his spelling is very weak, dah-dee-dah.'

Putting the issues of work and education together means that Louise feels discriminated against. As she concludes, 'These two key drivers mean that I want to come home to England: my work, and forging a path through for the future, given that I still think I have a lot to offer, and I don't want to be out to pasture, aged 48 and never do anything else. I haven't been able to fulfil my potential.'

Her husband is several years older than Louise and has now retired. He is, it appears, happy to support his wife's desire to return to England and, although for him it means leaving his own family and country behind, the family have decided that it is now time for Louise to be 'the fish to be put back into the water'.

Relations with others

In the ways that the British talk about and relate to others, race, ethnicity, nationality and un/belonging are made, remade and, very occasionally, unmade as key ways of seeing themselves and the world (Erasmus 2008). While most constitute themselves and others as racialised and ethnicised, through the diverse ways that colour and national heritage are drawn upon as meaningful categories and used, shorthand, to explain differences, group boundaries were constructed. While most positioned black South Africans as 'other' and were unable to identify with their lives or their politics, for some, such as Stephen, the perceived rifts between whites and blacks were imagined to be so deep as to prevent any vision of South Africa as unified or a place to which he could belong. For others, such as Louise, the divisions she felt were most salient were between whites, particularly between the British and the Afrikaners. Because she had assumed a certain commonality, that white people would be 'on the same wavelength', it came as some surprise to her that there were real differences in the ways in which white people understood and related to each other. The dawning recognition of this exacerbated her sense of unbelonging, as she explains:

> My friend Jane, who I'm also incredibly close with – so she is white, English-speaking South African, and I am British. So you have Afrikaners, you have people who've been born and brought up in South Africa but not Afrikaans, so they're white English-speaking. And then you have British people. And then you have a whole different other set, circles of people who come from different nationalities, either first- or second- or third-generation South Africans. So you have Portuguese, you know, and all the rest of it. And most of those, you'll find – because of South Africa being what it is – they come from different areas. You know, you don't have to go back through many generations to find out how many people have British heritage, you know. But they've been in South Africa for several generations, so they consider themselves born and bred South African, and they don't speak with British accents; they speak with South African

> accents. So the differences between Jane and myself, and we're completely on the same wavelength about such a lot of things, but just the things that you talk about and the outlook, she could never understand my difficulties with Afrikaners. She couldn't empathise with that at all. As far as she's concerned, she's working in a prevalently Afrikaans [workplace], which is Afrikaans in its heritage. She's fluent in Afrikaans herself. She talks and speaks and works with Afrikaans people all the time. She doesn't have an issue. It must be me...And then, you know, the sort of things that I say, like there's all sorts of nuances about British speech and British culture, which is completely different to white, English-speaking South African culture.

The distance and competition that Louise perceives to exist between the British and the Afrikaners is not only a mystery but a disappointment to her, working to augment her sense of estrangement. For others, it is more important to maintain the differences between the British and Afrikaners, and the sense of British 'unbelonging' to broader white South African society. Typically positioning the Afrikaners as more traditional and entrenched in the ideologies of the rural and/or apartheid past, an alternative British response was to emphasise the perceived boundaries between the two groups, as well as other communities within South Africa.

Norman has lived in the Johannesburg area since the early 1970s, coming out originally to undertake academic research. He gradually moved into management as he felt he 'could do their job as well as them', and was then headhunted by a sequence of high profile corporations. Making a considerable amount of money, he and his English-speaking South African wife have more recently become farmers and horse breeders. Norman is keen to tell Pauline that he believes that 'separate development is right' because the differences between the communities are such that there will never be a common sense of belonging:

> Well, the Afrikaner I'll start with; there's still many of them – well, you've got the problem again that many of them have almost been tribalised. If you go down into the real countryside, where you've got the Afrikaner farmers and things like that, as a woman you will sit quiet; you won't speak. Unless the man says, 'You may now speak.' It's as bad as that! I was at a farm right deep down in the bush on one occasion. Where the mother and the daughter sat silent. Until the son said they could converse...So there's that area, and there's the other who are still living deep in the Boer War. You know, the Boer

War was a pretty awful thing. I met the Afrikaans director of one or other company. We were at a cocktail party once, and he came over to me, and he'd had too much to drink! And he said to me, 'Why did you give my grandmother a broken glass to drink?' So there's certain of them where it's still strong... but mostly they're fine and super!

Despite the frequent positioning of the Afrikaners as farmers with a strong, historical entitlement to the land, their approaches to land management and, in particular, animal-keeping, were sometimes drawn upon to contest the legitimacy of this position. Other writers have also noted the ways in which animals have been used by humans to construct a distinctive range of identities for themselves within the African context, and an impressive body of literature exists that explores the ways in which domestic animals such as dogs and horses are drawn upon in support of race, identity and difference-making, particularly in South Africa (e.g., Swart 2003; van Sitter and Swart 2008). The horse, for instance, was first imported in 1652 and became integral to settler identities, 'used both symbolically and in a material sense to affirm white difference from the indigenous population' (Swart 2003: 48). In our research, we also found that relationships with animals and animal husbandry were often used to define British identity as well as to construct difference – and superiority – from the Afrikaners.

However, the attempt to unsettle the assumed bond between the Afrikaners, the land and its animals often only served to emphasise British unbelonging. For example, Moira and Ted excused their powerful commitment to the animals on their game park as being a particular facet of Britishness: 'I think it's only the Brits that get taken over by animals... There's not so many people with [our] sort of passion,' Ted informed Pauline as they bumped over the rutted bush. Further, it is not only passion that distinguishes the British relationship with animals and the land, but also the higher status that is given to their knowledge, especially in comparison to the perceived ignorance of the Afrikaners as Ted goes on to explain:

> We have this problem, and this misconception about here today, and the people of Afrikaner stock that live out here, they have this inbred belief that nobody can tell them – nobody will tell them what they can and can't do with their land and its – it is a problem. And the other thing is of course that – the words '5 hectares per large livestock units stocking level' mean absolutely nothing to them. You know they, 'Oh, you know, 20 hectares- oh, that's a big piece of

land. Oh, I could have had sheep – I can have sheep and cattle and I can feed myself and feed my family!' Wrong! 20 hectares is just big enough to go bankrupt on. So, of course, overgrazing becomes the norm and...it really is quite a problem.

A further point of difference often mentioned was the ways in which the British and Afrikaners relate to black South Africans. For Ruth, this was drawn upon as a metaphor to illustrate what being British in South Africa actually meant, her use of the word 'local' underscoring a prevailing sense of unbelonging, despite having lived in Johannesburg for nearly 50 years:

> What does being British here mean? Well, you have to realise you're foreign, but nobody really treats you as foreign. Nobody treats you as foreign. Strangely enough, black South Africans like to work for us because I think they find a fairness in, in the way they're treated to a great extent...perhaps more than they do with locals, with South Africans, although the farming community treat black people very differently...quite strong-handedly, but then Africans respect that as well. So there's two, two ways to...one is the, yes, the human dignity and human respect, and the other is the masterly, of being a bit patronising and managing...and it depends on how educated black people are as to which they will prefer.

Despite constructions such as these, we are not arguing that differences between the two 'groups' of whites were a constant or fixed construction, creating stable senses of unbelonging. Rather, respondents' narratives were highly contradictory, and relationships with Afrikaners were flexible, positioned simultaneously as sameness and difference, and reflections of both belonging (to the white community) and unbelonging (to the new black, South Africa). Although greater boundaries were usually perceived to exist between whites/the British and the black communities, here, too, multiple and fragmented positions were negotiated, such that senses of unbelonging were variable and transient, rather than stable or permanent. Thus to emphasise difference, a range of stereotypes were often drawn upon to accentuate the 'strangeness' of black practices and culture. For instance, Norman, who was very keen to position himself as an expert on South Africa, was concerned that, as researchers who did not belong, we would 'get it all wrong'. As such, his aim was to 'put us right', emphasising his credentials by the longevity of his residence and the opportunities he has had to participate in 'the real (black) South Africa'. As he sees it, his involvement in some activities, generally considered unusual for white people, underscores his belonging to the country. At the same time, however, the ways in which he constructs his narrative, and the aspects he chooses to focus on in order to define black South African life, only serve to underline his own unbelonging:

> I spent a lot of time out in the bush with people when I could... things had happened to me that I can't explain, how or why they happened.... because you're really dealing with magic and things like that. I mean, things like funerals and that are very interesting. A funeral for a black will take anywhere between two and three days. And it's really a big party, isn't it? The night before they have this enormous ceremony, where all the friends and that, you stand up and say something nice about the person who's dead. And then you go into a wail. Then the next person stands up, and this goes on for – all night. Then the next day you have the ceremony again, which lasts all day. And then there's a thing; there's ten bags of cabbages. There's the half a sheep or that, because anyone who goes has to be fed... The black people are very interesting.

Norman was not alone in fixing on the supposedly 'primitive' aspects of black culture. Those who were experiencing a change in the racial configuration of their local neighbourhoods, as members of the black middle class were moving into previously whites only areas, often commented on changes in community practices such as the playing of loud music or the slaughtering of cows in the back garden. While maintaining the 'otherness' of their new neighbours was primarily used as a means of emphasising the fact that they did not really belong, in the process this also reveals an unwillingness to converge with the broader vision of a multicultural South Africa. In the next chapter, we turn to examine more directly the extent to which the British are adapting to the social and political changes happening within South Africa.

7
Narratives of Continuity and Change: British Social and Political Attitudes in South Africa

> You know, here, the kids, they see it every day. We see children begging at traffic lights and my three-and-a-half-year-old, or my four-year-old daughter now, she says – or she understands that those children have got no Mummy and Daddy, and that's really sad, and she understands that, and you can't get that in schools. For me, I get quite emotional about it because it really is something that I only realised when I left. We have no grounding in the UK at all unless you come out here and do work. Lots of charities here, they build houses. There's a huge Irish building company that comes over here every year. They really are trying to help, but it's the people in South Africa that will make it change, not an organisation from Dublin, you know, as good as they are, and I think that there's a lot of what we call 'white guilt' as well, a lot of old South Africans who really genuinely feel bad about what happened, and they genuinely are trying to change it.
> —Shane, emigrated to Cape Town in 2001

The Guardian newspaper's South Africa correspondent, Rory Carroll (14/8/2006), published a valedictory article about his time living in the country, shortly before he moved to a different country. Carroll explained,

> This never really became home. Partly it was running to the airport every other week for overseas trips; partly it was being white and European; but mainly it was because South Africa was such a fraught

place to live. The anxiety about crime, the crunching on racial eggshells, the juxtaposition of first-world materialism with third-world squalor – it all added up.

The article caused considerable controversy in the country and beyond. Carroll's posting to the country continued: 'Everywhere I turned, South Africa presented difficult choices'. He had been a victim of crime, a romantic date with a black woman turned sour when a beer-drinking white man in the same bar called her a prostitute, and he came to realise that even self-styled white progressives were living in a bubble, alienated from the wider society around them. As a result, Carroll often felt more comfortable in other African countries, where 'whiteness is an issue but without South Africa's sting' (14/8/2006).

In our research, while we rarely encountered such antipathy, we did come across a wide range of responses to the dynamic politics and society of South Africa. These responses were mediated by the area of South Africa in which the respondents lived, time spent in the country (particularly for those who had emigrated during apartheid and those who moved to South Africa after 1994) and age.

For Shane, quoted above, South Africa's 'rawness' as a society, its obvious poverty and inequality, made it more 'real' and important for him and his children to experience. For others, this poverty 'on display' was a sign of the country's decline after 1994. A few continued to remain oblivious of the majority of South Africa's population and strangely naive about its past and contemporary challenges. The discourses that British migrants articulated to define the country and their place in it relate to broader white discourses and the 'white talk' (Steyn 2001) that continues to dominate understandings of South Africa. This 'white talk', which seeks to frame South Africa's history and politics in white self-interest and thereby to obscure ongoing white privilege, was not always the same as broader white discourses, however. The 'Britishness' of our respondents gave them a different perspective, the majority claimed, and South Africa was always (often favourably) compared to life in Britain. There was also the lived reality of daily life: where people worked, shopped, ate, drove and walked. These shaped perceptions of South African society and enabled our respondents to give starkly different accounts of their perceptions of society and politics in the country.

The transition from an apartheid state to a post-apartheid democracy acted as a 'tipping point' in many people's narratives. These were, in the main, structured around a 'before/after' temporality, whereby life 'now' was compared to the past, either from experience or imagination.

However, narratives about the political, social and economic changes happening in South Africa were not contained within that country alone; they intersected continually with what was perceived to be happening in the United Kingdom. This meant that attitudes towards, and decisions about, continuity and change within South Africa were often framed through a lens that included reflections on aspects of continuity and change at 'home'.

In this chapter, we turn to explore more directly these three themes, as they were constructed through the narratives of our respondents: apartheid South Africa, post-apartheid South Africa and the various discourses by which the United Kingdom was variously positioned. As we go on to show, this was usually in relation to the trope of 'Bad Britain' (O'Reilly 2000), whereby relations with and attitudes towards South Africa were framed simultaneously with a view of the United Kingdom as a nation in decline.

Remembering, negotiating and embodying apartheid

> In 1971, we made the decision to go back to the UK, and my reason was that I didn't know how to – I thought, how do I tell my child that I – you know, that man can't go into that lift because of the colour of his skin. Or he can't sit on that park bench. And also, I felt that the, you know, the children had more freedom in England. I suppose I was – well, I realised later that was being a little bit foolish, and I was thinking of the life I had as child, although I was brought up, you know, during the war years for part of – a lot of it. And we didn't have material things, but we, you know, we could go cycling miles around the countryside and things like that. We used to follow the sun on our bicycles [both laugh]. So we sold our house and packed up and shipped our belongings overseas. (Susan, emigrated to Johannesburg in 1963, now living Somerset West, Western Cape)

Susan and her family's return to England did not meet with success. They struggled to establish a new business and never settled back; by the mid-1970s, they had returned to Johannesburg. Daniel asked Susan what she told her daughter when (and if) she asked about the racism of apartheid. 'It never – I don't think it happened, actually', Susan replied, and she changed the subject.

Susan was not alone in leaving South Africa because of social and political factors (as we discussed in Chapter 5) and, as with other long-standing British residents whom we interviewed, downplaying or silencing the politics of apartheid were recurrent themes. Indeed, the ambiguous place of apartheid in British self-narratives about their lives is common for other white South Africans, who have also struggled to acknowledge or accept their role in sustaining white minority rule (Steyn and Foster 2008; Krog 1999). As was discussed in Chapter 2, encouraging British immigration to South Africa was a key tenet of apartheid governance from 1961 onwards and became increasingly politically controversial from the late 1960s onwards. British residents were part of a broader English-speaking white population who, although politically marginalised in many respects, actively participated and supported apartheid governance in economic, social, political and also operational terms.

In other former British Dominions with fraught racial histories, such as Australia, British immigrants' narratives about the past and changing present have also been considered politically significant. Wills characterises British immigrants to Australia as postimperial 'remembering posts' who have lived the country's journey from imperial outpost to postimperial multiculturalism as an 'embodied experience' (2005: 95). This is a broad experience expressed from conscious political views about the country, to more mundane and everyday practices and involvement in Australian life. British migrants to apartheid South Africa can also be conceptualised as 'remembering posts', as they have, like other white South Africans, been situated in and in relation to the country's very particular history and political present.

As discussed in Chapter 2, British migration to South Africa became politically controversial and an aspect of anti-apartheid campaigning from the late 1960s onwards. In contemporary South Africa, open acknowledgement by whites of their support or complicity in apartheid is now rare (Steyn and Foster 2008). There is also a growing tendency to give disproportionate focus and/or to exaggerate the contribution of whites who actively opposed apartheid to the achievement of non-racial democracy to the country (Conway 2008; Conway 2012; Steyn 2001; Steyn and Foster 2008). However, there is some useful research on British migrants' attitudes towards apartheid during the 1960s that gives us a sense of their political orientation towards, and complicity in, apartheid. In Stone's sample of 514 British residents living in South Africa in the late 1960s, few expressed extensive prior knowledge about the country before emigrating, but 76% had become either 'favourable' or 'very favourable' towards the apartheid system of government after having lived in South Africa, and only 10% were hostile (1973: 224). Many could think of no alternative political, social or economic arrangements, and some justified their views by comparing racial apartheid in South Africa to what they considered to be a form of class-based apartheid in the United Kingdom. Stone's survey also revealed the majority of British migrants had considerable hostility and prejudice towards black Africans, and a greater number of respondents held negative stereotypes about Afrikaans-speaking and Jewish white South Africans than positive (1973: 210). However, despite holding these strident social and political views, the majority of British residents professed a disinterest in, or disengagement from, South African politics more broadly. For some, this was because of fear of the consequences of being perceived as 'too political' in the oppressive context of National Party rule, for others because of lack of knowledge or information. More broadly, the 'apolitical' nature of English-speaking white culture encouraged British immigrants to turn away from the fraught reality of apartheid and towards their own private lives (Stone 1973: 174; Sparks 1997). Asking British migrants today about their own awareness of apartheid and their sense of complicity did not generate the full truth or recapture the full extent of what had been thought and experienced at the time, but it did demonstrate how the country's politics was an 'embodied experience' for many, and at times was decisive in shaping decisions to stay or leave and feelings of belonging and alienation. It also revealed how memories of apartheid were framed within key discourses of denial – either of apartheid's existence or that it was as problematic as certain representations purported – or difference: that is, that British people were somehow significant in apartheid's mitigation.

'A bit of an ostrich'

Joanna has lived in southern Africa since the early 1970s, having first moved to Rhodesia when in her early 20s. Today, she is retired and lives in a spacious and elegant home with her South African husband in a small and picturesque village outside Hermanus in the Western Cape. 'I suppose of I was a bit of an ostrich', she replies when asked about her knowledge of apartheid. 'I enjoyed the life out here so much. I enjoyed the scenery, I enjoyed the climate, and I guess I thought, you know, hopefully things will come right. A very naive feeling!'

Jane, who emigrated with her husband Barry in the 1960s, had a similar reply: 'I feel, when I look back on those times, I was a bit of an ostrich with my head in the sand. You know, I think we were so busy building this life of ours, so busy working, weren't we? I mean, I worked full-time. Barry worked full-time.' Barry interjects, 'Yeah, but, you know—' and

Jane continues: 'And I think that we – we knew what was going on, obviously. I mean, you've got news reports, newspapers and things, but you were so busy building this life of ours. I just felt at the time, well, sort of the authorities are there, and they're seeing to the whole thing. And you didn't take it all in, you know? I felt I didn't.'

White society during the apartheid era, until the 1980s at least, discouraged political scrutiny and debate about the nature of South African government and society. Without television until 1975, and then only television that was state-controlled and heavily censored, most whites were able to remain oblivious to the reality of the majority of black South African lives, and most were happy to leave the iniquity of the situation unquestioned. Yet even though whites were increasingly confronted with the extent of the repression and chaos of the apartheid system during the 1980s and the subsequent Truth and Reconciliation Commission laid bare the extent of the repression and suffering in the country, a surprising number of our respondents continued to seek to justify, or mitigate, apartheid as a political system.

The BBC is biased: It's not as bad as you think!

Apartheid could not be completely ignored, however, and it was clearly an embodied experience for British residents – both when in the country and when back for visits in the UK. 'What you'd see on BBC News, we wouldn't see,' says Jeremy who moved to Johannesburg in 1972. 'But then, what I can say is that when I did go over there [to the United Kingdom] and saw BBC News, I would say "That's so taken out of context!"' The notion that the BBC was biased, that it had created misperceptions of life in South Africa during the 1980s and misrepresented apartheid, was mentioned repeatedly in interviews and was often combined with personal experiences and confrontations with relatives, friends and complete strangers upon returning to Britain.

Daphne had moved to Durban in 1984 and was in London for a business trip in the later 1980s; she 'was asked to get out of a London taxi cab when he found out where I came from, when he found out where I was living. I was going back to the airport…and…he asked me to get out of his cab. My own sister said, "Are you going back to the land of slaves?" I found there was a mass ignorance in the UK, and it wasn't the people's fault, it was the media's fault.'

Catherine, who returned to the UK because of her concern for her family's future in the light of a national state of emergency in South Africa, found settling back difficult because of other British people's responses to the knowledge that she had been living in South Africa. 'I would become quite defensive, not of what was happening, but of their perception of what was happening.' Catherine recalled further:

> People [would] say, 'the way you treat the blacks' and things... I said, 'Oh well, we didn't feel it was bad, you know; if my maid didn't do things I wanted her to, then we just shut her in her hut for three days, and when she came out, she was much better.' And they'd look at me and things like that. And, well, 'I'd cut her wages, and she must work better.' And eventually they'd look at me and say, 'You're joking, aren't you?' I said, 'But that's what you're expecting me to say.' I mean, I'm an English person born and bred. I did have a maid who cleaned the house – a servant, if you like, and everything – [but] she was not a slave. She wasn't badly treated. I did pay what the going rate was; I didn't upset any apple carts or anything like that, probably wrong and everything. But I'm sitting here, we've had dinner, we've been out, and you think I could do that to somebody? You people criticise, but make sure you know what's going on. But they didn't... But yeah, they were quite aggressive. I found them quite aggressive, without much knowledge.

Catherine felt deeply alienated from other British people as a result of these encounters, and this feeling contributed to her decision to return to South Africa in the 1990s.

Jeremy also recalls having arguments with fellow train passengers about South Africa when on a visit back to the UK:

> The conversation just goes pear-shaped very, very quickly. You know, and they started telling me about South Africa, and I said, 'Well, have you ever been there?' 'No, but we've seen the pictures on the news.' I said, 'And you actually believe that shit?' You know, 'Do you really believe it? Do you actually believe there are – you actually believe that everything that's got on the news is absolutely 100% true?' 'Of course.' I said, 'Well, then, the BBC has got you brainwashed, I'm afraid. You are not a person. You are not a thinking person.'

That these encounters occurred is not surprising; South Africa had become an international cause célèbre by the 1980s, and Britain had a highly visible anti-apartheid movement. That the hostility directed to British migrants in the apartheid past is still remembered and continues to cause resentment is noteworthy, as is the sustained insistence that people in the United Kingdom had it 'wrong' about life in South Africa. These narratives relate to, and draw from, broader white narratives about apartheid and a denial of white South Africans' complicity in and awareness of it. They also draw from a belief that it is only white South Africans who 'know' the reality of South Africa, a reality that is misperceived abroad. They also reveal the narrative of the private, 'good' lives British migrants sought to build for themselves, a self-belief that leads to shock and resentment when complicity in the wider sociopolitics of the country is suggested, and their morality is questioned, as Joanna relates:

> One of my oldest friends, who I met when I was six years old, she has just been out here for six weeks, and it's not her first trip – she has been once before – but she was one of the very critical ones back in the '70s and '80s. When I went back there, you know, 'How can you live there?' and 'Isn't it dreadful?' and so on, and I think she had quite a liberal husband who sadly has died. This time, when she was here for a longer period, she saw things through such a different perspective – she couldn't believe some of the little idiosyncrasies that happened, and I can't even think of any, but she just sort of understood what – this is not going to sound right, but – what we've had to cope with all these years. But just, you know, how some people are, and how one needs to handle them. You know it's not plain sailing all the way; it really isn't.

Making a difference

A further theme across our interviews was the significance British immigrants had in South Africa, and the agency and ability they had to make a difference to South African society and to their own success. This significance was also invoked as a rationale for living in apartheid South Africa and the role they played in reducing the racism of the system. This claim, of course, depends on the assertion that apartheid was purely an Afrikaner creation, and that the individuals speaking, and British people more broadly, were not racist themselves. However, this was a claim that is not fully supported, either by Stone's 1973 research or by our research.

Jane recalls, 'You could have separate counters, and then somebody would bypass the black person, and say to you, and then I would say, "No, that black person was before me, you know, so they must be served before me." I mean, lots of people did things like that, which, I mean, in a very small way, helped to make changes in South Africa.'

Jeremy strongly believed the everyday experience of apartheid was different from international perspectives of it. He says he was surprised when he realised Soweto had no high walls around it, as he had been led to expect. Jeremy played in his company's soccer team, and they would regularly play against black, coloured and Indian teams. 'I was the first manager in [the information technology company] to employ a person of seriously dark colour into a technical position', Jeremy recalled.

> Not a cleaner, driver, whatever – into a technical position. And you know, the first objective I set myself was about finding out how he lived and what his issues were, and so, when he came to work on a Monday morning, and he was looking like he was looking, and I understood how his weekend had affected him – 'cause in those days, they literally lived two lives'.

Jeremy's belief that the BBC exaggerated and misrepresented apartheid casts doubt on the extent he really did understand the lives of his black employees, however. It was also, of course, a strategy of late apartheid government to advance certain black workers in the economy while at the same time denying them any political rights.

Julie lived in colonial Kenya as a teenager and moved to Johannesburg in the 1960s after having returned to London for a few years. When asked about whether she considered leaving South Africa during the state of emergency, she replied, 'I don't remember any emergency; was there a state of emergency?' After Daniel explained that there was, she added, 'No recollection of that whatsoever – so obviously I didn't feel threatened. No recollection whatsoever, and I mean, if you knew any black people that had problems, you did everything that you could to help them.'

Julie wanted to emphasise the difference she felt she had made to her community, being involved in the local library and in reading projects for children in the nearby squatter camp. She wanted to highlight white women's roles:

> What is perhaps not fully recognised is how much South African women helped their black employees, how much they did for them. Alright, to a certain extent, it was for their own benefit, but there were women who used to spend days in a pass office with their employees, trying to get their passes sorted out. The children would be sick, they'd take them to the doctor or to the hospital – they were like an extension of the family. Now I'm not saying they were all like

that, but there were a good number who were...who cared for their employees, and it wasn't uncommon to see a white women going shopping with her maid's child or children along with her own...but maybe, I'm thinking now, maybe this was the reason for there being so much good will in the country.

For some, their sense that they could and should more openly challenge the system came upon them gradually, as the realities of apartheid became more apparent. For example, Catherine's recollections of living in Durban from her late teens onwards in the 1960s reflect how her positioning changed as she became older and more aware of the consequences of the political system. She fully acknowledged the privileged and protected white life she had led at first: 'The race situation didn't seem to arise – and this, of course, is horrific in retrospect.' She explained that a relative of hers had warned her about apartheid before she arrived and that she had to be careful not to sit on the wrong bench or go into the wrong public toilet:

> 'No, no, you be careful, because you'll be breaking the law.' And I was very careful, and I wouldn't have noticed otherwise. I'd probably have just gone and sat on a bench. But in those days, the non-white population was kept so far away from the white population. I mean, at night, from six o'clock, there were no blacks in town at all. And we'd all go home and have a shower and then go out to movies or drinks or whatever you're doing, and the streets were yours. It's nothing to be proud of; you just accepted it. 'It's beautiful, it's a lovely country, there's no danger at night, I'm happy,' you know, and that's it.

In the late 1970s, however, Catherine was witness to apartheid's real modus operandi:

> I'd already had a run-in with the police about some definite beating up that was going on in a wood behind our house. I could hear the screaming and shouting, and my late husband came out with a torch and shone it across the stream, into the – 'Hey, what's going on there?' 'Mind your own business!' And I shouted, because I get very stroppy, and I said, 'Whatever it is you're doing, stop it! And everything went quiet. And 45 minutes later, we got a knock on the door it was about 12 o'clock at night – and three policemen, all plain clothes, came. 'Was it you that ...? We told you that we were the police and

go away!' And I said, 'Well, first of all, anyone can say that. I can't see in the dark who's doing the thing. And secondly, whatever you were doing, you have no right to do it.' And then, of course, my accent gets much – if I'm cross, it gets more and more English! And 'You're not South African, are you?' I said, 'None of your business.'

And they weren't used to being spoken to like this; they simply weren't. And my husband's going, 'Uh, uh, uh,' you know. I said, 'No, no – whatever you're doing there – '

'Oh, mind your own business.'

I said, 'Tell you what: who's your commanding officer?' I was all of 27 or something at the time, you know. And I phoned the man the next day, and I said, 'De, de, de,' and 'Oh, we'll look into it,' and what have you. But I just thought, no, I don't like this. I'm used to an English bobby who's there – you know, if in trouble go to the bobby, he'll help you. And I didn't think this was the way the police should act in the country.

This experience fed Catherine's growing belief that her young family's safety may be in doubt and, as mentioned previously, she left the country following the declaration of the state of emergency.

The significance of British migrants in mitigating the racism of apartheid rests on a number of claims: that the racism of apartheid was not as bad as internationally understood, that apartheid was an Afrikaner phenomenon, that British people, as culturally different, are not racist, and that individual acts of non-racism really could make a difference to what was a systemic and violent form of discrimination. These contentions, of course, are also aspects of 'white talk' that could serve to obscure broader forms of racism, and indeed the racism of the speaker in other spheres of their lives. We are not claiming that all respondents who claimed to be not racist were being disingenuous, for this is not the case. Rather, we are arguing that broader discourses of whiteness in South Africa exist to proclaim non-racism, while simultaneously allowing both structural and interpersonal racist acts to continue. Furthermore, only a small number of people we talked to supported the notions that British people 'made a difference' or were 'less racist'.

Joanna, for example, who has lived in southern Africa since the early 1970s and now lives outside of Hermanus, when asked whether she felt there was a tension between Afrikaans-speaking whites and herself as a British person, replied, 'I confess to knowing, and this goes back to Rhodesia as well as Johannesburg and Cape Town, English – true English people – were more racist than anybody I had met who was born in South Africa. You know, really horrendous.'

Daniel asked, 'Why do you think that is?' and Joanna replied, 'I think a lot of it is they were of an age where they hadn't been brought up with black people, and I think they were frightened. And they were aggressive, you know, attack is the best means of defence sort of thing. But you know, I can certainly think of a number of occasions when, you know, real English people behaved abominably to Africans.'

Other interviewees mentioned this assertion that British people lacked the knowledge and understanding of African people, an understanding that perhaps Afrikaans-speaking whites had. British positions towards apartheid were clearly multiple, multifaceted and complex, as well as subject to redefinition in their retelling. However, as the high apartheid period moved into the 1990s, it was also very clear to all that change was about to happen.

Transitional times

The transition that began with the release of Nelson Mandela in 1990 was a highly volatile and violent period in South Africa's history: many became concerned that the country could descend into civil war. For Roy, originally from northern England and a senior official in the Cape Town municipality from 1984, the only moment when he seriously considered leaving South Africa was when the senior ANC leader, Chris Hani, was assassinated in 1993 by white extremists. Roy remembers thinking, 'Fuck, I have put my family in danger by coming here,' and vividly recalled watching Nelson Mandela's television address that he (and others) credit with pulling the country back from civil war.

Apartheid framed every aspect of life in South Africa, for whites and British immigrants in particular. While trying to ignore the wider political situation was an option, this was not always an effective one. Witnessing the everyday doing of apartheid, the constant uncertainty, and the very real threat of a descent into civil war during the transition period raised serious doubts for some about the decision to migrate.

In the national referendum in 1992, which asked the white population whether they supported the negotiation process with the ANC begun by President De Klerk, British residents could vote for the first time. De Klerk also gave British residents the vote for the first democratic elections in 1994. These two votes were recalled as very significant moments in the lives of many of the people living in South Africa at the time. Jane, who lives with her husband Barry in Cape Town, explained emphatically:

> Obviously, you can't deny the fact that people were without their basic human rights. And I mean, being denied swimming on a beach and all the rest of it is – you know, it's just not on. I mean, I never agreed with any of those things. And I think when I felt the changes were coming, then I was happy with that, and we got the chance to vote. And I wish you could have seen the people, you know, not just Africans but everybody that went out there to vote. I mean, it was a day to remember, wasn't it, really!

Catherine, who now lives in Hermanus, had moved to a village in Kwa-Zulu Natal during the transition, one of the areas of the country that saw the worst levels of violence:

> And they organised – I don't think it was just in Eshowe – I think it was meant to be countrywide. At 12 o'clock on whatever day, everybody would like to stop and everybody must hold hands, come out into the streets. We're asking the office people to come out in the streets, and just hold hands with somebody else on the streets for five minutes. Now I'm not built like that, I mean, I don't hold hands with people. All this thing in church, shake – go away, leave me alone. But I thought, 'No, you've got to work for this thing.' And bearing in mind, we were committed here – our business was here, our livelihood was here. I wasn't working any more; I didn't have my pounds coming in, so it was everything here. So we had a vested interest in the country for selfish reasons.
>
> So out on the street, told all the staff, 'out on the street.' So we came out on the street, and we stood around. 12 o'clock: nothing – the traffic kept going, a few people were still standing around, and then I was pleased to see that the traffic light came and stopped all the traffic – stopped it. And they stopped all the traffic, and some elderly black gentleman came and stood beside me and took my hand. And we stood there for two or three minutes, whatever it was. And then everything went – and I think, yeah, you know, there's a chance. There is a chance that it could work!
>
> But then on the other hand, we were ducking bullets, literally ducking bullets. I mean, physically they were coming through our garden. And cops were running after them – pow, pow! We'd be down under the window, you know. But it was the Wild West. All the

road signs were shot up, and you'd just hear a gun from the reserve or the location. You'd just hear gunshots going all night.

These experiences were inevitably politicising, and those who felt involved in the country's transition held strong views about the current political direction of the country. Catherine commented further:

> We're so outnumbered in this country. We obviously could have been wiped out overnight. Everybody could have been wiped out. And no, I didn't think it was, 'That's it. It's done.' I just gradually came to the idea that you got your one man, one vote; hopefully, it's not one man, one vote, one time. Which usually happens in Africa. And Uhuru[1] didn't come. So in that way, yes, Uhuru didn't come the day after the election. But the worst was still to come, because the expectation of the black was now on the line, and I don't think anyone has really taken into account how disappointed these people must be. Whether they're right or wrong, I think the disappointment must be absolutely enormous.

As with the majority of the people we spoke to, Jane and Barry, who have lived in South Africa since the mid-1960s, have never taken South African citizenship.[2] In the late 1990s, they had to renew their British passport and have the 'permanent resident status' stamps reinserted. They were furious when the official at the Department of Home Affairs initially refused and suggested they go back to the United Kingdom. They speak at some length of their anger at that moment, and Barry explains how Jane really lost her temper. The story encompasses many of Jane and Barry's other attitudes towards the post-apartheid era, but it also underlines the ambivalent place British immigrants have always occupied in South Africa and how this ambivalence, reflected in their status, contribution to and attitudes towards South Africa, has nonetheless played a significant part in the broader politics and society of the country.

Engaging with post-apartheid South Africa

Saul, whose life history we first told in Chapter 3, volunteers in a township primary school, helping the children with literacy skills. It is an activity that takes up a considerable part of his week, gives him great personal fulfilment, and defines his attitudes towards the country. Saul explains:

> I've always felt that my going in is as much of an education for my white friends as it is for the children I try to go and help. I drive

a little open two-seater sports car...So first they say to me, 'You're not really going to Khayelitsha, are you?' Then, 'You're not going in your car?' Then, 'You're not going with the roof down, surely? You're going to get shot at!' is the general reaction.

Saul has tried to encourage his friends to come with him, but as of yet, no one has. He does admit the first time he took the trip he was very cautious:

> A lot of people crowded around the car, and all they wanted to do was see the car. They were not interested in doing anything they shouldn't have done. And I like driving in. I've driven in the odd day when I've had time. I've driven into areas I don't normally go into, and once or twice, I know I've got very funny looks from people, but not that would worry me particularly. They probably wonder what the hell a white guy is driving round in a car looking at them... [In Khayelitsha], I wave to people, they wave back. They've got used to seeing me now. If I pull up at a traffic light, road block, pull up at a traffic light, and there's a few guys standing there, so I always have got two gambits: either you want my car or 'What soccer club?' because I've got a big Arsenal sticker on my window, so soccer is a sort of common language. The car is mainly if I'm pulling up next to a taxi or a *bakkie* [a small truck], then there's always a bit of joshing going on. I even had a policeman one day stop me to say, 'Oh, can I drive your car, please?' Which we did, back to his depot.

Saul is disappointed that the school has too few teachers, and that they are of variable quality, but he is phlegmatic about South Africa's future. He recognises that South Africa has problems with corruption, but as a new democracy, he expects that to be inevitable and points out that corruption in Europe and elsewhere is often hidden and defined in different terms. Saul's partner's children were taken out of their private school because it was 95% white and sent to a mixed-race state school. He also supports race-based affirmative action and cites the United States as a society that has benefitted from this system since the 1960s. Saul's engagement with South African society, his attitudes, and his use of space are not unique, but are still unusual in our study.

He recalls the time he stopped on the motorway close to Cape Town and adjacent to Khayelitsha:

> We hadn't been stopped for 10 seconds when a policeman pulled up and said, 'Have you got a problem?'

'No!' We explained.

He said, 'I wouldn't stop here. I would move on.' That is instilling a prejudice in us. And that prejudice is there. I'm not saying it's unwarranted at all. I'm quite sure there are more than enough problems in townships, but it's to be expected. This country desperately needs gainful employment. It needs good education.

This rationalisation is not common. Many of the British residents we spoke to, in similar terms to the majority of white South Africans, regard the country in which they live with varying levels of apprehension, confusion, resentment and anger. Even those who claim to love the country and consider it home can have surprisingly little knowledge and engage with it in a somewhat superficial way.

As discussed in the previous chapter, for those in work, negotiating the changing racial politics of contemporary South African workplaces can become a key part of their everyday lives. Shane found his working life as a chef in Cape Town very different from London. He noticed that, 'if one of my staff has a problem, they wouldn't come and speak to me directly in my office because the assumption would be, 'Now that member of staff is talking about all the other members of staff,' so therefore you couldn't do it in a closed environment. 'All meetings had to be open, and everyone can see it.'

Shane finds South Africa's labour laws to be 'bloody ridiculous', because he feels it is now impossible to dismiss anyone, regardless of whatever misdemeanour they may have committed. He believes his whiteness, but not his Britishness, may have been a problem initially, but now 'the staff just – they don't worry or particularly care what colour I am, as long as I'm deemed to be fair, and I do everything according to the rules, and it's all above board, and I consult with the unions, then they're happy.'

When Daniel asks Shane if he socialises with anyone from work, Shane replies that no one from work has become a friend and pauses to think. He explains he had socialised with his colleagues in Britain, but he did not think it was because of race in South Africa, but lifestyle. Shane's colleagues have invited him to social occasions in their homes at times, but he has always declined.

> But that's fear, not because…I just wouldn't want to go out there. I would not feel comfortable going out there, although everyone tells you that it's fine to go to the bars and *shebeens* [township bars] and whatever. Just no – it's fine if you're a foreigner and on holiday, and you're on a guided tour in a bulletproof bus or whatever, but if I'm

driving out there in my car, I kind of would feel a bit...I think that's the reality for people that live here. You know, we understand the dangers more I suppose, so yeah, I have no friends from work at all. All my friends are through my [South African] wife and any expats I know.

Shane believes relations in his workplace have changed over the past ten years and now his whiteness is less of an issue. He explains that there may be a level of envy over his possessions and lifestyle, but he believes that because he is British, he cannot be blamed for benefitting from apartheid. Shane also feels that any comments made about his new car, or holiday plans or other aspects of his lifestyle are made in a jovial manner.

As discussed in the previous chapter, the existence of Black Economic Empowerment (BEE) policies, which include race-based affirmative action policies in employment, incentives and sanctions against companies that do not advance previously disadvantaged racial groups as managers and stakeholders in companies, and special BEE investment groups to increase black ownership of the economy, provoke sharp and widespread political debate in white society. For some, BEE typifies what they see as the discrimination against whites in the labour force after 1994 and the advancement of unqualified and undeserving black people (Steyn and Foster 2008). For others, BEE is an acceptable and necessary means to redress the racial economic imbalance left by apartheid.

During our period of research, BEE was a continual source of political controversy. In 2010, a report found that black economic advancement in the Western Cape province had advanced from 1994 until the early-2000s and then fallen back thereafter, provoking a sharp response from the province's governing Democratic Alliance party (Surtee and Hall 2010). In 2012 there was a furore over the (unproven) allegations that the Woolworths chain of shops were no longer hiring white staff, a claim that provoked a social media campaign for white South Africans to boycott the store (Pillay 2012). Our sample demonstrated that BEE formed a considerable social myth and, for some, acted as a metaphor for the state of South Africa. However, there were divergent views. Joanna, who had run a business with her husband until she retired in the 2000s, explains:

The BEE employment policy, which some have worked and some have failed abysmally, would have made our lives well-nigh impossible... Subsequent to selling our business, [Joanna's son] had opened another business with a group of companies which promised all sorts of BEE opportunities, and they were going to employ, you know, well, they did employ a very highly qualified black man who had a PhD and CA (Chartered Accountant), and you name it. He spoke fluent Italian and French, I think, and English – and he never lifted a finger. He never brought a single thing into the business. He was purely a figurehead, and he was off to fancy golf clubs and lunches every day and flying around the place and just, you know, he talked a good story. He said he would introduce us to all the, you know, these government organisations and so on, and he's got contacts everywhere, and so on, and he never did a thing. So you know that was a bit of an eye-opener and a big letdown. So yah, we've seen a lot of things change in that respect, and really it is not easy to run the sort of business that we had, and it was very successful in its day. It would have been impossible to run these days, absolutely impossible. Which is sad because the country needs small businesses; every country does.

James, who retired to South Africa in the 1990s, can understand why so many white South Africans have emigrated from the country because he believes BEE policies have made it impossible for them to get a job. He also believes it has allowed unqualified black people to perform jobs that they are not capable of doing, the consequences of which he feels frame his daily life:

Whenever you go to the bank or something, you go to the information desk, you ask a question, and they say, 'Oh! I must refer that to the manager!' And they leap up, and they go and interrupt the manager to get the answer. Well, if you go to the bank in England, HSBC or something, they're much better qualified; they can answer most of your questions themselves, and very sensibly answer them. They won't here. I'm sure you notice that things are quite inefficient now... To get anything done here, to get it done properly, or to rectify a mistake, is really quite a challenge.

Jeremy has worked in the information technology sector since he migrated to the country in 1973. When asked if he thinks young white people are disadvantaged because of BEE, he immediately replies, 'They're talking nonsense, honestly! Honestly. If you want to get a job, you can get a job anywhere, if you want it.' Jeremy explains he has recently hired people for nine new entry-level positions: eight were coloured, and one was white. He explains why there was only one white person:

> It's just because the white kid arrives here, and he wants 10,000 rand a month to start in a job that only pays 5,000 rand a month 'cause there's an entitlement problem, I guess, firstly. Secondly, you say to him, 'It's shift work.'
>
> Right, 'I only work Monday to Friday through 9 'til 4.'
>
> 'Oh, sorry, fella! Get a life!'
>
> 'Oh – no, I'll come back to you.' And then he complains he can't get a job. Then he complains about affirmative action and BEE. He's talking, you know, bullshit!

Although these accounts are based on the narrators' life experiences, and we are not suggesting they are fabricated, they still draw from a white social mythology that informs their perspective. The labour market evidence suggests BEE policies have not disadvantaged whites (Steyn and Foster 2008). The additional claim that BEE has led to a decline in services and standards is also politically controversial and relates to much broader social and political perspectives of a problem-ridden post-apartheid South Africa.

In Jeremy's anecdote above, a meritocratic non-racialism seems to be driving his recruitment policies. However, of the nine people he employed, none were black South Africans. 'How do you create a work ethic?' Jeremy wonders. 'It doesn't happen. You can't write a little note: "Tomorrow you are going to want to work hard!"' When asked if he thinks black South Africans lack a work ethic, Jeremy replies 'Absolutely. Yeah. Yeah. Big time.' He continues:

> And that's why – and I'm as guilty as anybody else – I employ a Malawian house boy who works hard, has – he's a really nice character. Honest as you could possibly get; I can leave him in my house with the doors open and have absolutely no concerns. But unfortunately, I can't say the same for a lot of the other indigent population in this country. I can't, 'cause it's not the reality. So, yeah. And he works. And I don't need to be standing over him. I do, occasionally, as you do – should do – with any person who's working for you. But I have to watch him all flippin' day and say, you know, sort of 'You've been doing that for the last year. Why didn't you do it today?' 'Sorry boss.' That – yeah.

The discourse that black Africans from countries other than South Africa are harder working, more trustworthy and/or intelligent is drawn upon in a number of our interviews and has also been heard by both of us in our conversations with other white South Africans. Further, the term 'house boy' continues an apartheid diminution of black domestic workers and qualifies Jeremy's claims of non-racialism. The extract reveals the extent to which expressed attitudes towards racial progress, employment and integration are not always consistent, as well as how British residents can continue to position themselves within the broader and resilient discourses of white racism. Further, these are often co-constituted with reference to the United Kingdom, which, in its contemporary form, is seen by many to symbolise the consequences of a full turn towards multiculturalism.

'An island that is about to sink'

> Jane's dad said, "You'll always be proud to be British," and I must be honest with you, when I see what's going on over there at the moment, I don't know whether I can honestly say I would be proud to be British. It's not the Britain that I can feel comfortable with. (Barry, emigrated to South Africa in the mid-1960s.)

As we saw in Chapter 3, in O'Reilly's study of the British in Spain (2000), one of the most striking ways migrants constructed home and belonging in the destination context was through the repudiation of the 'Bad Britain' they had left. Any positive attitudes towards Britain, from happy visits back to the country to the decision to return for good, were silenced and ignored. This 'bad Britain' discourse also arose in almost all of our interviews, often fed by media sources readily available in South Africa including *Sky News*, the *Express* and *Telegraph* weekly print editions, the *Daily Mail* website and also from anecdotes gained from friends and family. Stone's (1973) study revealed a similar set of discourses about the United Kingdom, neatly summed up by one respondent as 'the three Ws – the weather, Wilson[3] and the welfare state'. (232)

Contemporary British discourses are politically similar, albeit expressed in different terms and against new targets: multiculturalism, immigration, law and order, education and social values were contrasted between Britain and South Africa and often found wanting. The 'bad Britain' discourses were noteworthy for much more than the conservative social attitudes they revealed; they rested upon sometimes startling contradictions: hostility towards immigrants expressed by immigrants, opposition to multiculturalism and diversity from the vantage point of one of the most diverse societies in the world, and anger about a country that many claim is no longer home or a place they have any desire to return to.

Daphne has always felt South Africa has had a 'positive feeling', and she has never doubted the country would move in the 'right direction', even at the height of the State of Emergency. In contrast, after her last few visits to the UK, Daphne says, 'I find the change unbelievable. It's just not the same country that I left 25 years ago at all – more than 25 years ago.' She details this change:

> I think it's become too diverse. I think there are too many ethnic groups living in the UK. And there's not a lot of understanding or tolerance of each other's cultures and beliefs. The other impression – I travel quite a lot through Europe – is that England has become a dirty country. The hotels are dirty, the restaurants are dirty, there's a lack of respect in service, there's a lack of pride that the rest of Europe has. The English seemed to have just gone through a bit of a beating. That's the impression I get now when I go back.

Immigration was a near constant refrain in our research, a 'tap that had been left to run' in an island that was 'likely to sink' as a result, as one interviewee put it. 'I don't want to sound xenophobic, but you go into shops, and it's just awful,' Shane said. He continued:

> If I want to be a foreigner in my own country, yeah, it's bizarre to me. I don't understand it... English people seem to have become almost weak and accepting of everything, whereas here you can't be like that. You can't just accept it; if something affects your life, you can't just let it walk. We've kind of got to the stage where there's nothing we can do about it anymore in England; we just have to live with it. Well, what can I do? I can change nothing, so you know, that's what I think and feel about England now; it just seems, I always say it's gone to the dogs because it's still a very vibrant, economic – you know it's always on the edge of greatness, almost. It just never does seem to get over it.

Joanna, who has lived in southern Africa since the early 1970s and now lives in a spacious and comfortable home outside of Hermanus, remarked,

I think it's changed very sadly in a lot of ways. And again, some of them have to be – and one doesn't like to do it, but it's impossible to keep a racist tone out of it – I just see time after time, 'Oh, there's been another stabbing in southeast London,' and you know it's not going to be a white child, it's going to be a black child, and that's horrendous, you know. And ... I don't know, it's hard to really put into words, but a couple of the last times that we've been back to England, I've been horrified by the behaviour of some of the youth... Some of the laws that the Blair government passed – I mean, God, you're not allowed to do this... that's not the England I grew up in.

The notion that 'the England I knew' had changed reoccurred often in the narratives. In a long and increasingly impassioned discussion about the problems of the United Kingdom, ranging from the welfare state, crime and education standards, Barry and Jane conclude that immigrants are to blame. Jane remarks, 'I mean, we are immigrants here, but British immigrants have changed the country for the better. But immigrants to Britain have changed it for the worse.' And Barry adds, 'They're not there to contribute. They're there to screw the system, to put it bluntly.'

As previously discussed, these discourses of a United Kingdom in decline, similar to research conducted elsewhere, also mirror the social and political discourses British immigrants have expressed about Britain in previous decades in South Africa. They are perhaps informed to some degree by the social identity of those who emigrate to South Africa: a skilled white person during apartheid, an economically mobile or relatively wealthy retired person after apartheid. In South Africa, they may also be fed by more accessible conservative news sources than to left-leaning ones, and by a broader set of pervasive white discourses that continue to express racist and deeply conservative political positions, and which continue to be acceptable within many quarters of white society.

However, despite the predominance of negative social and political attitudes towards the United Kingdom, some respondents replied in very different terms. James, who was broadly negative about the changes in South Africa since the end of apartheid, and pessimistic about the future, told Daniel that 'quite a lot of my British friends have left South Africa... They've gone, and they refuse to come back as well, which is quite surprising. They wouldn't even come back on a holiday.' James thinks this is because of their perceptions of the future of the country and because they want to grow old in a society with a more supportive welfare state and National Health Service. James adds,

> I know a lot of English people are negative, but no, I'm happy in England. I visit quite often. In the winter, I normally go away – not necessarily to England. I sometimes go to Germany and Switzerland, but then you see how people live and how safe it all is in comparison, and when you initially come back here, you're a bit shocked, really, about dirt and the litter and the standards and the begging.

James' discourse about Britain helps construct a 'bad South Africa' positioning, not that he has any immediate plans to leave the country himself.

For Saul, the UK changing since he left was inevitable: 'Everywhere changes.' He observes:

> It's obviously economically going through a very difficult time. But don't forget, if I go for a week, I see it very superficially...I go round the shops. I go into the Apple shop to look at a computer. I go to the museum. I do the things I can't do very well here. The pleasure of waking up one Sunday morning and realising the Wigmore Hall was just down the road, and there was a little concert about to start, and going in and listening to a wonderful Czech quartet playing for an hour...Britain? Britain will carry on in its own sweet way. It will have a Conservative government or a Socialist government or whatever. The pendulum will eventually always swing the other way. Britain has – that's why Britain never used to worry about some of the problems. You go to America, and they're already panicking because there's a problem over in Korea. Britain would never worry about things like that because we've been here for thousands of years, or hundreds of years. We have a different attitude. Britain has a very, on the whole, a very liberal attitude towards other people. It's a very mixed society and happily a mixed society.

Conclusion

> I was involved in politics in England in the Conservative party...in the Young Conservatives, and also my background was that my parents had lived in Africa in the '50s, and I grew up in England with

Africa always discussed, always spoken about, [there] was always an opinion, and I had huge sympathy for Rhodesia. And it was both my political involvement and also I'd always wanted to work overseas. I hated the weather, even when I was younger, so that was a real motivation: Well, why don't I just go there? (David, moved to Rhodesia in 1978, returned to Britain after independence, moved to Cape Town in 1989)

David's overtly political motivations for moving to southern Africa were not matched in quite the same overt terms by any other of our interviewees. Neither is there much evidence of previous generations of British migrants moving to South Africa for expressly pro-apartheid reasons. Yet in spite of some denials to the contrary, all of our respondents can be seen to be political, if politics is taken to mean how individuals are situated in relation to other groups in society, how they define that society, and experience everyday political and social change (Stephenson and Papadopoulos, 2006: xviii). For migrants arriving in South Africa during apartheid, their awareness of and potential complicity in that oppressive and unjust social and political regime was a political issue both at the time and subsequently. As British immigrants, they were part of a broader white minority governance strategy and vital, if economic growth was to remain on white political terms. Yet at an individual level, many were trying to build a new and 'a good life' in a society they often knew little about and that was hidden from them.

Their present-day accounts of apartheid both reveal and conceal the extent to which they were aware, feel complicit and apportion blame. The embodied experiences of apartheid, seeing the reality of a racist society, being part of moments of high political tension and participating in the key moments of political transition, such as in the 1992 referendum and the 1994 elections, became key moments of pride in their life histories and acts of belonging. That they do not always feel they have been sufficiently rewarded or acknowledged for what they consider to be progressive political acts reflects and also engendered feelings of ambivalence towards South Africa.

The coexisting themes of continuity and change dominated the narratives of our respondents. On the one hand, South Africa was undoubtedly perceived by most as fundamentally changed, with the position of white people being constantly questioned and reconfigured. On the other hand, these dramatic political changes are being conducted against on ongoing backdrop of daily stability. Within the micropolitics of South African everyday life, social and political relations continue very much as they always did. It is this sustainability of white privilege that keeps many British within South Africa, as they are not quite ready for the multicultural realities of contemporary Britain.

8
The British in South Africa: Conclusion

We began this book posing the question of whether Britishness is a salient identity in contemporary South Africa. Of course, Britishness, Englishness, and of course, Irish, Welsh and Scottish identities, have always been constitutive parts of whiteness in South Africa, as well as a key dynamic in defining the colonial, cultural and institutional history of the country. These identities extend beyond those who were born in the United Kingdom to their descendants and the English-speaking white community. As Dubow argues, Britishness, as an identity or set of values, could be admired and incorporated by Afrikaans-speaking whites and black South Africans, as evidenced by Nelson Mandela's expressed admiration for English values and modes of behaviour (2009). But what of a British identity today? To what extent is it meaningful to identify a group as 'the British in South Africa'?

As was discussed in Chapter 1, we were initially somewhat surprised at the enthusiasm (and even insistence) by so many British-born residents that we should speak to them. Their desire to be 'heard' can firstly be seen as evidence that some South African residents continue to consider themselves 'British', but also that the story of their lives, their 'significance' and 'contribution' to South Africa is important to note and record. Of course, this desire to be 'heard' takes place against a backdrop where many white South Africans of all backgrounds feel increasingly threatened and alienated from South Africa's national story, and, as such, consider the reframing and defining of South African history, politics and society on their own terms to be an important social and political project. Our interviewees' senses of place, belonging or alienation are thus all part of a broader and ongoing process of shifting British, South African and white identities. The desire to be considered both the authority on South African society and to be placed at the 'centre' of events, a desire that characterises 'white talk' in South Africa (Steyn 2001; Steyn and Foster 2008), was very apparent when speaking to some of our interviewees. However, such discourses were never presented as coterminous to South African whiteness; rather, everyone we spoke to drew from their pasts in the United Kingdom – in relation to the attitudes, values and behaviours they considered to be British and in relation to the contemporary United Kingdom.

The desire to speak to us may also have been driven by the need to simply tell the story of making a new life – and a good one at that – in a country that has, for decades, been the subject of political controversy. In the past, this controversy equated emigration to South Africa with support and active participation in an unjust, immoral and racist political regime. More recently, perceptions of crime, political uncertainty and simple lack of knowledge have made many British residents in South Africa continue to feel misrepresented or ignored. In these circumstances, Britishness could never be successfully defined as apart from or different than broader social and political developments in South Africa.

During apartheid, British South Africans could face familial and social hostility from other British people when they returned 'home' because of the political role they were perceived as playing in upholding apartheid. Today, some still feel that their residence in South Africa means that the British back 'home' position them suspiciously. The narratives in this book are often attempts to rationalise this: to differentiate the individual talking from the broader political forces at work, and to justify what the narrator considered to be a just, individual life in the context of an unjust system they felt they had little control over. At the same time, the narratives are by those whose lives have been considerably influenced by the politics and society that surround them. For those who migrated during apartheid, their very circumstances of migration were influenced by the policies of the National Party government, which encouraged British migrants with generous assisted passages and benefits. The presentation of the country as Western and 'British', (the latter, by organisations like the 1820 Memorial Settlers Association), was premised on the racial discrimination and authoritarianism of the political system. Emigration to South Africa was therefore a latent political act, even if the realities of apartheid were not consciously understood or supported.

South Africa's fraught political history was also an embodied experience, one where the opportunity to vote presented itself, to witness police brutality, to become frightened about the chaos of the State of

Emergency. In contemporary South Africa, the politics of the country continue to define space and place, to make Cape Town and the Western Cape 'different' from the rest of the country – more desirable for some and best avoided for others. It was clear that the racial and spatial politics of South Africa fascinated our respondents, even if they did not always understand or agree on what these signified. As we have shown, spaces were feared, avoided and almost always considered highly dynamic; they were also explored and ventured into. It was both the imagination of space and the placed activities of everyday life that could profoundly change individuals' political and social views and their engagement with South African society.

Migration as a mistake or failure?

> I would have – you know, if I'd gone onto college or got a job or something in England and just done what everyone else is, go skiing and – I think it would have been easier on me as a human being, because I would have had roots in England, and I wouldn't have been so disturbed. And I have – I know I'm very disturbed about my tripartite relationship I have with countries now, because not only am I English, I'm also French and South African. It's good for rugby; I usually win, one way or another. But it is disturbing. I'm not settled, and I'm 61 years old now, and it's ridiculous; I should be settled somewhere, and I thought I was settling here. And I don't think I am...(Catherine, Hermanus, emigrated to South Africa in the late 1960s)

> Barry: Some people say Cape Town is the last stand. Do you know what I mean? Our backs are up against the sea.
> Jane: Yeah, well, we're going to be backed into the sea, aren't we, you know? (laughs)
> Barry: Yeah, yeah, that's right. We're going to be backed into the sea. But I mean, we're British, so backs up against the wall!
> Jane: Well, that's where they're trying to get us, you see. There's no wall; it's a sea! (laughs)
> Barry: That's it! (laughs) (Barry and Jane, Cape Town, emigrated to South Africa in the mid-1960s)

Catherine, Barry and Jane's comments reveal the liminal spaces the British in South Africa inhabit. There was a sense of irony in Barry and Jane's comments, but in describing their life histories, the metaphors used had considerable resonance for them. The couple left Johannesburg in the 1990s after Barry had been made redundant and the family had been the victims of violent crime. They lost money as the property values fell in the lower-middle-/working-class white area where they lived in southern Johannesburg, just as Cape Town's property prices increased.

Barry was made redundant again in the 2000s and is resigned to never working again. The couple are not living the glamorous lifestyle that tourist adverts promise of Cape Town. Now in their 60s, they live modestly, and although they say they have some money 'put aside', Daniel is surprised to hear they have no private health insurance in a country where that is necessary for adequate healthcare. On occasion, they have considered returning to Britain, but for financial and family reasons, they think it is impractical. As previously discussed, the couple believe South Africa has been good to them; theirs is a narrative of social mobility, and being present for and participating in the country's first democratic elections was a memorable and meaningful moment in their lives. Yet, at the end of the afternoon Daniel spends with them, Barry asks, 'What do you think our lives would be like if we had stayed in the UK?' It is an uncomfortable moment, because Daniel thinks that with a more extensive welfare state and a historically more stable economy, they would probably have fared better had they remained in the United Kingdom.

Few of the people that we spoke to were as frank or as poignant as Catherine about wishing they had chosen differently and *not* emigrated to South Africa. Catherine lived in a large property with a sea view in a sedate and beautiful coastal village. Hers should have been an account of lifestyle migration: of fulfilling an idyllic life in the sunshine. Yet her story was complicated by return to Britain in the 1980s because of the politics of South Africa, alienation from the country of her birth, time spent living in France in the 2000s, and now life in a town and society she felt puzzled by and largely excluded from.

Similarly, Louise, who we met in Chapter 6, also felt excluded by South Africa. Her failure to secure a good job for herself in Johannesburg or the educational support she desired for her son, were pushing her to regret her decision to persuade her South African husband to return to his homeland. That both their stories could be expressed through ambivalence and possible failure is perhaps testimony to the fracturing of the discourses of whiteness in South Africa: unlike in other locations such as Spain and France, British residents can express their disappointment, resentment and alienation freely, because so many other white

South Africans do, too. However, while most of the people we spoke to proclaimed love for and belonging to South Africa, their narratives and everyday lives were fraught with contradictions. Their life histories were framed as though South Africa was the inevitable and optimal place in which to enjoy and fulfil their lives, but, as we have shown through the chapters of this book, the 'decision' to go there was often entirely by chance, or the result of a haphazard process of elimination. Most enjoyed the country's magnificent landscape, but they often also feared it in equal (and even greater) measure. They could express no interest in the country's politics, yet hold forth about the country's history and society, often revealing how deeply implicated they were in the country's troubled past. They could proclaim their exaggerated wealth and status, enabled by a cheap currency and being part of a privileged white elite, yet worry about the cost of cable TV subscriptions, visa fees, healthcare, groceries and the expense of property in the UK that could remove any prospect of return. Many felt the 'Great Britain' they had left had vanished, to be replaced with a multicultural country that some felt 'ashamed' of; yet they also could feel loss of a cosmopolitan British lifestyle in their lives in South Africa, and followed events in the United Kingdom via television, newspapers and the internet assiduously. They could declare a deep sense of belonging to South Africa, but be unsure about the country they claimed to belong to, and their everyday lives could be framed by fear, suspicion and parochialism. The ambiguous and sometimes contradictory nature of these accounts raised the question: where exactly do white British residents in contemporary South Africa belong?

The British in South Africa have always existed in liminal spaces, not occupying the central, foundational place in the nation that they did in other 'old' Commonwealth states such as Australia, Canada and New Zealand, but not quite the linguistic and cultural outsiders that they are in countries such as France and Spain. British settlers and their descendants in the nineteenth century framed the 'master narrative' (Steyn 2001) of whiteness that legitimated colonial control and framed the South African nation in white British terms. This was never fully successful because of the intrawhite cleavages with the Boer/Afrikaner white population and the failure of South Africa to attract British settlers in large numbers. Throughout the twentieth century, the consequences of the Boer War included the rise of an exclusionary and anti-British Afrikaner nationalism. Restrictive immigration policies and political events restricted mass British migration to the country, but nevertheless British migrants were the most consistently significant groups of white migrants to the country throughout the twentieth century. The apartheid government increasingly viewed British migrants as an important means to aid economic growth without having to make political or economic concessions to the black majority, but the post-republic state considered British immigrants suitable for assimilation in the white state. As the accounts in this book demonstrate, this was by no means a seamless or inevitable process. Experiencing Afrikaner culture and the Afrikaner state could be deeply alienating, and one that reaffirmed a sense of 'Britishness'.

As Samantha recalls, arriving in South Africa in the early 1960s, she was told: 'Well, we don't want you, but we need you!' However, as with English-speaking South African whites more broadly, identifying the state and South African society as Afrikaner also enabled a disingenuous disavowal of any involvement or responsibility for apartheid. The narratives that continue to express anger at the BBC for 'misrepresenting' or 'exaggerating' the iniquity of apartheid, irritation at the criticisms of friends and relatives in the United Kingdom, the claims that apartheid was a lot of fuss about nothing, or that black South Africans did well out of it, may appear shocking to a reader outside of South Africa. Within the country itself, white social and political discourses normalise the claims. For this reason, conducting some of the interviews could be an uncomfortable experience for us, when the discourses our interviewees produced seemed so self-evident and commonsensical to them that they naturally assumed we would agree with them. The interviews also reveal how much of white society has not accepted responsibility for apartheid, and the extent to which British immigrants were implicated in its everyday operations.

However, both Pauline and Daniel *did* meet a few British people who recognised their role in the success, or derailment, of both apartheid and post-apartheid. In the beautiful gardens of the Johannesburg country club, Pauline drank coffee with Richard, a retired engineer now in his 70s, who had migrated to Port Elizabeth in 1975. As they watch peacocks wandering across the lawns and a few older white women playing croquet, Richard explains:

> I'm not one of those people who will shrink from that part of South Africa's history. It was brilliant! If you come to a country where you've got blue skies, and you've got sea, and you've got beaches, and you've got a wonderful way of life with a maid and a houseboy and everything, and it's quite zillion times cheaper than the UK? You know, you think, 'This is paradise!'

Conversely, we also met some who had been anti-apartheid, and had been instrumental in the movement against apartheid. In Pietermaritzburg for example, Pauline spent the day interviewing a group of political activists who, since the 1960s, had been concerned to challenge the ideologies of apartheid and undermine its modus operandi. As educational publishers, their central mission had been to 'rewrite' South African history and geography as it was typically represented in the textbooks that dominated the school curriculum, and to disseminate alternative versions across the educational system in both Afrikaans and Zulu.

While Malcolm, a publisher in his 60s who had migrated to Kwazulu-Natal with his South African wife, admitted that at first he had not been 'a political animal', his involvement in this kind of liberal politics soon changed him: 'My focus changed...I knew that I was working with a group of people that were seeking to make things better, and look for greater equality.' The work required considerable tactical skill: 'We walked a tightrope, there's no doubt in my mind, and we did it very cleverly. We walked a tightrope of dealing with the syllabus in an accepted way, but at the same time putting a new slant on it.'

As Pauline chatted with other members of the group, many now in their 80s, on the variances of a house in the Pietermaritzburg, she felt humbled by their ongoing sense of political engagement and the strength of their commitment now, in the post-apartheid space, to support the new black administration in Pietermaritzburg. Yet while we met other people who are similarly prepared to reach out to South Africa's different communities and engage with South African society in alternative ways, such people seemed to remain the exception, not the rule.

Belonging and the future

Contemplating the future was never far from the minds of the people we spoke to. In a country where approximately one in four of the white population has left since 1994, and in a continent where white citizens (and British citizens in particular) have been targeted for attack and rejection, as occurred in Zimbabwe in the 2000s, weighing up the future has become both a personal and a political preoccupation, where return or onward migration is a commonly discussed and enacted process. Some expected to stay in South Africa and could not envisage any circumstance in which they would consider leaving. Others were acutely aware that political circumstances could provoke, if not return to Britain, onward migration elsewhere. A few knew their futures would not be in South Africa and were actively planning to leave when we spoke to them.

Paul, an investment banker in his 40s, vividly evoked contemplating the future when he asked his wife Vanessa, 'Where do you want to die?'

She replied, 'Die? I want to be buried here. I already think that.'

Paul: Here?
Vanessa: Yeah...
Nigel: A tax consultant in the UK asked me that some years ago and said, 'Where do you want your bones to lie?' and it was the first time I'd actually thought about that. You know, it's – because, you know, a lot of my family, generations, are buried in a small churchyard and, you know –
Paul: You've broken that line.
Nigel: It's something that – yeah, it's something that you have to think about, I suppose, in the longer term. I mean, it's putting it crudely, but where do you want to spend your last few years?

Paul and Vanessa moved to South Africa in 2003; Nigel has lived in South Africa since 1986. Paul's stark question to his wife brought expectations of the future into sharp and personal focus. As at other moments in the morning Daniel spent with them, Paul seemed somewhat surprised by Vanessa's answers and less certain about his long-term commitment to remaining in South Africa. For others, the future remained absent from their narratives, which were embedded entirely in the present.

Thinking about the prospect of life in the future in South Africa was often deeply implicated in expectations of the country's political prospects. Joanna, now living in retirement in the Western Cape, replies that the prospect of the future 'worries' her: 'We [Joanna and her husband] quite often say to each other, Thank goodness we are the age we are, because we hopefully will not have to cope with some of the problems that I'm sure are coming, which is not a nice thing to say.'

Others expressed the same deeply pessimistic attitude toward the future that Catherine articulates:

Are we living in a fool's paradise here?...And you only have to say, how many million whites, how many million non-whites? And you think, Wow, how are we still here? Is it just waiting to shatter, thin ice? And all our friends, everybody, they're inclined to say now, because we're getting on a bit, 'It'll probably last us out.' But it might not. I don't think anybody that I know well has said that this country will not fall into Africa. It shouldn't, but I think that they believe that ultimately it will. It might take a long time to spiral out because of the big infrastructure, a lot of wealth, but they believe it will. It's going to unwind, and it will end up in Africa. And at the moment, they don't consider that they're in Africa, especially in the Cape.

James, also living in retirement in Cape Town, replies that he expects the future will result in 'an African state. They [the ANC] will eventually take over the Western Cape. They are not at all happy about it being run by the DA [Democratic Alliance]... We all feel it's going that way. I think 20 years is actually too far; I would say within 10 years. I will probably be gone by then.'

James' pessimistic view mirrors Catherine's concerns that the country will fall 'into Africa'. This perception that South Africa is not 'in Africa', or 'like Africa', is aided by the fact that Catherine and James live in the Western Cape, where the landscapes, demographics and politics enable the discursive framing of the landscape as white, European and even English ('England by the sea') to continue relatively unchallenged. Some base their enjoyment of the country entirely on this familiar landscape and would leave the moment it changed; others choose to disrupt this framing and live in different landscapes. That British residents in Johannesburg also identify Cape Town as 'too English' or 'too colonial' and not the 'real Africa' endorses the perception that to live in the Western Cape is to exist in a particularly white space.

The different spaces in which British migrants live reveal the multiple engagements they have with broader South Africa, however: choosing to live and enjoy life in Johannesburg because of its perceived multi-racialism, its 'African-ness', or its faster pace of life, demonstrates that British residents engage with South Africa's localities in diverse ways, and the country is not just an entirely blank canvas onto which they can project meanings. As we have argued, this complicates analysis of the British in South Africa as lifestyle migrants: they may claim that South Africa maximises their lifestyles and fulfils mythic ambitions for leisure in the sunshine, but contrasting perceptions of space and clear material engagements with the broader society mean that political and social perceptions, along with expectations of the country's future, have considerable impact on and mediate enjoyment of life in the country and plans for the future.

Whiteness

Whiteness clearly remains a salient and indeed dominant identity in South Africa. The British people we spoke to are continually reminded of their whiteness and the ambivalent and contested place in which this puts them within South Africa. In the contemporary state, British residents must also provide an explanation of race relations and how they believe they 'fit into' South African life. All the narratives explored in this book have in some way been about race and have had elements of 'white talk' (Steyn 2001). The unease expressed by Catherine, James, Barry and Jane, above, reflects their sense of dislocation and dissonance at being white in a context where they feel they do not quite belong (even if they believe their local area is, for the time being, different). Others felt South Africa has moved on in racial terms. Joanna, who lived in Rhodesia and then South Africa remarks, 'I think actually most white people have really come to the party of opening their lives to Africans and so on and really trying to just mix more and communicate more.'

It is clear that what constitutes whiteness in contemporary South Africa is still very much under construction and under debate (Distiller and Steyn 2004). Indeed, in contemporary South Africa, there is much ongoing debate on the issue of 'whiteness studies', and whether it is at all useful to pursue this enquiry in an allegedly 'post-race' South Africa (Hafferjee 31/3/2013). There have also been attempts to recuperate whiteness and white people in South Africa. For example, the Democratic Alliance party launched a political campaign in 2012 aimed at emphasising the apparent commitment of individual white South Africans, such as Helen Suzman and Helen Zille, to ending apartheid and claiming that the ANC had betrayed the ideals of the liberation struggle (M&G 18/4/2013). In this context, Joanna's 'post-racial' attitude of interracial understanding finds many supporters. Yet, as Steyn and Foster (2008) argue, this serves the political purpose of obscuring ongoing white privilege and racial inequality, as well as avoiding any responsibility for the apartheid past.

That British residents struggled to identify themselves as 'immigrants' who share commonalities with immigrants in the United Kingdom is also testament to the discursive power of whiteness in South Africa. Those British who commented on South African society, post-apartheid immigration to South Africa from other African states, and the resultant xenophobia, without any reference to themselves as migrants, attest to the ability of white discourses to frame the individual and society at large to suit personal interest. Similarly, defining oneself as progressive, liberal, non-racist and integrated did not have to relate to any meaningful evidence of this being the case: white South Africans are at liberty to define themselves as they wish, and the terms by which they and British immigrants are to be interpreted are no different. Similarly, hostility towards immigration in the United Kingdom and a desire for a return to an earlier, idealised age, was not just the influence of the predominantly conservative media sources the British in South Africa have access to, but also the white social and political discourses that many inhabit in their lives there.

The British in South Africa?

Our stories of the everyday lives and attitudes of the British in South Africa have demonstrated a complex social category that encompasses a broad range of identities, lifestyles, attitudes and social relations. However, across this diversity, our participants were steadfast in their ongoing sense of identification with British nationality and their sense of belonging, if not to the material and political landscape of the contemporary United Kingdom, to an imagined community with some shared characteristics and sense of culture. While the narratives represented in this book reveal that, for a whole range of highly diverse reasons, this is a group who chose to, and, of course, owing to their cultural capital, were able to, leave the United Kingdom and migrate to South Africa, once they arrive, it is clear that most are keen to retain their links with 'home' and their sense of belonging to it. In this regard, the British in South Africa can in some ways be conceptualised as diasporic: this is not a group of migrants keen to display 'authenticity' through separation with home and assimilation with local communities, but a group for whom sustained transnational and translocal connections provide valuable personal and social resources. While an actual return 'home' was not on the agenda for many – because they were now happily settled in South Africa, or their relationships with family and friends at home had dwindled, or they could not now afford to go back, or they decried the state of the contemporary UK – the landscapes of home still occupied an important place in the imagination of most people we talked to.

As a way of keeping this emotional support alive, many prioritised other British people in their social relations and embodied activities, sharing news, gossip and humour, helping with each other's problems and giving advice. The strength of this national attachment perhaps in part explains the lack of division *among* the British: unlike the lifestyle migrants of France or Spain, there were very few comments about class differences or attempts to distinguish themselves from other Britons through class terms. Of course this can be explained in part through the divisions within the broader white communities we have discussed in this book, whereby ethnicity and class were conflated. Distinction, for the British, was produced through their perceived difference from other whites. However, important as British social networks are, they do not preclude the British from forging meaningful relationships with South Africa and its people. Many of our respondents *also* claimed to feel they belonged in South Africa: through a love of its landscape 'It gets into your soul,' as many put it; through a love of its people – in friendships, marriage, partnership and the making of families; through work – some owned their own companies, or had jobs they were committed to; or even through a love of its politics – whether as an acknowledged beneficiary of the privileges accrued through whiteness or by a professed allegiance to the 'new South Africa'.

The myriad and nuanced intersections that exist here through both people and place mean that, without doubt, the British are an integral part of that broad group known as WESSAs: White English-Speaking South Africans. At the same time, however, many British would, partially at least, agree with Susan, when she succinctly explains, 'It's that birds of a feather fly best together. That pretty well sums it up.'

Notes

1 The British in South Africa: Continuity or Change?

1. We refer to the descendants of the original Dutch/German/Huguenot settlers whose first language is 'Afrikaans' as 'Afrikaners'. This group of mixed heritage Europeans were originally known as the 'Cape Dutch', of which the 'Boers' were a sub-group of mainly farmers (Giliomee, 2003).
2. In the early 2000s Rhodes, like many other former white universities, continued to have a majority of white students and academic staff, a matter that was increasingly the focus of debate and criticism. Furthermore, the purpose and identity of higher education in South Africa began to be debated in racial terms, with specific controversies and am attendant white 'backlash' politics (Makgoba, 25/03/2005; Morrell, 1/04/2005; Statman and Ansell, 2000; Southall and Cobbing, 2009).
3. We are grateful to The British Academy for funding this project

2 The Historical, Political and Social Dynamics of British Migration to South Africa

1. In 1919, the Society for the Overseas Settlement of British Women was founded to continue the encouragement of women's emigration to the Empire and Dominions. The Society was partly funded by the British state and at times obtained grants from the South African government. It was still operating in the 1960s. The Society encouraged and assisted women with emigration to South Africa, advertised job vacancies and assisted with the recruitment and assessment process of potential employees and migrants. It also owned hostels for newly arrived immigrants in Cape Town and Johannesburg (Smith 2013: 181–192).
2. Although the South African government did institute a national 'Settlers Day' holiday from 1952 onwards, to commemorate the arrival of the first 1820 British Settlers (Smith 2013: 210).
3. The slogan of a 1970s car advertisement in South Africa.

3 Transnational and Translocal Identities: Settling in South Africa

1. 'Geordie' is a regional nickname for a person from the Tyneside in North East England.
2. 'Brickie' is a British nickname for a bricklayer.
3. The television programme Moira is referring to was an American children's series called 'Daktari' about a fictional Animal Study Centre in East Africa.

4. 'Ten pound Pom' was an Australian expression given exclusively to British migrants to Australia between the 1940s and 1970s. During this time, the cost of British migrants' passage was assisted by the Australian government such that migrants themselves only had to contribute ten pounds sterling (see Hammerton and Thomson 2005).
5. Place name changed for anonymity.

4 Space and Place in South Africa

1. This is a pseudonym.
2. *Coronation Street* is a long-running and very popular British soap opera of northern working-class life.

5 Landscapes of Belonging: Negotiating Britishness in South Africa

1. British forces had established internment camps to house residents of the Boer Republics in 1900. This was part of the 'scorched earth' tactic of destroying farms, livestock and disrupting supply lines for Boer forces. Conditions in the camps were poor with starvation and disease commonplace. By some estimates over 26,000 Afrikaner women and children died in the camps. The existence of the camps and the tales of the suffering of the internees became a major tenet of Afrikaner nationalism after the Boer War.

6 The Landscapes of Un/belonging in South Africa

1. **Julius Sello Malema** is the leader of the Economic Freedom Fighters, a South African political movement, which he founded in July 2013.

7 Narratives of Continuity and Change: British Social and Political Attitudes in South Africa

1. Uhuru is the Swahili word for freedom. It characterises the African nationalist and Pan-African movements for liberation from colonialism and also various political organisations that advocate Pan-Africanism and African socialism.
2. Two thirds of Stone's 1973 sample said they would never take out South African citizenship (215). At that time it was not possible to hold dual nationality. In 1984, citizenship laws were tightened, and white immigrant men between the ages of 15 and 25 were obliged to be military conscripts in return for citizenship or face losing their permanent residents status. In the post-apartheid era, dual nationality is possible, but most of those we interviewed have not taken the opportunity to be dual citizens. Many continue to view holding a British passport as an important aspect of life in South Africa and a form of 'insurance'.
3. Harold Wilson, leader of the Labour Party and United Kingdom Prime Minister 1964–1970 and 1974–1976.

Bibilography

Adepoju, Adedayo (2002) 'Issues and recent trends in international migration in sub-Saharan Africa' *International Social Science Journal* 52 (165), 383–394.
Ahmed, Sara (1999) 'Home and away: narratives of migration and estrangement' *International Journal of Cultural Studies* 2 (3), 329–347.
Alexander, Claire (2009) 'Stuart Hall and "race"' *Cultural Studies* 23 (4), 457–482.
—— (2010) 'Diaspora and hybridity' in Patricia Hill Collins and John Solomos (eds) *The Sage Handbook of Race and Ethnic Studies*, London, Sage.
Alexander, Claire and Knowles, Caroline (2005) *Making Race Matter: Bodies, Space and Identity*, Basingstoke, Palgrave Macmillan.
Alibhai-Brown, Yasmin (2000) 'Muddled leaders and the future of the British national identity' *The Political Quarterly* 71 (1), 26–30.
Amit, Vered (2002) 'The Moving "Expert": a study of mobile professionals in the Cayman Islands and North America' in Sorensen, N. N. and Olwig, K. F. (eds) *Work and Migration: Life and Livelihoods in a Globalizing World*, London, Routledge.
—— (ed.) (2011) *Going First Class? New Approaches to Privileged Travel and Movement*, New York, Berghan Books.
Anderson, Ben and Harrison, P. (eds) (2010) *Taking Place: Non-Representational Theories and Geography*. Farnham, Ashgate.
Andruki, Max (2010) 'The visa whiteness machine: Transnational motility in post-apartheid South Africa' *Ethnicities* 10 (3), 358–370.
Appadurai, Arjan (1995) 'The Production of locality' in Fardon, R. (ed.) *Counterworks: Managing the Diversity of Knowledge*, London, Routledge.
Armbruster, Heidi (2012) 'Realising the self and developing the African: German immigrants in Namibia' in Fechter, Anne-Meike and Walsh, Katie (eds) *The New Expatriates: Postcolonial Approaches to Mobile Professionals*, London, Routledge.
Armbruster, Heidi (2010) '"Realising the self and developing the African": German immigrants in Namibia' *Journal of Ethnic and Migration Studies* 38 (8) 1229–1246.
Atkinson, Will (2010) 'The myth of the reflexive worker: class and work histories in neo-liberal times' *Work, Employment and Society* 24 (3), 413–429.
Back, Les and Solomos, John (2000) *Theories of Race and Racism*, London, Routledge.
Ballard, Richard (2004) 'Assimilation, emigration, semigration, and integration: "white" peoples' strategies for finding a comfort zone in a post-apartheid South Africa' in Distiller, Natasha and Steyn, Melissa (eds) *Under Construction: 'Race' and Identity in South Africa Today*, Pietermaritzburg, Heinemann.
Ballard, Richard (2005) 'When in Rome: claiming the right to define neighbourhood character in South Africa's suburbs' *Transformation* 57, 64–87.
Ballard, Richard and Jones, Gareth (2011) 'Natural neighbours: indigenous landscapes and eco-estates in Durban, South Africa' *Annals of the Association of American Geographers* 101 (1), 131–148.

Barclays Bank (1971) *Emigrating to South Africa: A Guide to Procedure and an Introduction to Life in the Republic* London, Barclays Bank.
Basch, L., Glick Schiller, N. and Blanc, C. S. (1994) *Nations Unbound: Transnational projects, Postcolonials Predicaments and Deterritorialized Nation-States*, London, Routledge.
Basler, Carleen (2008) 'White Dreams and red votes: Mexican Americans and the lure of inclusion into the Republican Party' *Ethnic and Racial Studies* 31 (1), 123–166.
Bauman, Zygmut (2005) *Liquid Life*, Cambridge, Polity Press.
—— (2008) *The Art of Life*, Cambridge, Polity Press.
Baumann, Martin (2010) 'Exile' in Kim Knott and Sean McLoughlin (eds) *Diasporas: Concepts, Intersections, Identities*, London, Zed Books.
Beaverstock, Jonathan (2002) 'Transnational elites in global cities: British expatriates in Singapore's financial district' *Geoforum* 33, 525–538.
Beaverstock, J. V. (2005) 'Transnational elites in the city: British highly skilled inter-company transferees in New york city's financial district' *Journal of Ethnic and Migration Studies* 31 (2), 245–68.
Beck, U. and Beck-Gernsheim, E. (2002) *Individualization*, London, Sage.
Beinart, William (2001) *Twentieth Century South Africa*, Oxford, Oxford University Press.
Bender, Barbara (1993) *Landscape: Politics and Perspective* London and New York, Berg.
Benson, Michaela (2011) *The British in Rural France: Lifestyle Migration and the Ongoing Quest for a Better Way of Life*, Manchester, Manchester University Press.
Benson, Michaela and O'Reilly, Karen (eds) (2009a) *Lifestyle Migration: Expectations, Aspirations and Experiences*, Farnham, Ashgate.
Benson, Michaela and O'Reilly, Karen (2009b) 'Migration and the search for a better way of life: a critical exploration of lifestyle migration' *Sociological Review* 57 (4), 608–625.
Bennett, Tony, Savage, Mike, Silva, Elizabeth, Warde, Alan, Modesto, Gayo-Cal and Wright, David (2009) *Culture, Class, Distinction*, London, Routledge.
Bhengu, Ruth (2010) 'Romance' in Heidi Holland and Adam Roberts (eds) *From Joburg to Jozi: Stories about Africa's Infamous City*, South Africa, Penguin.
Bickers, Robert (ed.) (2010) *Settlers and Expatriates: Britons over the Seas*, Oxford, Oxford University Press.
Blunt, Alison (2007) 'Cultural geographies of migration: mobility, transnationality and diaspora' *Progress in Human Geography* 31, 684–694.
Bond, John (1956) *They Were South Africans*, Cape Town, Oxford University Press.
Bourdieu, Pierre (1977) *Outline of a Theory of Practice*, Cambridge, Cambridge University Press.
—— (1984) *Distinction*, London, Routledge, Kegan & Paul.
—— (1986) 'The forms of capital' in J. Richardson (ed.) *Handbook of Theory and Research for the Sociology of Education*, New York, Greenwood.
Bousiou, Pola (2008) *The Nomads of Mykonos: Performing Liminalities in a 'Queer' Space*, Oxford, Berghahn.
Braziel, Jana Evans (2008) *Diaspora: An Introduction*, Malden, MA, Blackwell.
Brah, Atvar (1996) *Cartographies of Diaspora: Contesting Identities*, Abingdon, Routledge.

Brickell, Katherine and Datta, Ayona (2011) *Translocal Geographies: Spaces, Places, Connections*, Farnham, Ashgate.
Brownell, Josiah (2008) 'The hole in Rhodesia's bucket: white emigration and the end of settler rule' *Journal of Southern African Studies* 34 (3), 591–610.
Brubaker, Rogers (2005) *Ethnicity Without Groups*, Cambridge, MA, Harvard University Press.
Bryman, Alan (2001) *Social Research Methods*, Oxford, Oxford University Press.
Burawoy, Michael (ed.) (2000) *Global Ethnography: Forces, Connections and Imaginations in a Postmodern World*, Berkeley, University of California Press.
Bureau of Information RSA (1989) *South Africa 1988–89: Official Yearbook of the Republic of South Africa*, Pretoria, Government Printer.
Butler, Anthony (2009) *Contemporary South Africa*, Basingstoke, Palgrave Macmillan.
Butler, Guy (1976) 'The nature and purpose of the conference' in Andre de Villiers (ed.) *English speaking South Africa Today: Proceedings of the National Conference July 1974*, Cape Town, Oxford University Press.
Callan, H. and Ardener, S. (eds) (1984) *The Incorporated Wife*, Beckenham, Croom Helm.
Callewaert, Staf (2006) 'Bourdieu, critic of Foucault: the case of empirical social science against double–game–philosophy' *Theory, Culture and Society* 23 (6), 73–98.
Chambers, I. (1994) *Migrancy, Culture, Identity*, London, Routledge.
Clark, A. & Emmel, N, 2010. Using walking interviews. *Realities*, 13, 1–6.
Clarke, Nick (2005) 'Detailing transnational lives of the middle: British working holiday makers in Australia' *Journal of Ethnic and Migration Studies* 31 (2), 307–322.
Clifford, James (1994) 'Diasporas' *Cultural Anthropology* 9 (3), 302–38.
Cohen, E. (1972) 'Towards a sociology of international tourism' *Social Research* 39, 164–82.
Cohen, Robin (1994) *Frontiers of Identity: The British and the Others*, London, Longman.
Coles, Anne and Fechter, Anne-Meike (2008) (eds) *Gender and Family among Transnational Professionals* New York, Routledge.
Coles, Anne and Walsh, Katie (2012) 'From 'trucial state' to 'postcolonial' city? The imaginative geographies of British expatriates in Dubai' in Fechter, Anne-Meike and Walsh, Katie (eds) *The New Expatriates: Postcolonial Approaches to Mobile Professionals*, London, Routledge.
Coles, Tim and Timothy, Dallen J. (2004) *Tourism, Diasporas and Space*, Abingdon, Routledge.
Conradson, David and Latham, Alan (2005) 'Friendship, networks and transnationality in a world city: antipodean transmigrants in London' *Journal of Ethnic and Migration Studies* 31 (2), 287–305.
Conway, Daniel (2012) *Masculinities, Militarisation and the End Conscription Campaign: War Resistance in Apartheid South Africa*, Manchester, Manchester University Press
Conway, Daniel (26 July 2010) 'The changing lives of expats in South Africa', *The Telegraph*. Accessed 9 February 2014. http://www.telegraph.co.uk/expat/expatlife/7903228/The-changing-lives-of-expats-in-South-Africa.html.

Conway, Daniel (2009) 'Queering apartheid: the National Party's "gay rights" election campaign in Hillbrow' *Journal of Southern African Studies* 35 (4), 849–863.

Conway, Daniel (2008) 'Masculinities and narrating the past: experiences of researching white men who refused to serve in the apartheid army' *Qualitative Research* 8 (3) 347–354.

Crush, Jonathan (2008) *The Perfect Storm: The Realities of Xenophobia in Contemporary South Africa,* Cape Town and Kingston, Ontario: Southern African Migration Project.

Dagut, Simon (1997) 'Paternalism and social distance: British settlers' racial attitudes, 1850s–1890s' *South African Historical Journal* 37 (1), 3–20.

—— (2000) '"Women's history" and the construction of social distance: middle-class British women in later nineteenth-century South Africa' *Journal of Southern African Studies* 26 (3), 555–572.

Davies, Rebecca (2009) *Afrikaners in the New South Africa: Identity Politics in a Globalised Economy,* London, I. B. Tauris.

Distiller, Natasha and Steyn, Melissa (2004) 'Introduction: under construction' in Distiller, Natasha and Steyn, Melissa (eds) *Under Construction: 'Race' and Identity in South Africa Today,* Pietermaritzburg, Heinemann.

Drake, Helen and Collard, Susan (2008) 'A case study of intra-EU migration: 20 years of 'Brits' in the Pays d'Auge, Normandy, France' *French Politics* 6, 214–233.

DuBois, William E. B. (1977) *Black Reconstruction in the United States 1860–1880,* New York.

Dubow, Saul (2009) 'How British was the British world? the case of South Africa' *Journal of Imperial and Commonwealth History,* 37 (1), 1–27.

Dunn, Kevin (2010) 'Embodied transnationalism: bodies in transnational spaces' *Population, Space and Place* 16, 1–9.

Durrheim, Kevin (2005) 'Socio-spatial practice and racial representation in a changing South Africa' *South African Journal of Psychology* 35, 444–459.

Dyb, Kari and Halford, Susan (2009) 'Placing globalizing technologies: telemedicine and the making of difference' *Sociology* 43 (2), 232–249.

Dyer, Richard (1997) *White: Essays on Race and Culture,* London, Routledge.

Easthope, Hazel (2009) 'Fixed identities in a mobile world? The relationship between mobility, place and identity' *Identities: Global Studies in Culture and Power* 16, 61–82.

Edwards, Isobel (1934) *The 1820 Settlers in South Africa: A Study in British Colonial Policy,* London, Longmans, Green and Co.

Elder, Catriona (2007) *Being Australian: Narratives of National Identity,* Crows Nest, NSW, Allen and Unwin.

Erasmus, Zimitri (2008) 'Race' in Nick Shepherd and Steven Robins (eds) *New South African Keywords,* Johannesburg, Jacana.

Erklank, Natasha (1995) 'Thinking it wrong to remain unemployed in the pressing times': the experiences of two English settler wives' *South African Historical Journal* 33, 62–82.

Essed, Philomena and Trienekens, Sandra (2008) 'Who wants to feel white? Race, Dutch culture and contested identities' *Ethnic and Racial Studies,* 31 (1), 52–72.

Farrer, James (2012) 'New Shanghailanders' or 'New Shanghailanese': Western expatriates narratives of emplacement in Shanghai' in Fechter, Anne-Meike and Walsh, Katie (eds) (2012) *The New Expatriates: Postcolonial Approaches to Mobile Professionals,* London, Routledge.

Fechter, Anne-Meike (2007) *Transnational Lives: Expatriates in Indonesia,* Aldershot, Ashgate.

Fechter, Anne-Meike and Walsh, Katie (2010) 'Examining "expatriate" continuities: Postcolonial approaches to mobile professionals' *Journal of Ethnic and Migration Studies* 36 (8), 1197–1210.

Fechter, Anne-Meike and Walsh, Katie (eds) (2012) *The New Expatriates: Postcolonial Approaches to Mobile Professionals,* London, Routledge.

Fedorowich, Kent (1991) 'Anglicization and the politicization of British immigration to South Africa, 1899–1929' *Journal of Imperial and Commonwealth History* 19 (2), 222–46.

Field, S. and Swanson, F. (2007) 'Introduction' in Field, S., Meyer, R. and Swanson, F. (eds) *Imagining the City: Memories and Cultures in Cape Town,* Cape Town, HSRC Press.

Finch, Tim, Andrew, Holly and Latorre, Maria (2010) *Global Brit: Making the Most of the British Diaspora,* London, IPPR.

Findlay, Allan, Hoy, Caroline and Stockdale, Aileen (2004) 'In what sense English? An exploration of English migrant identities and identification' *Journal of Ethnic and Migration Studies* 30 (1), 59–79.

Fine, Michelle, Weis, Lois, Powell, Linda, Wong, Mun (1997) *Off White: Readings on Race, Power and Society,* New York, Routledge.

Foster, Jeremy (2008) *Washed with Sun: Landscape and the Making of White South Africa,* Pittsburgh, PA, University of Pittsburgh Press.

Foucault, Michel (1972) *The Archaeology of Knowledge and the Discourse on Language,* London, Routledge.

Foucault, Michel (1980) *Power/Knowledge,* Brighton, Harvester Press.

Frankenberg R (1993) *White Women, Race Matters: The Social Construction of Whiteness,* London, Routledge.

—— (ed.) (1997) *Displacing Whiteness: Essays in Social and Cultural Criticism,* Durham, NC and London, Duke University Press.

Franklin, Adrian and Crang, Mike (2001) 'The trouble with tourism and travel theory' *Tourist Studies* 1 (1), 5–22.

Frederikse, Julie (1986) *South Africa: A Different Kind of War* James Currey, Oxford.

Frey, William H. (1979) 'Central City white flight: racial and non-racial causes' *American Sociological Review* 44 (3), 425–448.

Gaitskell, Deborah (1983) 'Introduction' *Journal of Southern African Studies* 10 (1), 1–16.

Garson, Noel G. (1976) 'English-speaking South Africans and the British connection 1820–1961' in andre de villiers (ed.) *English Speaking South Africa Today: Proceedings of the National Conference July 1974,* Cape Town, Oxford University Press.

Giddens, Anthony (1991) *Modernity and Self-Identity: Self and Society in the Late Modern Age,* Cambridge, Polity Press.

Giliomee, Hermann (2003) *The Afrikaners: Biography of a People,* University of Virginia Press.

Gilroy, Paul (1997) 'Diaspora and the detours of identity' in Kath Woodward (ed.) *Identity and Difference,* London, Sage.

Gielis, Ruben (2009) 'A global sense of migrant places: Towards a place perspective in the study of migrant transnationalism' *Global Networks* 9 (2), 271–287.

Goldberg, David (2009) 'A political theology of race' *Cultural Studies* 23 (4), 513–537.

Graham, E. (2000) 'The past, present and future of population geography: reflections on Glenn Trewartha's address fifty years on' *Population, Space and Place* 6, 257–272.

Guarnizo, L. E. and Smith, M. P. (1998) 'The Locations of Transnationalism' in Smith, M. P. and Guarnizo, L. E. (eds) *Transnationalism from Below*, New Brunswick, NJ, Transaction.

Gurney, Christobel (2000) '"A Great Cause": The origins of the anti-apartheid movement, June 1959–March 1960' *Journal of Southern African Studies* 26 (1), 123–144.

Hafferjee, Ferial (31 March 2013) 'The problem with whiteness' *City Press*. Accessed 9 February 2014. http://www.citypress.co.za/columnists/the-problem-with-whiteness-ferial-haffajee/.

Halford, S and Leonard, P (2006) *Negotiating Gendered Identities at Work: Place, Space and Time* Basingstoke, Palgrave.

Hall, C. Michael and Williams, Allan M. (eds) (2002) *Tourism and Migration: New Relationships between Production and Consumption*, Dordrecht, Kluwer Academic Publishers.

Hammerton, A. James and Thomson, A. (2005) *Ten Pound Poms: Australia's Invisible Migrants*, Manchester, Manchester University Press.

Hatfield, Madeleine E. (2011) 'British families moving home: translocal geographies of return migration from Singapore' in Brickell, Katherine and Datta, Ayona (eds) *Translocal Geographies: Spaces, Places, Connections*, Farnham, Ashgate.

Hetherington, Penelope (1993) 'Women in South Africa: The historiography in English' *The International Journal of African Historical Studies* 26 (2), 241–269.

Hobsbawm, Eric (1990) *Nations and Nationalism Since 1780*, Cambridge, Cambridge University Press.

Holland, Heidi and Roberts, Adam (eds) (2010) *From Jo'burg to Jozi: Stories about Africa's Infamous City*, London, Penguin.

Hoy, David Couzens (1991) *Foucault: A Critical Reader*, Oxford, Wiley-Blackwell.

Hughes, David McDermott (2010) *Whiteness in Zimbabwe: Race, Landscape, and the Problem of Belonging*, New York, Palgrave Macmillan.

International Defence Aid Fund (1975) *Southern Africa's Immigration from Britain: A Fact Paper*, London, IDAF.

Jackson, Peter (1998) 'Constructions of whiteness in the geographical imagination' *Area* 30 (2), 99–106.

Jeffrey, Anthea (2010) *Chasing the Rainbow: South Africa's Move from Mandela to Zuma*, Johannesburg, SAIRR.

Johnson, R. W. (2009) *South Africa's Brave New World: The Beloved Country Since the End of Apartheid*, London, Allen Lane.

Jupp, J. (2004) *The English in Australia*, Cambridge, Cambridge University Press.

Kalra, Virinda, Kaur, Raminder and Hutnyk, John (2005) *Diaspora and Hybridity*, London, Sage.

King, Russell (2012) 'Geography and migration studies: retrospect and prospect' *Population, Space and Place* 18, 134–153.

King, Russell, Warnes, Tony and Williams, Allan (2000) *Sunset Lives: British Retirement in the Mediterranean*, Oxford, Berg.

King, Russell, Mai, N. and Schwander-Sievers, S. (eds) (2005) *The New Albanian Migration*, Brighton, Sussex Academic Press.

Klein, Genevieve (2007) 'The Anti-Apartheid Movement (AAM) in Britain and Support for the African National Congress (ANC), 1976–1990'. Unpublished PhD thesis, University of Oxford.

Knott, Kim (2010) 'Space and movement' in Kim Knott and Sean McLoughlin (eds) *Diasporas: Concepts, Intersections, Identities*, London, Zed Books.

Knott, Kim and McLoughlin, Sean (eds) (2010) *Diasporas: Concepts, Intersections, Identities*, London, Zed Books.

Knowles, Caroline. (2003) *Race and Social Analysis*, London, Sage.

Knowles, Caroline (2008) 'The landscape of post-imperial whiteness in rural Britain' *Ethnic and Racial Studies* 31 (1), 167–184.

Korpela, Mari (2009) 'When a Trip to Adulthood becomes a Lifestyle: Western Lifestyle Migrants in Varanasi, India' in Benson, Michaela and O'Reilly, Karen (eds) (2009a) *Lifestyle Migration: Expectations, Aspirations and Experiences*, Farnham, Ashgate.

Kothari, Uma (2006) 'Spatial practices and imaginaries: experiences of colonial officers and development professionals' *Singapore Journal of Tropical Geography* 27, 235–253.

Krog, Antjie (1999) *Country of my Skull* London, Vintage.

Kumar, Krishnan (2003) *The Making of English National Identity*, Cambridge, Cambridge University Press.

Laing, Aislinn (20 May 2013) 'South Africa considers £80 visas for Britons as diplomatic "tit for tat" escalates' *The Telegraph*. Accessed 18 August 2014 http://www.telegraph.co.uk/news/worldnews/africaandindianocean/southafrica/10069229/South-Africa-considers-80-visas-for-Britons-as-diplomatic-tit-for-tat-escalates.html.

Lambert, John (2009) 'An unknown people': reconstructing British South African Identity' *The Journal of Imperial and Commonwealth History* 37 (4), 599–617.

―― (2010) '"The Last Outpost": The Natalians, South Africa, and the British Empire' in Bickers, Robert (ed.) *Settlers and Expatriates: Britons over the Seas*, Oxford, Oxford University Press.

Lefebvre, H. (1991) *The Production of Space* Oxford, Blackwell.

Leonard, Pauline (2010) *Expatriate Identities in Postcolonial Organizations: Working Whiteness*. Farnham, Ashgate.

―― (2013) 'Landscaping privilege: being British in South Africa' in Twine, France Winddance and Gardener, Bradley (eds) *Geographies of Privilege*, New York, Routledge.

Lemanski, Charlotte (2004) 'A new apartheid? The spatial implications of fear of crime in Cape Town', *South Africa Environment and Urbanization* 16 (2), 101–111.

―― (2006) 'Residential responses to fear (of crime plus) in two Cape Town suburbs: implications for the post-apartheid city' *Journal of International Development* 18, 787–802.

―― (2007) 'Global Cities in the South: Deepening social and spatial polarisation in Cape Town' *Viewpoint Cities* 24 (6), 448–461.

Lemanski, Charlotte, Landman, Karina and Durington, Matthew (2008) Divergent and Similar Experiences of 'Gating' in South Africa: Johannesburg, Durban and Cape Town *Urban Forum* 19, 133–158.

Lester, Alan (2012) 'Forward' in Fechter, Anne-Meike and Walsh, Katie (eds) *The New Expatriates: Postcolonial Approaches to Mobile Professionals,* Abingdon, Routledge.
Lester, Alan (2001) *Imperial Networks: Creating Identities in Nineteenth Century South Africa and Britain,* London and New York: Routledge.
Ley, D. (2004) 'Transnational spaces and everyday lives' *Transactions of the Institute of British Geographers* 29, 151–164.
Levitt, Peggy (2001) *The Transnational Villagers,* Berkeley, University of California Press.
Levitt, Peggy and Schiller, Nina Glick (2004) 'Conceptualizing simultaneity: a transnational social field perspective on society'. *International Migration Review,* vol 38, no 145, 595–629
MacCanell, D. (1999) *The Tourist,* New York, Schocken.
Makgoba, Malegapuru (25 March 2005) 'Wrath of dethroned white males' *Mail and Guardian.* Accessed 18 August 2014 http://mg.co.za/article/2005-03-25-wrath-of-dethroned-white-males.
Macmillan W. M. (1929) *Bantu, Boer and Briton: the Making of the South African Native Problem* London, Faber and Faber.
Mail and Guardian (18 April 2013) 'DA's Mandela, Suzman Pamphlet Raises ANC's Ire', *Mail and Guardian.* Accessed 9 February 2014. http://mg.co.za/article/2013-04-18-das-mandela-suzman-pamphlet-raises-anc-ire.
Marks, R. and Bezzoli, M. (2001) 'Palaces of desire: century city, Cape Town and the ambiguities of development' *Urban Forum* 12 (1), 27–47.
Massey, Doreen (1994) *Space, Place and Gender,* Cambridge, Polity Press.
Massey, D. (2005) *For Space,* London, Sage.
McAleer, J. (2010) *Representing Africa: Landscape, Exploration and Empire in Southern Africa, 1780–1870,* Manchester, Manchester University Press.
McClintock, Anne (1991) '"No longer in future heaven": women and nationalism in South Africa' *Transition* 51, 104–123.
McKenzie, Kirsten (1997) '"My own mind dying within me": Eliza Fairbairn and the reinvention of colonial middle-class domesticity in Cape Town' *South African Historical Journal* 36 (1), 3–23.
Merleau-Ponty, Maurice (1962) *Phenomenology of Perception,* London, Routledge and Kegan.
Micklethwait, J. and Wooldridge, A. (2001) *A Future Perfect: The Challenge and Hidden Promise of Globalisation,* London, Random House.
Miller, Daniel (ed.) (1998) *Material Cultures: Why Some Things Matter,* London, Routledge.
Mills, C. Wright (1997) *The Racial Contract,* Ithaca, NY, Cornell University Press.
Mills, Sara (2003) *Michel Foucault,* London, Routledge.
Mitchell, Katharyne (1997) 'Different diasporas and the hype of hybridity' *Environment and Planning D: Society and Space* 15, 533–553.
Mlambo, Alois (1998) 'Building a white man's country: aspects of white immigration into Rhodesia up to World War II' *Zambezia* 25 (2), 123–146.
Morrell, Robert (1 April 2005) 'White, male, democrat, African', *Mail & Guardian.* Accessed 18 August 2014. http://mg.co.za/article/2005-04-01-white-male-democrat-african.
Morris, Alan (1994) 'The desegregation of Hillbrow, Johannesburg, 1978–82' *Urban Studies* 31 (6), 824–834.

Murray, Martin (2011) *City of Extremes: The Spatial Politics of Johannesburg*, Durham, NC, Duke University Press.
Neocosmos, M. (2010) *From 'Foreign Natives' to 'Native Foreigners': Explaining Xenophobiain Post-Apartheid South Africa*, Dakar, CODESRIA.
Nowicka, Magdelena (2008) 'Heterogeneity, borders and thresholds: how mobile transnational professionals order the world' *Journal of Borderlands Studies* 23 (2) 41–58.
Nowicka, Magdelena. (2006) *Transnational Professionals and Their Cosmopolitan Universes*, New York, Campus Verlag.
Nudrali, Ozlem and O'Reilly, Karen (2009) 'Taking the risk: the British in Didim, Turkey', in Benson, Michaela and O'Reilly, Karen (eds) *Lifestyle Migration: Expectations, Aspirations and Experiences* Farnham, Ashgate.
Nuttall, Sarah (2001) 'Ways of seeing: beyond the new nativism' *African Studies Review* 44 (2), 115–140.
—— (2004) 'City forms and writing the "Now" in South Africa' *Journal of Southern African Studies* 30 (4), 731–748.
Nuttall, Sarah and Michael, Cheryl Ann (2000) *Senses of Culture: South African Cultural Studies*, Oxford, Oxford University Press.
Oliver, Caroline (2008) *Retirement Migration: Paradoxes of Ageing*, London, Routledge.
—— (2011) 'Imagined communities: older migrants and aspirational mobility' in Vered Amit (ed) *Going First Class? New Approaches to Privileged Travel and Movement*, New York, Berghan Books.
Oliver, Caroline and O'Reilly, Karen (2010) 'A Bourdieusian analysis of class and migration: habitus and the individualizing process' *Sociology* 44 (1), 49–66.
Ong, Aihwa (1999) *Flexible Citizenship: the Cultural Logics of Transnationality*, Durham, NC and London, Duke University Press.
O'Reilly, Karen (2000) *The British on the Costa del Sol: Transnational Identities and Local Communities*, London, Routledge.
Parekh, Bhiku (2000) 'Defining British national identity' *The Political Quarterly* 71 (1), 4–14.
Pearce, Malcolm and Stewart, Geoffrey (1992) *British Political History 1867–1990: Democracy and Decline*, London, Routledge.
Peberdy, Sally (2009) *Selecting Immigrants: National Identity and South Africa's Immigration Policies, 1910–2005*, Johannesburg, South Africa, Wits University Press.
Pillay, Verashni (5 September 2012) 'Woolworths: You Like No Whites?' *Mail and Guardian*. Accessed 18 December 2013. http://mg.co.za/article/2012-09-05-woolworthss-racist-jobs-advert.
Ponte, Stefano, Roberts, Simon and van Sittert, Lance (2007) '"Black economic empowerment", Business and the State in South Africa' *Development and Change* 38 (5), 933–955.
Popke, E. Jeffery and Ballard, Richard (2003) 'Dislocating modernity: identity, space and representations of street trade in Durban, South Africa' *Geoforum* 35, 99–110.
Prasad, Pushkala (2005) *Crafting Qualitative Research: Working in the Postpositivisit Traditions*, New York, M. E. Sharpe.
Robins, Steven (2002) 'At the limits of spatial governmentality: a message from the tip of Africa' *Third World Quarterly* 23 (4), 665–689.

Roediger, David (2005) *Working Toward Whiteness: How America's Immigrants Became White: the Strange Journey from Ellis Island to the Suburbs*, New York, Basic Books.

Rotberg, Robert (1987) 'The ascendency of Afrikanerdom' in Mermelstein, D. (ed.) *The Anti-Apartheid Reader: South Africa and the Struggle against White Racist Rule*, New York, Grove Weidenfield.

Said, Edward (1979) *Orientalism*, New York, Vintage Press.

Sassen, Saskia (1998) 'The De Facto Transnationalizing of Immigration Policy' in Joppke, C. (ed.) *Challenge to the Nation-State: Immigration in Western Europe and the United States*, Oxford, Oxford University Press 49–85.

—— (ed.) (2002) *Global Networks, Linked Cities*, New York, Routledge.

Saldanha, Arun (2007) *Psychedelic White: Goa Trance and the Viscosity of Race*, Minneapolis, University of Minnesota Press.

Salusbury, Tess and Foster, Don (2004) 'Rewriting WESSA identity' in Distiller, Natasha and Steyn, Melissa (eds) *Under Construction: 'Race' and Identity in South Africa Today*, Pietermaritzburg, Heinemann.

Saunders, Christopher (2006) 'Britishness in South Africa' *Humanities Research* 13 (1), 1–7.

Scott, S. (2006) 'The social morphology of skilled migration: the case of the British middle class in Paris' *Journal of Ethnic and Migration Studies* 32 (7), 1105–1129.

Shields, Rob (1990) *Places on the Margin*, London, Routledge.

Shaw, Mark and Gastrow, P. (2001) 'Stealing the show? Crime and its impact in post-apartheid South Africa' *Daedalus* 130 (1), 235–258.

Simone, AbdouMaliq (2004) 'People as infrastructure: intersecting fragments in Johannesburg' *Public Culture* 16 (3), 407–429.

Silvey, Rachel and Lawson, Victoria (1999) 'Placing the Migrant' *Annals of the Association of American Geographers* 89 (1), 121–132.

Sklair, L. (2001) *The Transnational Capitalist Class* Oxford, Blackwell.

Smith, Jean (forthcoming) '"Transformation to paradise": wartime travel to southern Africa, race and the discourse of opportunity, 1939–50' *Twentieth Century British History*.

Smith, Jean (2013) 'Settler Colonialism after Empire: Race and the Politics of British Migration to Southern Africa, 1939–1980'. Unpublished PhD thesis, University of California, Santa Barbara.

Smith, Michael Peter (2001) *Transnational Urbanism: Locating Globalisation*, Malden, Blackwell Publishers.

Smith, Mick, Davidson, Joyce, Cameron, Laura and Bondi, Liz (2009) *Emotion, Place and Culture*, Farnham, UK, Ashgate.

Soja, Edward, (ed.) (1996) *Thirdspace: Journeys to Los Angeles and Other Real – and – Imagined Places*, Oxford, Blackwell.

South African Tourism, Official Site (SAT) (2012; accessed 1 December 2012). http://www.southafrica.net/country/uk/en/.

Southall, Roger (2004) 'Political change and the Black middle class in democratic South Africa' *Canadian Journal of African Studies* 38 (3), 1–20.

Sparks, Allistair (1997) *The Mind of South Africa: The Story of the Rise and Fall of Apartheid*, London, Arrow.

Sriskandarajah, Dhananjayan and Drew, Catherine (2006) *Brits Abroad: Mapping the Scale and Nature of British Emigration*, London, IPPR.

Statman, James and Ansell, Amy (2000) 'The rise and fall of the Makgoba Affair: a case study of symbolic politics' *Politikon* 27 (2), 277–295.

Stephenson, N. and Papadopoulos, D. (2008) *Analysing Everyday Experience: Social Research and Political Change* Basingstoke, Palgrave Macmillan.

Steinberg, Jonny (2008) 'Crime' in Nick Shepherd and Steven Robins (eds) *New South African Keywords*, Johannesburg, Jacana.

Stock, Femke (2010) 'Home and memory' in Kim Knott and Seán McLoughlin (eds) *Diasporas: Concepts, Intersections, Identities*, London, Zed Books.

Steyn, Melissa (2001) *Whiteness Just Isn't What it Used to Be: White Identity in a Changing South Africa*, Albany, NY, State University of New York Press.

Steyn, Melissa (2012) 'The ignorance contract: recollections of apartheid childhoods and the construction of epistemologies of ignorance' *Identities: Global Studies in Culture and Power* 19 (1), 8–25.

Steyn, Melissa and Foster, Don (2008) 'Repertoires for talking white: resistant whiteness in post-apartheid South Africa' *Ethnic and Racial Studies* 31 (1), 25–51.

Stone, John (1973) *Colonist or Uitlander?: A Study of the British in South Africa*, Oxford, Clarendon Press.

Sugrue, T. (2005) *The Origins of the Urban Crisis: Race and Inequality in Post-War Detroit*, Princeton, Princeton University Press.

Surtee, Sabie and Hall, Martin (2010) *Transformation: African People in the Western Cape, An Overview* Cape Town, Development Policy Research Unit Working Paper 10/141, University of Cape Town.

Swart, Sandra (2003) 'Riding high: Horses, power and settler society c. 1654–1840,' *Kronos* 29, 47–63.

Swart, Sandra (2008) 'High Horses' – Horses, Class and Socio-Economic Change in South Africa *Journal of Southern African Studies* 34, 1 193–213.

Thompson, Leonard (2001) *A History of South Africa*, New York, Yale University Press.

Tilley, Christopher (1997) 'Performing culture in the global village' *Critique of Anthropology* 17 (1), 67–89.

Time Magazine (1962) 'South Africa: Honorary Whites' Friday January 19th Hall.

Tölölyan, Khachig (1991) 'The nation state and its others: in lieu of a preface' *Diaspora* 1 (1), 3–7.

Tomlinson, Richard, Beauregard, Robert A., Bremner, Lindsay and Mangcu, Xolela (2003) *Emerging Johannesburg: Perspectives on the Postapartheid City*, New York, Routledge.

Trundle, Catherine (2009) 'Romance Tourists, Foreign Wives or Retirement Migrants? Cross–cultural Marriage in Florence, Italy' in Benson, Michaela and O'Reilly, Karen (eds) *Lifestyle Migration: Expectations, Aspirations and Experiences*, Farnham, Ashgate.

Tuan, Yi-Fu. (1977) *Space and Place: The Perspectives of Experience*, Minneapolis, MN : University of Minnesota Press.

Tuan, Yi-Fu (1974) *Topophilia: A Study of Environmental Perception, Attitudes, and Values*, Englewood Cliffs, NJ, Prentice-Hall.

Turok, Ivan (2001) 'Persistent polarisation post-apartheid? progress towards Urban integration in Cape Town' *Urban Studies* 38 (13), 2349–2377.

Turner, V. and Turner, E. (1978) *Image and Pilgrimage in Christian Culture*, New York, Columbia University Press.

Twine, France Winddance and Gallagher, Charles (2008) 'The future of whiteness: a map of the third wave' *Ethnic and Racial Studies* 31 (1), 4–24.
Urry, John (1995) *Consuming Places*, Abingdon, Routledge.
Urry, John and Larsen, Jonas (2011) *The Tourist Gaze 3.0*, London, Sage.
Van der Westhuizen, Christi (31 March 2013) 'The problem with Whiteness' *City Press*. Accessed 9 February 2014. http://www.citypress.co.za/columnists/the-problem-with-whiteness-christi-van-der-westhuizen/.
van Hear, Nicholas (2010) 'Migration' in Knott, Kim and McLoughlin, Seán (eds) *Diasporas: Concepts, Intersections, Identities*. London, Zed Books.
van Helten, Jean Jacques and Williams, Keith (1983) '"The Crying Need of South Africa": The emigration of single British women to the Transvaal 1901–10' *Journal of South African Studies* 10 (1), 17–38.
van Sittert Lance and Swart, Sandra (eds) (2008) *Canis Africanis: A Dog History of Southern Africa*, Leiden.
Vertovec, Steven (1999) *Migration and Social Cohesion*, Aldershot, Edward Elgar.
—— (2001) 'Transnationalism and identity' *Journal of Ethnic and Migration Studies* 27 (4), 573–582.
Vertovec, Steven and Cohen, Robin (1999) *Migration, Diasporas and Transnationalism*, Cheltenham, Elgar.
von Lieres, Bettina and Robins, Steven (2008) 'Democracy and Citizenship' in Nick Shepherd and Steven Robins (eds) *New South African Keywords*, Johannesburg, Jacana.
Waldren, Jacqueline (1996) *Insiders and Outsiders: Paradise and Reality in Mallorca*, Oxford, Berghahn Books.
Walker, Cherry, l. (1991) *Women and Resistance in South Africa*, Claremont, David Philip Publishers.
Walsh, Katie (2006) 'British expatriate belongings: mobile homes and transnational homing' *Home Cultures* 3 (2), 123–44.
Walter, Bronwyn (2011) 'Whiteness and diasporic Irishness: nation, gender and class' *Journal of Ethnic and Migration Studies* 37 (9), 1295–1312.
Western, John (2001) 'Africa is coming to the Cape' *The Geographical Review* 91 (4), 617–640.
Wills, S. (2010) 'Diasporic dialogue among the British in Australia', in Knott, K. and McLoughlin, S. (eds) *Diasporas: Concept's, Intersections, Identities*, London: Zed.
Wills, S. (2005) 'Passengers of memory: constructions of British immigrants in post-imperial Australia' *Australian Journal of Politics and History*, 51 (1), 94–107.
Wills, S. and Darian-Smith, K. (2004) 'Beefeaters, bobbies, and a new Verangian guard? negotiating forms of "Britishness" in suburban Australia' *History and Intellectual Culture* 4 (1), 1–18.
Williams, Allan M. and Hall, C. Michael (2002) 'Tourism, Migration, Circulation and Mobility: The Contingencies of Time and Place' in Hall, C. Michael and Williams, Allan M. (eds) *Tourism and Migration: New Relationships between Production and Consumption*, Dordrecht, Kluwer Academic Publishers.
Williams, Glyn, Meth, Paula and Willis, Katie (2009) *Geographies of Developing Areas: The Global South in a Changing World*, London, Routledge.

Wise, Amanda (2010) 'Sensuous multiculturalism: emotional landscapes of inter-ethnic living in Australian suburbia' *Journal of Ethnic and Migration Studies* 36 (6), 917–937.

Zournazi, Mary (1998) 'Out of bounds: inauthentic spaces and the production of identities – Ang, Ien in *Foreign Dialogues: Memories, Translations, Conversations*, Annandale, Pluto Press.

Index

accidental migrants, 10, 60
Act of Union (1910), 18, 35
affirmative action, 128, 133, 143, 144, 166, 168, 170
Afrikaans, 19, 24, 41, 92, 111, 113–14, 128, 142, 145–9, 183
Afrikaners, 1, 189n1
    attitudes towards British, 114
    differentiation from, 111–15
    discrimination by, 42, 145
    language, 74, 114, 146, 189n1
    nationalism, 18–19
    relations with British, 147–51
    whiteness, 74
Aliens Act (1937), 37
Aliens Control Act, 47
ANC (African National Congress), 2, 20–1, 141, 163, 185, 186
Anglican Church, 31, 83
animals, 28, 64, 84, 85, 87, 130, 139–40, 149, 183
Anti-Apartheid Movement (1960), 42
apartheid, 1–2, 27, 120, 133, 140
    alleged perceived bias of BBC, 157–9
    Anglican Church, 31
    British narratives, 154–6
    British South Africans during, 178
    embodied experiences of, 154–6, 175
    negotiating, 154–6
    oblivious to reality of, 156–7
    remembering, 154–6
    segregation laws, 81
Assisted Passage scheme, 25
Auf Wiedersehen, Pet! (TV series), 50

Ballard, Richard, 81, 87, 94, 99, 134
Bantustans, 19, 80, 81
Barclays Bank, 45, 107
BBC News, 157–9, 160, 182
belonging, 12, 29
    British-born immigrants, 126

British migrants, 115–20
British sense of, in Africa, 88
differentiation from Afrikaners, 111–15
future in South Africa, 183–5
home, 96–9, 105–9
national and ethnic, 132–3
South African, and Britishness, 109–11
see also un/belonging
Benson, Michaela, 9, 10, 54–5, 59–60, 64, 66–8, 87, 142
Biko, Steve, 31
biographies
    migrating to South Africa, 50–2, 55–9, 64–7, 179–83
    see also narratives
Black Economic Empowerment (BEE), 51, 143, 145, 168–9
Blair government, 173
Boer Republics, 35
Boers, 17–18, 34, 35, *see also* Afrikaners
Boer War (1899–1902), 7, 18, 19, 35, 36, 115, 181, 190n1
Boycott Movement (1959), 42
brickies, 50, 189n2
BRICS (Brazil, Russia, India, China and South Africa), 3
British, term, 4
British Dominions, 18, 31–2, 35–6, 57, 155, 189n1
British expatriates, 2, 25, 58, 66–7, 91, 96
British migrants
    belonging, 115–20
    belonging and future in South Africa, 183–5
    children of, 123–7
    future for, 123–7
    making a difference in South Africa, 159–63
    in South Africa, 21–3, 187–8

British migration
  history, 31–2
  politics of, to South Africa, 42–6
  white immigrants, 41–2
Britishness, 5, 16, 76, 77, 177
  embodied practices of, 98
  South African belonging and, 109–11
British settlement, history of, in South Africa, 32–8
British Telegraph Travel Awards (2004), 82–3
Broederbond, 19
Butler, Guy, 76

Cape Town, 28, 72, 80, 110, 120
  belonging in, 115–19
  British settlement, 32–3
  migration to, 55–8, 107–8, 179–80
  the Mother City, 82–3
  space and place, 81, 87
  spatial organization of, 102–3
Carroll, Rory, 152–3
Catholicism, 42
children, future for, 123–7
citizenship, 12, 29, 54, 105, 128
  belonging and, 55, 71, 72
  British, 40
  New South Africa, 138–40, 139
  South African, 11, 19, 38, 39, 131, 165, 190*n*2
Citizenship Acts, 38, 47
Cohen, Robin, 13, 16, 31, 32
colonialism, 16
Conway, Daniel, 6, 47, 81, 100, 155
Coronation Street (soap opera), 97, 190*n*2
corruption, crime, security and, 134–6
crime
  corruption, 134–6
  fear of, 94–5
  security, 93–6, 134–6

Daily Mail (online), 171
Daily Telegraph (online), 6, 130
de Klerk, F. W., 20, 163
democracy
  New South Africa, 75, 138–42, 166
  non-racial, 47, 155

parliamentary, 45
post-apartheid, 28, 153
Democratic Alliance, 141, 168, 185, 186
desegregation, 99
diamonds, 34
diasporas, 13–15, 73
discrimination, 19, 42, 137, 143, 145, 162, 168, 178
distinction, transnational identities, 67–71
Drake, Sir Frances, 32
Dutch East India Company, 32
Dutch Reformed Church, 19

East India Company, 82
eco-estates, 78, 87, 100
education, post-apartheid period, 143–7
Empire Settlement Act, 36
employment, migration for, 53
Englishness, 69, 109–11, 177
English-speaking
  language, 36, 74, 76, 114
  whites/community, 3, 5, 22, 31, 42, 109, 112, 123, 155, 156, 177
eugenics, 37
Evening Standard (newspaper), 45
expatriates, 2, 6, 11–12, 14, 16, 25, 58, 66, 73, 91, 96, 129, 131
Express (newspaper), 171

faux serendipity, 63, 64, 70
fear, security and crime, 93–6
Female Middle-Class Emigration Society, 34
FIFA World Cup, 6, 110
food, 8, 64, 72, 77, 117
fool's paradise, 116, 184
freedom, 10, 75, 95, 98, 117, 122, 131, 154

game estates, 87
gated communities, 10, 25, 51, 58, 79, 81, 83, 87, 93–6, 115
Geordie, 50, 189*n*1
global Brits, 132
global economy, South Africa, 48, 49
global ethnography, 72

gold, 34
Grahamstown, 5, 30, 33, 36, 114
Group Areas Act, 20
Guardian, The (newspaper), 152

Hani, Chris, 163
Hawker Siddeley aircraft factory, 43
Hermanus, 15, 46, 114, 115, 156, 162, 164, 172, 179
Hertzog, J. B. M., 36
home, 12, 13, 75–6, 83
  belonging, 96–9
  green and pleasant land, 96–9
  landscapes of, 133–4
  sense of belonging, 96–9, 105–9
Home Affairs, 51, 137–8, 144, 165
Homelands, 19, 80
Hopetown, diamonds, 34
Huguenots, 32, 189n1

IDAF (International Defence Aid Fund), 43, 62, *see* apartheid
immigration policy, 49
international migration, 8–10

Johannesburg, 20, 21, 24, 28, 92, 94
  belonging, 115–16
  City of Gold, 18
  landscapes of un/belonging, 129, 131, 148, 150
  migration to, 56, 58, 60, 64, 69, 71, 79, 107, 185, 189n1
  space and place, 81, 86, 89–90, 95, 99–102
  spatial and racial divisions, 81–3
John II (King), Portugal, 32

Kenya, 64, 113, 160
Knowles, Caroline, 14, 16, 55, 73, 74, 84, 118
Kwa-Zulu Natal (Natal), 1, 6, 20, 34–5, 44, 65, 78, 81, 83, 87, 99, 101, 116, 120, 164, 183

labour migration, 22–3, 60–2
Land Acts, 20
land reform, people/space, 81
landscapes
  emotional connection to, 84–8

opportunity and mobility, 120–3
leisure, 15, 24, 25, 45, 80, 82, 83, 87, 98, 185
Leonard, Pauline, 8, 9, 11, 15, 26, 32, 48, 55, 60–1, 74, 81
Lemanski, Charlotte, 81–3, 93–4, 103, 134
lifestyle choice, 54, 117
lifestyle migrants, 8–9, 59–60, 87, 108, 185

Macmillan, William, 3
Malan, Dr. D. F., 38
Malema, Julius S., 129, 190n1
Mandela, Nelson, 20–1, 51, 69, 75, 126, 163, 177
Merriman, John X., 31
migration
  biographies, 50–2, 55–9, 64–7, 179–83
  everyday lives, 54–5
  international, 8–10
  labour, 22–3, 60–2
  lifestyle, 59–60
  as mistake or failure, 179–83
  privileged, 2–3, 7–12
  strategic decision, 62–7
migration processes, 27–8
Mills, Charles W., 64
mobility, 53, 66, 73, 80, 124
  social, 8, 18, 88, 91, 121, 180
  international, 117
  South Africa, 120–3
  transnational, 63
  white entitlement, 63–4

Napoleonic War, 33
narratives
  apartheid, 154–6
  'bad Britain' discourses, 171–4
  BBC bias, 157–9
  British making difference in South Africa, 159–63
  engaging with post–apartheid South Africa, 165–71
  migration, 50–2, 55–9, 64–7, 179–83
  oblivious to reality of apartheid, 156–7
  transitional times, 163–5

Index

Natal (Kwa-Zulu Natal), 1, 6, 20, 34–5, 44, 65, 78, 81, 83, 87, 99, 101, 116, 120, 164, 183
National Health Service, 57, 174
nationalism, Afrikaners, 18–19, 42, 181, 190n1
National Party (NP), 1, 19, 22, 36, 38, 41, 45, 156, 178
nationhood, landscape and identity, 83–4
nature estates, 87
Nazism, 37, 69
New South Africa, politics and, 138–42
new South Africa speak (NSAS), 75

opportunity, South Africa, 120–3
Orange Free State, 35
O'Reilly, Karen, 9–12, 14, 22, 28, 32, 54–5, 59–60, 66–8, 87, 107, 142 154, 171

paradise, 78, 85, 87, 126, 182
  fool's, 116, 184
parliamentary democracy, 45
Paton, Alan, 76
Peberdy, Sally, 8, 30, 33–4, 36–9, 41–2, 48
Pietermartzburg, 1, 15, 24, 28, 34, 183
  belonging, 115–16, 130
  migration, 50, 67
  space and place, 81, 83, 91, 94, 97–9
place, space and, 15, 24, 28, 54, 78, 103–4, 133, 179
police, sense of unbelonging, 136–7
politics
  New South Africa, 138–42
  racial, 18, 27, 167, 179
Population Registration Act, 19
positionality, 12, 13
post-apartheid, 23, 27, 134
  democracy, 28, 153
  dynamics, 46–9
  education, 143–7
  engaging with, 165–71
  work, 143–7
post-colonialism, 16
power, whiteness as form of, 74, 118

privileged migration, 2–3, 7–12, 53, 54, 60–2
professional migrants, 8, 9
public service, 136–8

Quota Act (1930), 37

race, 1, 10, 12, 13, 16, 17, 22, 24, 34, 68
  affirmative action, 128, 133, 143, 144, 166, 168, 170
  race relations, 17, 47, 114, 147–51, 186
  racial politics, 18, 27, 138–42, 167, 179
  racial privilege, 80–2, 85
  segregation by, 80–2, 84
  transnationalism, 71–3
  white immigrants, 28, 41–2, 73–7, 126, 186
racism, 19, 55, 75, 133, 141–2, 154, 159, 162, 171
Rainbow Nation, 2, 20
Rand Club, 89, 90
re-tribalisation, 19
Rhodes, Cecil, 89
Rhodesia (Zimbabwe), 35, 40, 48, 55, 82, 90, 130, 140, 183
Roman Catholics, 42
rooineks (rednecks), 112

Samorgan (South African Immigration Organisation), 39, 40, 43, 57–8, 63
Schreiner, Olive, 76
seasonal migrants, 11
Second World War, 42
security
  crime, and corruption, 134–6
  fear of crime, 94–5
  gated communities, 93–6
  wealthy estate, 78–9
segregation
  racial, 17–21, 28
  spatial, 80–1, 93, 104
Settlers, (1820), 33, 35–8, 40, 44, 85, 178
Settlers Memorial Association (1820), 36, 40, 44, 178

Sharpeville massacre (1960), 31
shopping, 25, 79–81, 97–8, 100–1, 103–4, 117–18, 127, 131, 135, 161
short-term migrants, 11
Sky News (media), 171
Smith, Jean, 37–8, 189*n*1–2
Smuts, Jan, 30, 37, 38
Society for the Overseas Settlement of British Women (1919), 34, 189*n*1
Somerset, Lord Charles, 33, 85
Somerset West, 79, 105–6, 154
South Africa
  British in, 21–3, 187–8
  context of, 17–21
  future for, 123–7
  history of British settlement in, 32–8
  politics of migrating to, 42–6
  post-apartheid dynamics, 46–9
  post-republic, 126–7
  republic and immigration, 39–41
  transitional times, 163–5
South Africa House, 43, 45, 58
South African Atlas Aircraft, 43
South African Citizenship Act (1949), 38, 47
South African Defence Force, 31, 47
South African Institute of Race Relations, 47
South African Journal (newspaper), 35
soutpiel, 22, 24
Soweto, 82, 92–4, 160
  Uprising (1976), 20, 22, 41
space
  of change, 99–104
  fitting into a, 88–93
  management of, 80
  and place, 15, 24, 28, 54 78, 103–4, 133, 179
  segregation, 81
  social and spatial outcomes, 84
  white, 6, 18, 80, 89, 90, 92, 141, 185
sport, 42, 45, 98, 106, 113, 142
State of Emergency, 20, 22, 46, 119, 157, 160, 162, 172
Steyn, Melissa, 1, 2, 6, 23, 63, 68, 73–5, 137, 153, 155, 168, 170, 178, 181, 186
Stone, John, 35, 49

Sun, The (newspaper), 45
Suzman, Helen, 186

Table Mountain, 82, 87
Telegraph (newspaper), 171
Telegraph Online (newspaper), 52
Telegraph Weekly World Edition (newspaper), 6, 25
television, 45–6, 64, 76, 105, 131, 157, 163, 181
thirdspace, 71
This England (magazine), 97
Times, The (newspaper), 33
tourism, 2, 12, 22, 48, 49, 59–60, 64, 82, 106
translocalism, 13–15, 55, 70, 72, 73
translocality, 97
transnational identities
  distinction, 67–71
  space and place, 81–2
  transnationalism, space and race, 71–3
  whiteness, 73–7
transnationalism, 13–14, 15, 54, 71–3
Transvaal (South African Republic), 35
Transvaal National Party Congress (1967), 42
Treaty of Paris (1814), 32
Trollip, A. E., 39
Tutu, Desmond, 21

un/belonging, 12, 98
  biographies, 128–31
  British senses of, 133–4
  crime, security and corruption, 134–6
  education, 143–7
  politics and New South Africa, 138–42
  public service and sense of, 136–8
  relations with others, 147–51
  work, 143–7
  see also belonging
unemployment, 22, 33, 36, 59, 72, 122
Union Castle Line, 38, 41, 58
Union of South Africa (1910), 35
Urban Areas Act (1923), 80

van Riebeck, Jan, 32
Verwoerd, Dr. H. F., 39
Viljoen Commission, 39
VOC (*Vereenigde Oost-IndischeCompagnie*), 32
voluntariness, 10

Walter Sisulu Botanical Gardens, 90
Walsh, Katie, 8, 9, 11, 55, 61, 72, 96
wealth, 8, 45, 50, 69–70, 78, 87, 89–90, 94, 100, 108, 115, 117, 122, 173, 181, 185
weather, 8, 11, 45, 59, 68, 98, 117–18, 171, 175
WESSAs (White English-Speaking South Africans), 3, 76–7, 188
white entitlement, 63–4
white flight, 56, 82, 100–1, 121
whiteness, 16, 55
  belonging, 107
  identity, 186–7
  power, 74, 118
  spaces, 127
transnational identities, 73–7
white immigrants, 41–2
white unulation, 75
white space, 6, 18, 80, 89, 90, 92, 141, 185
white talk, 68, 75, 141, 153, 162, 178, 186
Wilson, Harold, 171, 190n3
Witwatersrand, gold, 34
women, 25, 27, 30, 34, 44, 62, 89, 103, 113, 143, 160–1, 182, 189n1, 190n1
work, post-apartheid period, 143–7
work permit, 143, 144
World War One, 36

Xhosa population, 33

Zille, Helen, 141, 186
Zimbabwe (Rhodesia), 35, 40, 48, 55, 82, 90, 130, 140, 183
Zuurveld (sour land), 33

Printed and bound by CPI Group (UK) Ltd, Croydon, CR0 4YY